ANDREW CONWAY started his career as an astrophysics lecturer and researcher and has a degree and PhD in astrophysics from Glasgow University, which awarded him its Faraday medal. He also has an award for work on NASA's RHESSI mission and is a Fellow of the Royal Astronomical Society. On leaving academia, he spent time as an entrepreneur, founding two companies. As Chief Scientific Officer he touched on the world of politics, being responsible for the data engine behind the UK government's ActOnCO2 campaign. Whilst teaching at the Open University he honed his skills in explaining difficult concepts to people from all backgrounds. This experience led him to his current work on bringing clarity to essential information about our society. He is the co-author o *A Beginner's Guide to the Universe* (2002) and *An Introduction to Astrobiology* (2003).

How Scotland Works

A GUIDE FOR CITIZENS

ANDREW CONWAY

Luath Press Limited
EDINBURGH
www.luath.co.uk

First published 2018

ISBN: 978-1-912147-36-6

The paper used in this book is recyclable.
It is made from low chlorine pulps
produced in a low energy, low emissions
manner from renewable forests.

Printed and bound by
Bell & Bain Ltd., Glasgow

Typeset in 11 point Din by 3btype.com

Contents

Why should I read this book?

But facts are chiels that winna ding,
An' downa be disputed.

– From *A Dream* by Robert Burns, 1786.

Have you felt frustrated when politicians and pundits juggle facts and figures leaving you baffled by a mess of complexity and opinion? Have you felt aggrieved when during a debate in the media – either traditional or social – opponents make contradictory claims on a point and you wish you could be sure who was correct, or at least closest to the truth? Or do you suspect a particular party – one you oppose, or perhaps one you favour – of cherry picking information or distorting the numbers?

My aim with this book is to share an understanding of the information and data that should underpin the political debate in Scotland. If you just want some facts and figures then you'll find them within, but the intention is not just to list statistics about Scotland; it is to highlight sources, dismantle barriers of jargon and place information in a context where you can relate them to your morals and politics. In short, to assist anyone who wants to improve their knowledge of our society.

A single voice can carry far in the right circumstances. You can choose to be passive and just nod or shout at the TV, or you can choose to become active. The most common forms of activity are to join with others in a political party or a one-off protest rally or, at the very least, just to feed the ballot box on election day every few years.

It is a fact that many people do not engage in any of these ways. At the last election for the Scottish Parliament in 2016, 44% of people who could vote, did not. That's a turnout of 56%. Although Scotland was widely touted as being much more politically engaged following the 85% turnout in the 2014 referendum, the Scottish turnout of 71% in the 2015 election was only a little higher than the UK-wide 66% turnout, and the 2017 general election saw the Scottish turnout falling to 66%, slightly below the 69% for the whole UK. Non-voters are so common – roughly one in three adults – that you've almost certainly heard their reasons for yourself: it doesn't matter who's in power; the parties are all the same; my vote won't make a difference; the system is too flawed; and perhaps the most common, and unsaid: people are too busy just getting on with their lives.

But there is another form of engagement, and one which doesn't require you to align with a political party or even vote: improve your understanding of the society in which you live. Learn to question which facts are known with some certainty, and to recognise where uncertainty lies. Learn to separate what is a technical issue, for example how tax is calculated, from what is a moral and political issue, such as why higher incomes are taxed at a higher rate.

At the very least you'll gain a satisfying insight into your society. Even if you still choose not to be politically active you will very likely feel the need to share your insights with others. Whether you do so directly with friends or family, on Twitter or Facebook, at public debates or with your MP, MSP, MEP or councillors, you can make a difference.

Anyone who is honest about advertising knows that the best way to spread a message is not a TV advert in Coronation Street, nor on a fancy billboard at the busiest road junction, but by word-of-mouth. And these days, word-of-mouth is greatly augmented by word-of-type across the internet.

But, word-of-mouth's (and type's) problem is that it can spread falsehoods as efficiently as truths. If you want to insulate yourself from the falsehoods and help stem their flow, then the first pre-requisite is that you know how to check facts, and as time is valuable, it's important to be able to do so efficiently. With smart phones and tablets and ubiquitous internet access this has never been easier.

Politics is society's attempt to make sense of a jumbled nest of moral and factual issues and as such is a tremendously difficult business. The aim of this book is to help you untangle and identify some of the certain and uncertain facts. What you then do with them is entirely up to you.

How should I read this book?

You may of course read this book however you wish, but it is structured so that the earlier chapters deal with more familiar concepts and straightforward topics. Chapter 1 deals with the population whereas Chapter 6 delves into the complexity of the political economy. Important concepts are mostly explained as they are needed but a few key points are briefly summarised later in this introduction.

Sections highlighted in grey indicate they are about potentially contentious topics where subjectivity (of both the author and the reader) may come into play. Discussion still hinges around the facts and their uncertainty but they become harder to separate from issues of politics, morals and identity.

Do not be put off by the numbers. If you can add, subtract, multiply and divide then you have all the mathematical skills that are required to tackle anything in this book. The difficult bit is understanding the words I've put around the numbers. I've done my best to try and make the explanations clear, in fact at times I've agonised over it, but I will not always have succeeded, sometimes due to my own limitations, but also because reality itself is complex.

If you're tempted to say 'I don't really do numbers' then think again. I have met people who have said that with conviction, but then after an afternoon in the lab I have helped them calculate the wavelength of light to a fraction of nanometre (a billionth of metre) from measurements they themselves made. And the help I gave them was not doing the calculation for them, instead it was to build their confidence and nudge them into forgetting that they couldn't 'do' numbers. Get pen and paper out, use a calculator or challenge yourself to learn how to use a spreadsheet. You never know, it might even come in handy in managing your own finances.

With each chapter we wade deeper into politics. Chapter 1 is relatively free of politics, but Chapter 7 is concerned specifically with electoral, party politics. I only mention specific politicians and parties when the need arises. There is no shortage of political analysis and that is deliberately not the focus of this book. But neither can it be ignored as it is at times inseparable from the subject under discussion. The debate around public debt and the deficit is a prime example of where politics, moral values and technicalities merge into a perplexing guddle.

A repeated, though mostly implicit theme in this book is that many trends and events under examination seem to occur *despite* the actions of politicians, not because of them. Only rarely is it clear that a particular outcome can be linked to a deliberate government policy. For much more evidence on this point see the book *Blunders of Our Governments* by Anthony King and Ivor Crewe, and *Who Governs Britain?*, also by Anthony King.

Particular politicians and parties are mentioned fairly infrequently, but on completing the book I noticed that the SNP and the Conservatives receive more attention than other parties, notably Labour. This is simply because the SNP have been in government for a decade, and the Conservatives since 2010.

Uncertainty is another recurring theme in this book. So recurrent that you, like me, will soon yearn for certainty and hope never again to see the words 'probably' or 'likely' or 'one possible reason...' (Or maybe you won't). Although constantly qualifying every statement makes writing good prose difficult at times, and can even paralyse thinking, it is vital to embrace uncertainty. At the end of the book I'll suggest how that might be done.

Language, and in particular the ambiguity that gives English its colour for humour and drama, can hinder non-fiction writing, and creates a particular problem around cause and effect. For example, in Chapter 4, we see that police numbers have risen in the last decade and that crime has fallen. Simply stating these facts in proximity tempts the reader to conclude that the latter was caused by the former, but there is no clear-cut evidence to back this up. When you read that part of the book you should be able to form an opinion on that point and I deliberately try not to direct your thinking on it. If you are left feeling that such a point is unresolved, as you will throughout this book, and as I do myself, then scratch that itch. Type a few words into a web browser, or visit a library, or consult some more knowledgeable individual. If this book causes you to do that, then I will have achieved one of my aims.

References are indicated throughout the text and my rule for including them is simple: either a point is explained in the text, or I provide a reference that directs you to an explanation or the source of information under discussion. Most of the references are links to websites and are listed by chapter at the end of the book. You do not need to type them into your browser. In almost all cases you can find them just by entering a few choice words into a search engine. I will also make a clickable list of references on the book's website howscotlandworks.org that will be updated to correct some links that will inevitably break over time.

I've chased references back to primary sources wherever possible, and in this book that usually means official government publications, or respected bodies such as the Office for National Statistics, the National Records of Scotland, or academic literature. Sometimes it is necessary to refer to (non-opinion laden) media reports. I have avoided any that are paywalled or have web links that may break. For this reason, the BBC and Guardian are most often used. Wikipedia is not listed as a reference directly, but it is very useful for finding lists of information and links back to primary sources.

Can we trust government sources? In my opinion, the sources mentioned above are reliable. That is because they are not really provided by the government as such but by skilled civil servants who are, in theory, working free from political interference. I have corresponded with many civil servants in writing this book and met a few in person too. They usually responded to my queries, sometimes on quite technical points, in anywhere from minutes to 24 hours, and were quick to correct mistakes that I found, or otherwise provide clear explanations to my questions or misunderstandings. Only once out of perhaps a 100 or so such enquiries in the last couple of years did I suspect a question was being evaded for political reasons. I intend to chase that instance until I have a satisfactory response and as it still ongoing as it write this, I do not want to go into further here. (OK, OK... I'll give you a clue, it relates to something in Chapter 3.)

All that said, I approach information from any source with some scepticism. Do the numbers add up to stated totals? Is information missing and if so is it explained? Are uncertainties identified and addressed correctly? The reason I say that government sources are reliable is because I found the answers to these questions are almost always 'yes', though sometimes it took hours of work to convince myself of it. I urge you to read this book with equal scepticism. If you find I have made an error, I will thank you for alerting me to it.

I make no claim to being objective. I would like to be of course, but I have my influences and opinions much like anyone else. I do perhaps differ in that I've trained myself to be quicker to say 'I don't know' and to recognise when I'm confronted with a subject where my knowledge is lacking. The act of doing that, and then spending hours searching the web, reading reports, blogs and books to educate myself is the reason why I ended up writing this book. So I make no stronger claim than I *try* to be honestly subjective, which, in my opinion, is as near to objective as a human can hope to be. My main advice, therefore, in reading this book – or indeed anything – is to wear your opinions lightly and check yourself if you notice that you *want* a particular claim to be true.

Conventions and jargon

I try and avoid using jargon but to help you with understanding information in other sources and contexts it is important to engage with some of it. Mostly, terminology and conventions are explained when they are first used, with some repetition throughout the book to save flicking back on forth. The most common ones are listed here:

- Mention of a year such as '2014' represents a calendar year, from 1 January to 31 December 2014 inclusive, but '2014–15' represents the financial year from 1 April 2014 to 31 March 2015 inclusive.

- The abbreviation pp stands for percentage points and means a change in a percentage. For example, if the Naughty Party see their share of the vote increase from 10% to 15% then their vote share has increased by 50% (5% is half of 10%), but the increase is 5pp (the difference between 10% and 15%).

- Use of 'real terms' indicates that some attempt has been made to account for inflation when quoting an amount of money from a past year. For large economic numbers this will be done with standard HM Treasury deflators (see Chapter 6), but for smaller amounts relating to individual spending the CPI or CPIH indices published by the Office of National Statistics or ONS will be used (see Chapter 3). Unless otherwise stated, the September 2017 editions of deflators and ONS indices are used throughout this book with links given in the references.

- I generally try to quote numbers to three significant figures or one decimal place, eg 68.1, but sometimes because of uncertainty or to avoid cluttering up the prose with distracting detail I will only quote two significant figures, rounding to the nearest whole number, eg 68.1 becomes 68. In performing calculations behind the scenes I use whatever precision the spreadsheet or calculator or source data will permit, which is usually more than three significant figures, and round only at the last step. For this reason, you may notice rounding errors and percentages that do not add to exactly 100% or other stated totals.

- In labelling the axes of graphs, you'll noticed the use of a slash '/'. For example, in discussing Scotland's GDP we deal with figures of 150 billion pounds or so. On the graph axis you might see the number '150' and the label will include something like '/ £ billion (real 2016–17 prices)'. This means I've divided the figures by £1 billion, and also they're expressed in real terms to be in prices of the financial year 2016–17.

Acknowledgements

Most of the information in this book comes from reports published by the Scottish and UK governments and so I would like to thank the various statisticians, economists and other civil servants and academics who curate and publish this valuable body of public information.

Links are given throughout the book if you want to read these reports yourself. In most cases they come with spreadsheets which were used to prepare data for the graphs and tables in this book. Almost all the graphs were generated using scripts I wrote using d3 which is available from d3js.org and used to great effect in Max Rosers's web publication ourworldindata.org.

At Luath Press, I'd like to thank Alice Latchford for her encouraging yet constructively critical editorial comments, and Gavin MacDougall for suggestions that helped greatly in shaping this book into its final form. I'd also like to thank Alastair Brian (of the Ferret Fact Checking Service), Gerry Hassan and Fraser Whyte for useful discussions along the way. There's a long list of others who have helped me to see information about Scotland in different lights. You can find me on Twitter as @mcnalu having discussions with many of these people, and, yes, constructive discussion on Twitter is possible!

My interest and understanding of public finances and economics was kindled through numerous conversations with Dr Andrew Berkeley, many of them over a traditional Scottish lunch of roll and sausage washed down with a coffee. More importantly, he helped me shed many of the restraining preconceptions that I had unwittingly held about politics, money and society. I also thank him for reading drafts of this book and making many constructive suggestions on how to improve and clarify its content.

And I am immensely grateful to my wife, Emma Conway, for her love, support and patience, especially during the final stages of writing this book. Not only that, but she found time to proof read the book for me. There is no one who is more adept at spotting my typos or grammatical mistakes, and no one who takes such great delight in pointing them out to me.

My children also deserve some thanks (even though they frequently interrupted my writing with requests for food, to play or to fix an errant electronic gadget) because they do more than anyone else to keep my mind open.

And I thank the many others who provided feedback on the book and provided words of advice along the way. Any mistakes that remain are entirely my own.

Website howscotlandworks.org

The howscotlandworks.org website contains a number of resources relevant to this book. It has a blog where certain subjects are explored in more depth and there will be updates and corrections. All the spreadsheets and other materials used to create this book will be placed there for people to reuse, inspect and check. I welcome any comments, questions and constructive criticisms you may have. You can email me on andrew@howscotlandworks.org or find me on Twitter as @mcnalu.

Chapter 1

Who are we?

I'm not aiming to answer this in some existential sense, but in a practical one with questions such as: How many people are there in Scotland? What's the age distribution? Where do they live? How are these things changing through time?

The stuff in this chapter, unlike some later chapters, is relatively free from controversy and is only weakly influenced by current political actions. But, information on people, often called **demographics**, is vital in planning many essential public services, such as education, transport and care for the elderly.

Probing population

What's the population of Scotland? This sounds like a simple question, and the answer is just one number, but estimating that number is not simple.

No one knows the precise population of Scotland *right now*. The census[1] is the most accurate estimate we have, but it relates to who was resident in Scotland on one day. The last census day was 27 March 2011 and the census is only performed once every ten years.

For the latest official population data on Scotland, look to the The National Records of Scotland which releases population data in April each year, giving an estimate of the population in the middle of the previous year. Their most recent release published in April 2018[2] is for mid-2017 and puts Scotland's population at 5,424,800 which is an increase of 0.4% on 5,404,700 in mid-2016.

Figure 1.1 gives an overview of Scotland's population in mid-2016.

Scotland, like most other developed countries, has more females than males. In the population of the whole world, males slightly outnumber females and the gap has been slowly widening in recent decades.[3]

Just under two-thirds of the population are aged 16 to 64 years old, with the remaining third split about evenly between under 16 and over 64. We'll look at the age distribution in more detail later.

What's a Scot?

Someone once said to me 'You're not very Scottish, are you?' and I replied, 'True, apart from being born here and having lived in Scotland for almost all my life.' Although it is true that neither of my parents are Scottish, it is also true that I'm the first Scot in my family. To avoid such

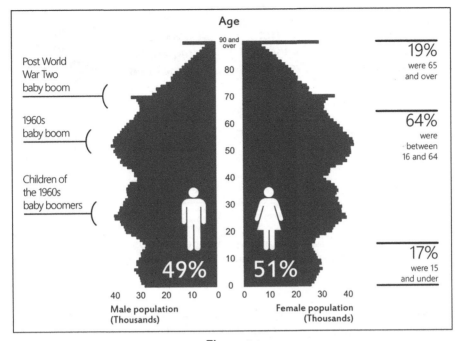

Age

Post World War Two baby boom

1960s baby boom

Children of the 1960s baby boomers

90 and over

80

70

60

50

40

30

20

10

0

40 30 20 10 0

Male population (Thousands)

49%

0 10 20 30 40

Female population (Thousands)

51%

19% were 65 and over

64% were between 16 and 64

17% were 15 and under

Figure 1.1

Population by sex and age 2016.

National Records of Scotland, Open Government License.

ambiguities it's important to have a precise definition of who should be counted as being part of the population.

As far as the census is concerned, you are in the population if you are a **usual resident** on the day of the census. To be a usual resident you need to have stayed in Scotland for 12 months or have the intention to stay for 12 months. But that doesn't mean you're Scottish of course, as you may specify your identity as you wish (though Picts and Jedis often feel left out).

A moment's thought reveals that there are only four ways for the population of Scotland to change: a person comes to live in Scotland; someone leaves; a baby is born to residents; or a resident dies. That's it.

Figure 1.2 shows how the population of Scotland has changed between mid-2016 and mid-2017. **Migration** refers to the number of people coming to live in Scotland and **net migration** is that number less the number leaving to live elsewhere.

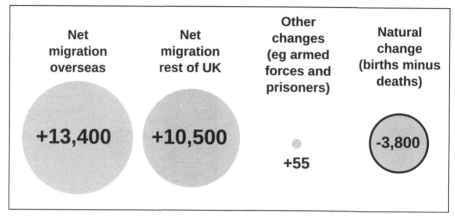

Figure 1.2
Why has Scotland's population increased?
National Records of Scotland, Open Government License.

You can work out the **net migration** figure by adding up the numbers in the first two circles to give 23,900. In the year to mid-2016, 23,900 more people came to live in Scotland than left. The other main cause of population change is **natural change** – the number of birth minus deaths – which contributed a decrease of 3,800.

Making sense of the census

A wealth of information from Scotland's census can be found at its website www.scotlandcensus.gov.uk.[4] You can quickly get lost in the detail, but the Results at a Glance[5] section provides a good starting point.

The raw data of the census come from questionnaires completed by millions of households across the country. Processing such a huge volume of data is a time consuming business. The fruits of this labour were released in stages[6] starting with Release 1A in December 2012, followed by Release 1B in March 2013 continuing on until Release 3N in January 2015. The later releases are concerned with more detailed and specific aspects, so for many purposes, and much of what's discussed here, the first few releases are most relevant.

The centre piece of each release is a document containing numerous charts and tables with a narrative that explains how the data was processed and highlights interesting features. All data presented in that document is available separately in spreadsheets so that you can work with the data yourself. This is true for almost all the data shown in this book. It's worth looking out for revisions and corrections which may be issued after the release was first made. And even where no mistake is made it's important to be aware of uncertainties in the data, of which, more later.

Censuses have taken place in the second year of each decade from 1801 to 2011 with only a few exceptions, the last being due to the Second World War in 1941. The census takes place in all four countries of the UK at the same time but under different legislative and administrative arrangements.

Population density

Scotland covers an area of 77,900 square kilometres,[7] which is about a third of the UK, whereas its population at the time of the 2011 census was 5,295,000 or 8.4% of the UK's. This tells us that Scotland's population is, on average, far more spread out over its land area than for the UK as a whole.

The **population density** is used to quantify this and can be calculated as follows for the population at the time of the 2011 census:

Scotland's population density = 5,295,000 divided by 77,900 = 68.0 per sq km

This means that if you were to draw a square of side 1 km in Scotland, then you would, *on average*, find about 68 people living it. Of course, people do not spread themselves evenly over the land so there are big differences in population density, with the highest being Glasgow with 3,395 people per square kilometre, and the lowest being the Highland and Western Isles council areas at nine people per square kilometre. For comparison, the population density of Greater London is higher even than Glasgow's at about 5,500 people per square kilometre.

Figure 1.3 shows population densities of EU countries.[8] (Malta has a population density of 1,305 people per square km and is omitted to avoid compressing the graph's scale.)

Ireland has a similar population density to Scotland whereas England's is much higher at 407 people per square kilometre and is the third highest in Europe, after the Netherlands and Malta. Most countries in Europe lie somewhere between Scotland and England.

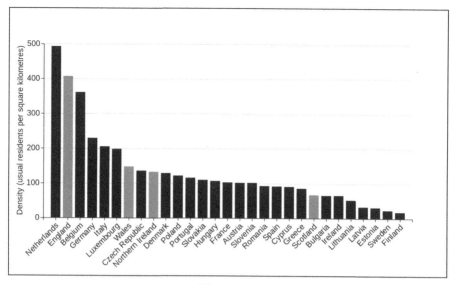

Figure 1.3
Population density of EU countries.

Geography and regions

Scotland is often divided into three large geographical regions: the southern uplands, the central lowlands and the highlands & islands. The division between the lowlands and highlands is arguably the most significant natural boundary on the British mainland as it is a major fault line, running from Helensburgh, through Loch Lomond and Crieff, reaching the east coast just south of Aberdeen at Stonehaven.

This division is not just of geological interest, but has influenced how the population has spread itself across Scotland. The mountainous terrain to the north and west of the fault line, which gives the highlands its name, makes transport more difficult and costly. The east coast of Scotland is much better served by railways and roads because of its flat terrain, and so there you have sizeable settlements such as Dundee, Aberdeen and Inverness, much larger than any north of Glasgow on the west coast.

Figure 1.4 shows how population density varies by council area, reproduced from the first release of the 2011 census.[9] Notice that higher population density areas are confined to the central belt of Scotland and the cities of Dundee and Aberdeen on the east coast.

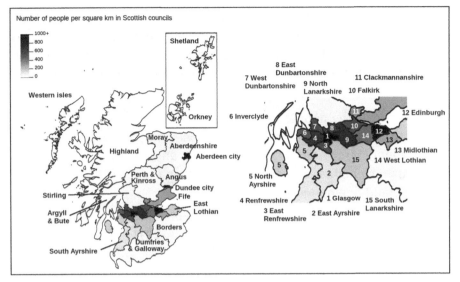

Figure 1.4
Population density of Scotland's council areas.

The majority of Scotland's population – some 3.8 million people – live in the central lowlands, and most of them are concentrated in the central belt, stretching from Greater Glasgow in the west, to Edinburgh, Fife and Lothian in the east, and extending from Lanarkshire in the South, to Stirling in the north.

The flat terrain of the central lowlands together with the natural location of ports in the firths of Clyde and Forth explains why population has concentrated there historically. The Forth and Clyde canal was built to connect the two firths together and formed the first major transport artery for cargo in Scotland at the dawn of the industrial revolution.

Communities grew up around the canal and provided the workforce for the coal and iron mines dotted along its length, as well as for the factories and ports at either end. Grangemouth at the eastern end remains an important industrial centre for chemical and oil and gas industries. Other areas, such as Maryhill in Glasgow have become more residential as heavy industry faded through the 20th century. A number of smaller settlements have disappeared altogether, such as Mavis Valley to the east of Glasgow. The canal was superseded by the railway network which largely determined the shape of suburban sprawl around Glasgow and Edinburgh.

The southern uplands is bounded to the north by a less well-known fault line that stretches from Ballantrae on the Ayrshire coast to Dunbar on the east coast. As with the highlands, the southern upland's undulating terrain makes transport less easy and so it has a much lower population density than the central belt.

Table 1.1 shows the population changes for the three regions between the last two censuses.[10] (The figures are based on council groupings and so Aberdeenshire, Angus, Argyll & Bute and Perth & Kinross are included in the highland & islands region even though they straddle the highland fault line boundary.)

Region	2001	2011	change
Southern uplands	254,600	265,200	4.2%
Central lowlands	3,670,200	3,805,900	3.7%
Highlands & islands	1,137,100	1,224,400	7.7%
Total	5,061,900	5,295,500	4.6%

Table 1.1
Regional population changes between the 2001 and 2011 censuses.

Population growth was most pronounced in the highlands & islands where it has increased by almost 8% between 2001 and 2011 compared to about 4% in the rest of the country.

Uncertain uncertainties
Uncertainty must be understood and accepted but should not be feared or ignored. Be wary of dismissals of information on vague accusations of its uncertainty. When you wake in the morning there is no certainty that you will survive to nightfall but few of us cower under the duvet all day waiting for better information. In fact, an awareness of our uncertain fate helps us survive routine tasks such as crossing the road. Similarly, a government minister deciding on a policy affecting society must do so using information that is uncertain. The outcome, which will have implications for their political survival, depends on a mix of luck and judgement. Understanding the uncertainty in weighing risks against benefits is vital.

The census is one of the least uncertain data-sets describing society, but it is not free from uncertainty. Notice the precision of the above population estimates: they are stated to the nearest 100. This suggests they could be as much as 50 higher or lower than the true value, often denoted by ±50. So, for example, this suggests that the actual population for 2011 lies between 5,295,450 and 5,295,550.

However, closer reading of the census (first release Appendix 4)[11] shows that the uncertainty is much higher, being estimated at ±23,000, which is ±0.4% of the population. The uncertainty arises because not every household returns a properly completed census questionnaire which means estimates have to be made to fill in the missing data – a process known as imputing the data. For example, if a census questionnaire was not submitted for a particular house, values can be imputed for it by averaging data returned from similar houses in that area.

In addition to the uncertainties in the census itself, further ones are introduced when updating the population for the years after the census. For example, to estimate the population for 2002, the number of births and immigrants are added to the 2001 census's population estimate, and the number of deaths and emigrants are subtracted. This will be done again every year until the next census. Births and deaths are carefully recorded, but there is some uncertainty in the immigrant and emigrant numbers. As a result, the uncertainty in the country's population will be greatest for the year just before the next census.

When the results of the 2011 census were compared with the 2001 results rolled forward ten years,[12] it was found to be 49,000 below the 2011 census result; about 0.9% of the population. Most of this error can be understood as uncertainty in the census results themselves (both 2001 and 2011 combined), but the rest is due to underestimation of immigration, especially between Scotland and the rest of the UK.

And, of course, estimates of uncertainties are uncertain themselves, but dwelling too much on such a recursive problem can lead to the intellectual equivalent of cowering under the duvet.

Council areas

In addition to having a parliament in Edinburgh, Scotland has 32 seats of local government – the councils. Figure 1.5 shows the populations of the council areas according to the 2011 census.

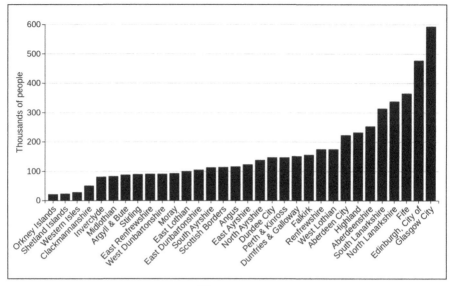

Figure 1.5
Population of council areas in 2011.

The three smallest council areas are for the islands. Clackmannanshire is the smallest council on the Scottish mainland with 51,442 residents and Glasgow is the largest with 593,245. Despite Glasgow being more than ten times larger in population it covers an area of 175 square kilometres which is not that much larger than Clackmannanshire's 159 square kilometres.

Ethnicity

The census questionnaire asks people to identify their own ethnicity. Before reading further, try and guess what fraction of the population state their ethnicity as something other than *White*.

Of the 5,295,000 people listed in the 2011 census, 5,084,000 identified themselves as being *White*. That's 96% of the population. In other words, 4% of Scottish residents say they are non-*White*. It's likely that, in common with many people, myself included, you guessed a percentage larger than 4%.

Of the White population, 4,446,000 million, 84% of the population, said they were *White: Scottish* and 417,100, or 7.9%, *White: Other British*. (Note that the use of italics is to emphasise these are the exact terms used in the census questionnaire itself.)

There are significant variations across Scotland, with cities and urban council areas having the largest non-*White* proportions; the top four being Glasgow with a 12% non-*White* population, Edinburgh and Aberdeen at 8% and Dundee at 6%.

The total increase in the population between 2001 and 2011 was 233,000, or 5%. Almost all of this – 229,000 – is from four ethnic groups, namely *White: Other British*, *White: Other*, *Asian* and *Black*. The *Black* group (including Africans and Caribbeans) has more than quadrupled in size and the *White: Other group* has doubled in size, mainly due to people of Polish ethnicity. Nevertheless, the *White: Scottish* group remains the largest by far even though it has decreased by 13,000 or -0.3%.

National identity and place of birth

The 2011 census was the first one to ask people to specify their national identity. The results are shown in Table 1.2. This differs from ethnicity because it needn't be dictated by place of birth nor your parents' background. For example, a young child that arrives from Nigeria may grow up to identify with a Scottish nationality whilst reporting a Nigerian ethnicity.

Scottish only	Scottish and British only	Scottish and other	British only	English only	At least one other UK identity	Other
62.4%	18.3%	1.9%	8.4%	2.3%	2.3%	4.4%

Table 1.2
National identity in the 2011 census.

Just over three fifths of the Scottish population see themselves as Scottish only, with another fifth seeing themselves as Scottish and British. Just over a quarter of the population say they have some kind of British identity. A little under 1 in 10 people say their identity is something other than Scottish or British.

Table 1.3 gives percentages on place of birth, also from the 2011 census.

Between 2001 and 2011 the percentage of residents born in Scotland dropped by 4pp (percentage points) whilst those born in England rose by 1pp. The much smaller percentages for Northern Ireland and Wales

Census	Scotland	England	N Ireland	Wales	Non-UK
2001	87%	8%	0.7%	0.3%	3.8%
2011	83%	9%	0.7%	0.3%	7.0%

Table 1.3
Places of birth.

remained the same. This means that the percentage born in the UK has decreased from 96% to 93% whilst the percentage born outside the UK has risen from 3.8% in 2001 to 7.0% in 2011. These people came from many countries, but the single biggest group were born in Poland, and they now make up 1% of residents.

Most Scottish residents born outside the UK arrived between 2001 and 2011 and the majority of them were under 30 on arrival. Around 64,000 or 17% of people not born in the UK arrived in Scotland before they were five.

Language
Language questions in the 2011 census applied only to the 5,118,000 people aged three or over. Unsurprisingly, a very high proportion of that population – 98% – say they are able to speak, read, write and understand English. This figure shows little variation throughout Scotland.

The census also asked which language was used in the respondent's home, to which 93% answered English. The prevalence of other languages is shown in Table 1.4.

	Gaelic	Scots	British Sign Language	Polish	Other language
Number	25,000	55,800	12,500	54,200	230,200
% of population	0.5%	1.1%	0.2%	1.1%	4.5%

Table 1.4
Numbers of people using languages other than English
in the home in the 2011 census.

By far the biggest concentration of Gaelic speakers is in the Western Isles where 40% of its 28,000 residents reported that it was the main language used at home. The number of people who can speak, read and write Gaelic in 2011 was 32,000 which is 0.6% of the population aged three or over and is little changed from 2001. If widened to those who speak, read, write *or* understand Gaelic then the figure is 87,000 (1.7%) in 2011 which is down from 92,000 (1.9%) in 2001.

Scots – is it a language?

The European Charter for Regional or Minority Languages recognises Scots as a language and it is accepted as such, along with English and Gaelic, by the UK and Scottish governments. There is an argument that Scots is merely a dialect or a collection of related dialects but debate on the issue is difficult to resolve because no consensus exists on the definition of what constitutes a language as distinct from a dialect. Neither is the question free of politics. As the quip credited to Max Weinreich goes: 'A language is a dialect with an army and a navy.'

The 2011 census included questions on the Scots language for the first time,[13] but this was not straightforward. Research leading up to the census found that what was understood by the term 'Scots language' varied significantly across Scotland, and responses to census questions generated some amusing inconsistencies: a significant number of people reported they could understand, speak, read and write Scots but said they had no corresponding skills in English, but then answered that they spoke English 'well' or 'very well' in a later question.

Historically, the Scots language shares its roots with English and developed as its linguistic sibling until the 1707 Act of Union which formed the United Kingdom. Those in power and with influence, which included many prominent Scots, such as philosopher David Hume, were keen to enhance a cultural identity across the newly formed UK by promoting English and discouraging the use of Scots in education, relegating Scots words to slang status. This attitude changed towards the end of the 20th century and today Scots is actively promoted in Scottish schools. Against the backdrop of political polarisation following the 2014 referendum, some people fear that promotion of Scots and Gaelic has motivations beyond a desire to preserve a cultural heritage.

If you use words such as dreich, glaikit, scunner, stooshie or wean in everyday language then you are, to some extent, speaking Scots.

Population through time

The National Records of Scotland provides data on Scotland's population for every year back to 1855, shown in Figure 1.6.

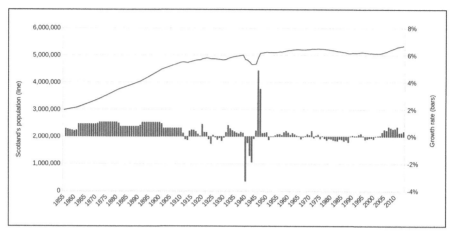

Figure 1.6
Population and its growth rate 1855–2015.

The population rises very rapidly during the late 19th century, but falters just before the First World War. There is some growth through the 1920s and 1930s, but this comes to an abrupt end at the start of the Second World War in 1939.

The bars on the graph show the growth rate. For much of the 19th century the population grew at an annual rate of about 1%. This doesn't sound like much, but if the trend between 1855 and 1905 had continued into the 20th century, the population would have exceeded 6 million by 1950 (it would literally be off the chart). In fact, an annual growth rate of 1% would result in a population doubling in less than 100 years. In reality, Scotland's growth rate fell after 1900 and was negative at many times during the 20th century, with a prolonged negative period from 1975. Scotland's population returned to growth from 2004 with the annual rate averaging at 0.5% over the last ten years.

Figure 1.7 shows data from the UK's Office of National Statistics (ONS) on how Scotland's population has changed as a percentage of the UK, Great Britain, and England.[14] **Great Britain (GB)** includes England, Scotland and Wales, to which Northern Ireland is added to make the **UK**, or to give it its full title, the United Kingdom of Great Britain and Northern Ireland.

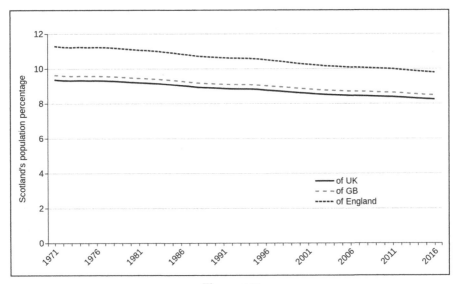

Figure 1.7
Scotland's population as a percentage of the UK,
GB and England 1971–2016.

All percentages are falling over time because the population of England, the largest UK country, has been growing throughout this time, and even though Scotland's population started growing in 2004, England's population has grown more rapidly.

From 1971 to 2016, England's annual, average growth rate has been 0.4%, compared to Scotland's 0.1%, whereas Wales grew at 0.3% and Northern Ireland 0.5%. Population growth has been higher since 2004, with England averaging 0.9%, Scotland 0.5%, Wales 0.5% and Northern Ireland 0.8%. We'll discuss immigration's role in this later on.

For mid-2016, Scotland's population share of the UK is 8.2% and of GB it is 8.5%. About 1 in 12 UK residents are in Scotland. Keep these figures in mind because they are handy benchmarks that become useful in later chapters, particularly when discussing the economy, public revenue and spending.

Growth

Growth is a recurring concept in politics, whether it means growth of the economy, growth in the number of jobs or demographic growth, which is just the technical term for population growth. In these contexts it is often used as a shorthand for **growth rate** – the percentage change over a given period, usually a year. If you're comfortable with numbers then you can skip this section, but if you're unsure on how to calculate a growth rate I urge you take some time to read it to make the most of what follows in this book, and indeed many other sources of information.

First, let's calculate Scotland's change in population between two years:

Change between from 2013 to 2014 = 5,347,600 – 5,327,700 = 19,900

That is, Scotland's population has increased by 19,900 in that one year. Now to calculate the growth rate we divide by Scotland's population in 2013:

growth rate = 19,900 divided by 5,327,700 = 0.0037351953

This is a decimal fraction, but we want the growth rate in percent, so we just multiply by 100:

growth rate = 0.37351953%

and finally, given that we started with a change of 19,900 in which only the first three figures are significant, we shouldn't be quoting all those decimal places, so we round it to

growth rate = 0.374%

In the discussion of the previous section, the fine details weren't important so growth rates were rounded further. To two decimal places this rate is 0.37% and to one decimal place it is 0.4%. The two rules of rounding are: round at the last step of calculation so as to minimise rounding errors, and don't quote the result using more figures than necessary to avoid giving the impression of false precision.

To illustrate the meaning of this growth rate, and check we calculated it correctly, we can multiply it on to 2013's population to find:

check = 0.374% × 5,327,700 = 0.00374 × 5,327,700 = 19,926

which is 19,900 to the nearest 100.

If you do this for every pair of years on the population graph, then you'll get the bars shown on Figure 1.6. Strictly we should call these *annual growth rates* because they express the growth from year to year. You may also come across monthly or quarterly (i.e. a quarter of a year) growth rates.

Birth, death and the bit in between

Figure 1.8 shows census data on changes in broad age groups[15] for the last 100 years. No census was carried out in 1941 because of the Second World War.

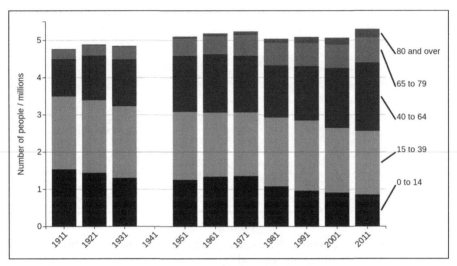

Figure 1.8
Age distributions in censuses from 1911 to 2011.

The number of people aged under 40 has been declining in Scotland throughout the 20th century, and those aged 40 and over have increased in number. The most striking change has been in the older age groups: *80 and over* increased from 30,000 in 1911 to 230,000 in 2011, and those between 65 and 79 increased from 228,000 to 660,000.

The age distribution of Scotland is similar to that of England, and in fact all European countries show a similar pattern:[16] two thirds of the population are in the range 15 to 64 with the remaining third roughly evenly split between 0 to 14 and 65 and over. This situation is set to change, however.

Detail on Scotland's age distribution and projections for the next two decades are provided in the National Records of Scotland's Population Pyramids publication[17] (so-called because it's used to produce charts like Figure 1.1). Figure 1.9 draws on this data to show three age groups that we'll return to in more detail in Chapter 4 in discussing Education and Health.

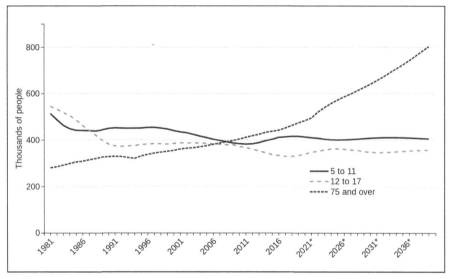

Figure 1.9
Numbers of people in three age groups: 5 to 11 (primary school),
12 to 17 (secondary school) and 75 and over. Projections are made
for 2017 and onwards.

The two younger age groups are relevant to primary and secondary education. They both show a declining trend until 2011 when the number of primary age children started to increase. Unsurprisingly, the projections show that secondary numbers will also rise with a lag of about seven years.

The striking feature of this graph is the rise of the 75 and over group. In 1981 it was just over half the size of either of the younger age groups, but by 2038 it will be more than double their sizes if these projections are accurate.

There are two certainties in life: birth and death (we'll come to tax in chapter 5 and for which, despite the popular saying, the data is a little less certain). Births and deaths are difficult to hide and must be registered so they produce a dataset that beats the census in uncertainty. For Scotland, it is available back to 1855[18] and is plotted in Figure 1.10.

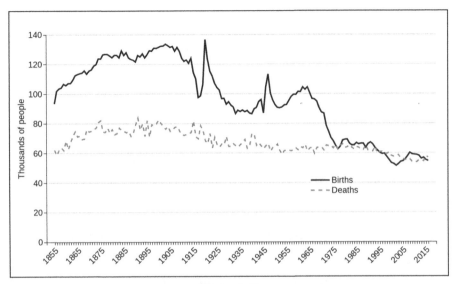

Figure 1.10
Numbers of births and deaths 1855–2015.

After rising during the latter half of the 19th century, the birth rate declined through the 20th century with peaks following the two world wars and the baby-boom around 1960. It fell dramatically until 1975, then remained relatively stable through the 1980s and has varied between 50,000 and 60,000 births per year since 1995.

The death rate remained well below the birth rate until 1975 and shows a steady declining trend through most of the 20th century and into the current century. It's notable that the rises in death rates at the time of both world wars is relatively small compared to the spikes in the birth rate just after each war.

Immigration and emigration
A person who comes to Scotland to become a usual resident (see earlier) is called an immigrant. A usual resident who leaves Scotland to live elsewhere is an emigrant. The number of immigrants less the number of emigrants is called **net migration** (sometimes net immigration).

Figure 1.11

Numbers for natural change in the population and net migration 1955–2016.

Figure 1.11 shows data on natural change (births minus deaths) and net migration from 1955.[19]

Net migration was negative until the late 1980s, and the net number of people leaving Scotland exceeded natural change (births minus deaths) in most years from the late 1960s until the end of the century. This explains the population decrease evident in Figure 1.6. Since 1980, natural change has remained close to zero, but, from 2004 onwards, net migration has risen significantly, driving Scotland's recent increase in population.

Figure 1.12 shows estimates of migration in and out of Scotland[20] to elsewhere in the UK and overseas. Note that movements to and from armed forces are not included and that there is some uncertainty in tracking movement of residents within the UK.

This graph shows that Scotland's migration used to be mostly within the UK, but since 2004 emigration to the rest of the UK has slightly decreased and immigration from outside the UK has noticeably increased.

In 2004, the European Union expanded considerably, admitting ten states: Cyprus, the Czech Republic, Estonia, Hungary, Latvia, Lithuania, Malta, Poland, Slovakia and Slovenia. In 2007, Bulgaria and Romania

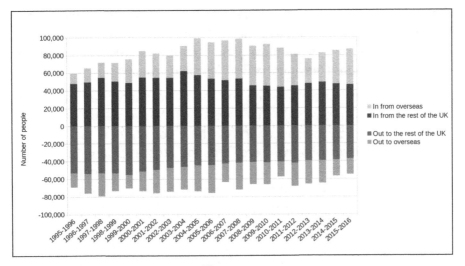

Figure 1.12

Migration in and out of Scotland to overseas and the rest of the UK
1995–96 to 2015–16.

joined the EU with Croatia joining in 2013. These new members, plus the EU's principle of free movement, are the main reasons for the increase in net migration which has driven Scotland's recent population increase.

Immigration and politics

When does immigration become a political problem? Equally, one could ask what benefits immigration can bring to a society. Such questions may have come to the fore in the EU referendum of 2016 and the ensuing machinations over Brexit, but they are not new.

To answer the first question: immigration becomes a political problem when the public perceive it to be one and politicians react to that at the ballot box. This was a factor in the rise of the United Kingdom Independence Party, and although they saw less electoral success in Scotland, they did manage to win one of Scotland's six MEPs with 10.5% of 2014 EU election vote, albeit on a 33% turnout (see Chapter 7).

Immigration has caused dramatic changes in culture, language and even ethnicity, and Scotland is no exception to that (ask a Pict what they feel about the Scots, if you can find one). However, on electoral timescales, it is the perceived rate of change caused by immigration that may generate disquiet, and a sizeable minority with a strong sense of national identity and associated cultural values will be most concerned about it. Ipsos Mori estimates that about 10% of the UK population favoured leaving the EU[21] for such reasons.

Separate to questions of identity and values are more practical issues on the impact of immigration on the workings of society and its economy. As an increasingly large cohort of the population enter old age, immigration can provide workers to do jobs that residents are either unwilling or unable to do. Further, the elderly cohort requires more services from the NHS and from council-level social care and so this creates a demand for a larger workforce in these areas. And, if these services are insufficiently provided, then sons, daughters and other younger relatives may find their ability to work restricted as they become carers for struggling elderly relatives. These issues are not unique to Scotland, but are present to varying degrees across the UK and also in other countries such as Germany and Japan.

A common argument against immigration is that immigrants will take jobs and so deprive existing residents of them. An extension of this argument says that an oversupply of workers will cause wages to fall. This is possible but depends on the assumption that there is a fixed number of jobs in the country. Historical evidence does not support such an assumption: an increase in population, whether from immigration or natural increase (more births than deaths), can lead to the creation of more jobs. Whether this is true in the current economic climate and while Brexit is proceeding is far from clear, however.

It has become common to see the pro-immigration view as being 'progressive', perhaps being combined with vaguer claims of being an 'internationalist'. But being pro-immigration solely because of the benefits it brings to *your* country ignores the effect on countries from which immigrants are coming. In the case of Scotland and the UK, the immigrants are mostly from Eastern European countries where demographic and economic problems either exist or are being created because young people are emigrating.[22] In fact, the problem is not just an international one: Scotland has experienced similar problems with rural and island communities suffering from excessive emigration to the central belt.

In the 2016 EU referendum, 62% of the Scottish electorate voted to Remain in the EU, whereas 48% of the UK electorate voted Remain. This is often cited as evidence that Scots are more pro-European and also more comfortable with immigration. However, more in-depth studies that go beyond the simple, single question nature of the referendum show that the views of Scots on Europe and immigration do not differ as much as the brexit result suggests[23] from other residents of the UK.

Households and home prices

According to the 2011 census,[24] 98% of Scotland's population lives in a household, such as a house or a flat, and 2% in communal accommodation, such as university residences, care homes or prisons.

The number of households has increased 8% since 2001 to reach 2,372,780 in 2011, whereas the population living in households has only risen by 4% to 5,196,400. If you divide the latter number by the first you'll find that the average number of residents per household is 2.19. This is down from 2.27 in 2001.

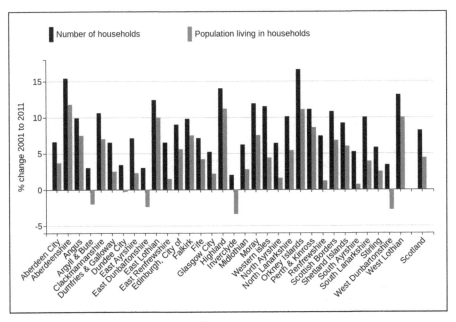

Figure 1.13
Changes in numbers of households and population by council between the 2001 and 2011 censuses.

Figure 1.13 shows that for all council areas the number of households has increased, even for those with a declining population, namely Inverclyde, Argyll & Bute, East and West Dunbartonshire and Dundee.

Further, the growth in the number of households exceeds population growth in every area too. With this in mind, let's take a look at how home prices have changed.

Statistics on property prices are published by Registers of Scotland [25]. Figures 1.14 and 1.15 show the history of median, inflation-adjusted residential property prices for certain council areas in Scotland. By definition of the median, half of properties in each area will have a greater price and half a lower price. The Consumer Price Index (CPI) is used to adjust prices for inflation. We could have chosen another index, but using CPI means that we calibrating home prices according to changes in the cost of a basket of common household goods.

Almost all areas in Scotland show the same pattern: strong growth until 2007 and then a drop in price following the financial crisis. Most areas have seen a recovery in price since then but more affluent areas such as East Renfrewshire and Edinburgh have seen bigger rises than

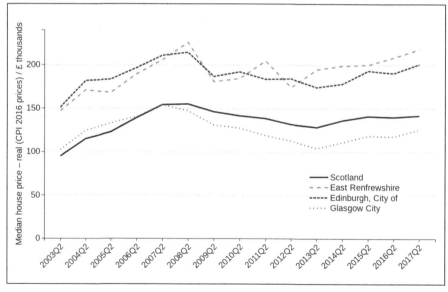

Figure 1.14
Median inflation-adjusted residential property prices for certain central belt Scottish council areas for Q2 (Apr-Jul) 2003 to 2017.

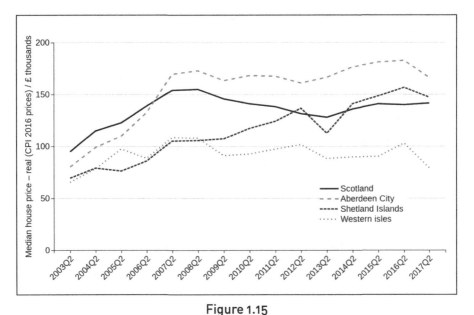

Figure 1.15

Median inflation-adjusted residential property prices for certain Scottish council areas outwith the central belt for Q2 (Apr-Jul) 2003 to 2017.

Glasgow or the Western Isles. In fact, Aberdeen City, Shetland and the Western Isles show significant drops in 2017. This is most likely because these areas provide services and employees for the North Sea oil and gas industry which has suffered following the drop in oil price in 2014–15 (see Chapters 5 and 6).

Figure 1.16 shows the percentage change for each council area from 2003 to 2017, and the change from the pre-crisis peak in 2007.

Without exception, there was significant home price growth in all council areas over the 14 years, and, in real terms, the median home price in Scotland increased by 50%. But only three council areas show an increase since 2007: East Renfrewshire, Shetland and Orkney.

The fact that the number of households grew faster than the population to 2011 (Figure 1.13) is part of the explanation of rising prices. It's likely that this is driven by the ageing population, because older home owners are less likely to have children living with them and more likely to live alone due to the loss of a partner. The result is that, on average, there are fewer people per home and so more homes are needed even if the

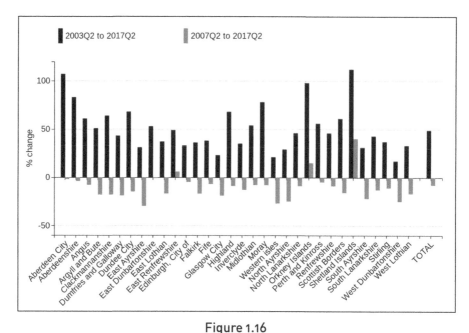

Figure 1.16
Median, inflation-adjusted residential property price changes for all Scottish council areas between 2003 and 2017, and also 2007 and 2017.

population remains unchanged. Prior to 2008, easy availability of mortgages fuelled the growth in home prices, and although conditions on mortgages were tightened after the crisis, interest rates fell to a historic low and that allowed those with sufficient incomes to take on larger mortgages, thus helping to grow or at least sustain home prices.

The continued rise in house prices has also been a factor in the shortage of *affordable* housing to buy or rent, especially for younger people. The cost of housing relative to income and its relation to poverty are separate questions that we'll return to in discussing inequality in Chapter 3, and the household expenditure in the whole economy in Chapter 6.

The Scottish Household Survey (SHS)

The census provides an invaluable body of data, but it only takes place once a decade. For more up-to-date information we have to rely on surveys; they are cheaper and quicker to perform and process. A survey involves interviewing a small but carefully selected sample of the population that are representative in terms of sex, age, location and many other attributes. The difference between a survey and the census is much like the difference between a poll of voting intentions which involves at most a few thousand or so people, and a general election which involves millions.

The survey approach introduces a new type of uncertainty that is common to almost all information you'll come across: statistical uncertainty from sampling. In fact, the census is unusual in being (almost) free from this kind of uncertainty.

The Scottish Household Survey (SHS)[26] has run since 1999 and is designed to provide the Scottish government and other bodies with information on the life of people living in Scotland. The type of information it gathers from over 10,000 annual household interviews overlaps with the census but goes into more detail. The results of each annual survey is published as a report in August or September of the following year.

Statistical uncertainty and bias

In any attempt to gather information about the population of a country, it is inevitable that a survey will be necessary. That is, you need to choose a sample of the population to interview. A statement you may hear such as 'that's not what I hear on the doorstep' should be viewed with suspicion, as should a debate in the pub when you hear something like 'All ma pals say aye, so I'm no wrong'. Both statements are in fact based on survey evidence if we take them at face value, but they doubtless suffer both from statistical uncertainty and bias arising from very poor sampling.

Let's start with statistical uncertainty. Imagine you suspect a coin of being loaded in that you think it is more likely to give heads than tails. If you toss it and see a heads then you may think you have some evidence for your suspicion, but the statistical uncertainty is so large that the evidence is near worthless. Why? Because there is a 50% (or 1 in 2, or 0.5 probability) chance of seeing a heads when tossing a normal coin. To build up more certain evidence, you toss the coin another nine times and get only one tails. Intuitively, you would agree that it is very likely this coin is loaded in favour of heads, but we can put a number to this. The chance of getting this result with a normal coin is 1%. So we can say that we are 99% (100% less 1%) certain that this result is not simply down to chance. Or, to put it the way statisticians often do: the result is statistically significant at the 99% confidence level.

In short, **statistically significant** means that the result appears to be real given the adopted level of statistical confidence. What confidence is accepted depends on the subject of study. In opinion polling, differences or changes in voting intention are usually accepted with a confidence of 90% or better. In scientific experiments a confidence greater than 99% is often required before a result is accepted. A confidence above 90% sounds quite impressive, but it is subjective: would you cross the road if you were 95% confident of surviving? Or 99%?

The term bias has a more precise meaning than the colloquial one in which someone might say 'I don't trust the mainstream media, it is biased'. In statistics, **bias** occurs when the sample you are working with is not representative of the whole population. This could occur if you recruited participants in the survey using an advert in one newspaper with a particular political leaning, or if you posted your advert only in old peoples' homes. It can also occur due to the way questions are worded or ordered in a questionnaire. Good polling companies work hard to make sure their samples are representative of the population and as free from bias as possible.

Later chapters will draw more on the Scottish Household Survey but here we will compare its results for 2011, which had a sample of 31,885 people, with that year's census. Reassuringly, both agree on the male: female ratio being 48%: 52%. The age distribution is also similar, as shown in Figure 1.17.

The apparent differences are not statistically significant and are consistent with chance variations that are expected given the sample size of the SHS. (The broad range of 0 to 24 is used because the census and SHS uses different age boundaries below 24 years old.)

From 2007, the SHS has asked a question on ethnicity that's similar to the one in the census; results are shown in Table 1.5

There is some disagreement here between the 2011 census and the SHS. For example, the census has *White: Scottish* at 84.0% whereas the SHS has it at 80.3%. Given that the SHS sample size for the ethnicity question is 12,886, this is a statistically significant difference. It is most likely due to differences in the way the question is asked. Whatever the reason, both the census and SHS do agree that there is a decreasing trend in *White: Scottish*, with the census showing a 4pp (percentage

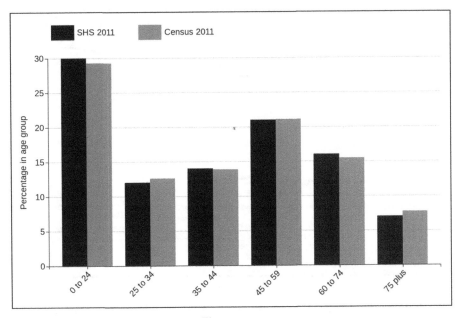

Figure 1.17
Comparison of age distributions between the census and the
Scottish Household Survey for 2011.

point) decline from 2001 to 2011, and the SHS showing a 6pp drop from
2007 to 2016.

Figure 1.18 shows the change in religious identification from the Scottish
Household Survey.

	2007	2007 -8	2009	2009 -10	2011	2012	2013	2014	2015	2016
White	97.9	97.4	96.8	96.8	96.8	96.3	96.4	96.7	96.3	96.0
Scottish	85.2	84.4	82.1	81.5	80.3	78.8	79.7	78.2	78.9	78.9
Other British	9.0	8.9	11.4	11.7	12.6	13.1	12.1	13.2	12.1	11.9
Other white	3.7	4.1	3.3	3.6	3.9	4.4	4.6	5.3	5.3	5.2
Non-white	2.1	2.6	3.2	3.2	3.2	3.7	3.6	3.3	3.7	4.0

Table 1.5
Self identified ethnicity in the Scottish Household Survey 2007–2014.

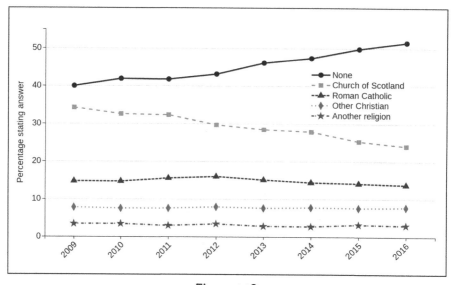

Figure 1.18

Religious identification from the Scottish Household Survey 2009–2016.

The answer None has increased from 40% to 51% between 2009 and 2016 which also saw a decline for *Church of Scotland* from 34% to 24%. *Roman Catholic* has shown a slight decline too from 15% to 14%. Other religions make up the remaining 11% which has remained constant within statistical uncertainties.

The 2011 census's answers on religion[27] found that 37% of the population stated they had *No religion*, which is 5pp lower than the SHS. However, the census also has a separate entry for *Religion not stated* for 7% of the population. Together these come to 44% which is 2pp above the SHS value which is still a statistically significant difference.

Church of Scotland and *Roman Catholic* are the same in both the census and the SHS 2011, at 32% and 16% respectively. The same is true for the total for all non-Christian religions which is 3% in both. The extra 2pp in *No religion* plus *Religion not stated* seem to have come from *Other Christian* which is 2pp lower in the census.

Some thoughts

At the start of the chapter I said that the issue of demographics was relatively controversy-free and only weakly influenced by current politics. This is true, or at least has been true recently, but there is good reason to believe we are moving into a new era where this will no longer be so.

Changes in population are mostly gradual, but a change in the growth rate of a fraction of one per cent can compound over decades to alter demographics greatly. In fact, the change is extraordinary over the century between the censuses of 1911 and 2011. The numbers from Figure 1.8 are worth emphasising:

- The population aged 80 and over has increased by 770%.
- The population aged between 65 and 79 has increased by 290%.
- The population under 65 has decreased by 2%.
- The total population has increased by 11%.

And the trends behind these changes show no sign of abating as the post-war, baby boomer generation now move into old age. Predictions made on reliable trends – that we age by a year each year – say the older cohorts will double in number in the coming 30 years. The number of children, and so future adults, looks set to stagnate, though, as seen in recent years, migration into Scotland offers a possibility of slight increase.

The pressure of the complex health needs of many older folk are already being felt on our health and social care services (see Chapter 4), but there are implications for the economy and wider society too as working age adults fall as a proportion of the population.

Questions to ponder:

- How will the tax base be affected?
- How do we fund the rising numbers claiming the state pension?
- Who will staff the health and social care services?
- How will Brexit affect immigration and in turn the working-age population?
- Should Scotland have a different immigration policy from the rest of the UK because its demographics differ?
- Scotland has suffered from emigration in the past in which young people have left to pursue careers elsewhere, but is it troubling that Scotland's population boost from immigration is made possible by an emigration drain on other countries, particularly in eastern Europe?
- What social solutions are feasible, such as schemes in which a younger person chooses to live with an older person with potential personal and financial benefits for both?
- Must we limit care based on what the government can spend given tax revenues and prevailing economic circumstances?

- Or can we insist that our ageing population, and others needing help in our society must receive a basic level of care and amend our economic and fiscal plans accordingly?
- How do we help politicians to see beyond electoral cycles and take a longer term view of these issues, especially thorny issues such as immigration and taxation?
- Much of Scottish history and culture is intwined with religion but the share of the population saying they have no religion has steadily increased and recently exceeded 50%; are people now finding new outlets for the human need for faith, perhaps in politics?

Chapter 2

Networked society

Our society relies on networks of infrastructure such as roads, railways, pipes and wires. Without them our time would be occupied by fetching water, lighting fires, collecting fuel, washing clothes by hand, and travelling using horse-power or on foot. In other words, we would return to a way of life of two or more generations ago.

This chapter is concerned with information on energy, water, transport and the internet. Unlike the aspects of population considered in the last chapter, the extent and quality of infrastructure is more obviously influenced by decisions made by various governments stretching back over several decades.

That said, most of the services provided *using* our infrastructure are managed by private companies. Current exceptions are Scottish Water and Calmac ferries which are owned by the Scottish government, though parts of both have recently been put out to tender to private companies.

The technology that supports our infrastructure has brought efficiencies to the work place, such as instantaneous global communications and robots in factories, and saved us valuable time in the home thanks to washing machines and central heating. In fact, we hardly appreciate these as efficiencies now because we take them for granted in daily life. Nevertheless, supporting our current way of life requires constant investment to maintain infrastructure and to upgrade it as technology develops, as witnessed in the last 20 years with the growth of the internet.

Underlying all of this progress is innovation which is easy to see with hindsight but difficult to identify at the time, and near impossible to predict. It can sometimes be traced to seemingly esoteric subjects in academia – our modern electronic devices owe much to quantum physics and linear algebra, for example – but it can sometimes emerge at the coal-face, quite literally in the case of steam power and the industrial revolution.

Energy and power

Before going into any detail, it's important to make clear the difference between an amount of energy and a power. Here's an example of a common kind of mistake:

> I got a huge bill for using 1000 kW of energy last quarter.

This makes as much sense as saying:

I got done for speeding last week for driving 90 miles.

A speed tells you the rate at which you cover distance. Likewise a power tells you the rate at which you use amounts of energy. Part of the confusion lies in how units of power and energy are defined.

The unit of power is the watt denoted by W, and is named after the Scottish steam engine pioneer James Watt. The usual unit of energy is the kilowatt-hour or kWh. Note the use of capital letters, KWH and KwH are both common mistakes. When written in full the unit is the watt with a lower-case 'w' (just in case someone thinks there are lots of little James Watts running around inside our wires).

The watt is too small when talking about kettles or power stations, so a number of other units are used, as shown in Table 2.1.

Power	Unit	In Watts	Example
1 W	watt	one	An LED
1 kW	kilowatt	one thousand	Electric fire
1 MW	megawatt	one million	Wind turbine
1 GW	gigawatt	one billion	Hunterston B nuclear power station
1 TW	terawatt	one trillion	Lightning strike

Table 2.1
Units of power.

All of these can be multiplied by a time in hours to give their corresponding energy unit, so a 1 kW electric fire uses 1 kWh in an hour, or a 1 GW nuclear power station could generate 24 GWh in a 24 hour period. And you can divide an amount of energy by a time to calculate the average power involved. If your house uses 48 kWh in a day then your average power consumption is 48 divided by 24 hours, that is 2 kW (and you'd best check you haven't left an electric fire on).

Unimaginable energy

The numbers describing energy and power we'll encounter below suffer from the double whammy of being both being unimaginably huge and somewhat abstract. To help with that let's deconstruct Scotland's total energy consumption into something more intelligible.

In 2014, Scotland used a total of 142 TWh of all types of energy, added up over all types of use. You can think of 142 TWh or 142,000 GWh as the energy produced by 142 large power stations in a month, but unless you're a very unusual sort of person this will be of no help to your intuition.

If we divide 142,000 GWh by Scotland's mid-2014 population of 5,347,600 we end up with a figure of 0.0266 GWh per person. Now we've got a number that's irritatingly small, but Table 2.1 is our friend. We can switch to MWh by multiplying by 1000, to get 26.6 MWh, and to help our intuition in a moment (bear with me), let's multiply by 1000 again to get a figure in kWh, that is 26,600 kWh. You could, if you wish, multiply this number by the number of people in your house and compare it with the numbers given on your own household's energy bills for a year, but if you use this much energy you either live in a mansion or are spectacularly energy inefficient.

A year is still too long a time for us to imagine, so let's divide 26,600 kWh by the number of hours in a year which is 365×24=8760 to get the average amount of energy that's used per person per hour, which is 3.04 kWh per person per hour. Remember, this average includes all household and business usage in all types of energy.

Now, the 'h' in kWh stands for hour so we can say that on average we use about 3 kW of *power*. This is an imaginable amount. For example, Scotland's total energy usage is equivalent to leaving 3 electric fire bars on 24/7 all year long for every person in the country. If you were to do this, at typical domestic electricity rates of about 15p per kWh you'd get a bill of about £4000.

A fit person on an exercise bike can generate about 0.1 kW of power. This is well short of the 3 kW average per person (including babies), and gives you some idea of how heavily we rely on energy generation to sustain our modern daily lives. Even if each Scottish resident owned a horse which could work 24/7 without rest, we'd still only have a quarter of energy needs met. One 'horse power' is only 0.73 kW.

If you want to learn more about how the availability of energy has transformed human civilisation then it has been documented in terms of the cost of producing light over the last four millennia.[1] Scots get a mention because they used to make economical lamps by putting a wick down the mouth of a dead, oily bird.

Energy usage

Scotland accounts for about 10% of the UK's total energy consumption and has just over 8% of the UK's population. This includes all energy used in transport, industry, homes and in all forms including electricity, and burning of oil, gas, coal and other fuels.

When energy usage is mentioned in everyday life, it's common for people to think first of electricity. Perhaps this is because it is associated with an image of large power stations or wind farms, but also because almost every room in a modern house will have mains electric lights and sockets. But it's important to remember that the majority of energy end use – about 80% of it – is *not* in the form of electricity, but from burning fossil fuels, such as gas for heating, and petrol or diesel used in vehicle engines.

The information on energy in this chapter comes from the Scottish government's Energy in Scotland 2017 report.[2] The '2017' refers to the date of publication but the data within it extends to 2015 or in some cases only to 2014.

Figure 2.1 shows how annual energy usage has changed in Scotland between 2005 and 2014. The graph tells us that in 2014 about 142,000 GWh of energy was used in Scotland. Note that the solid *Total* line uses the right hand axis and the breakdown of the total is shown by the other lines which use the left hand axis.

There's an evident decreasing trend with total consumption being 15% lower in 2014 than 2005. However, much of this decrease occurred as a sharp drop between 2008 and 2009 in *Industry & Commercial* usage and is likely a result of the 2008 financial crisis.

The main reason for the gradual declining trend is use of more efficient technology. For example, households have benefited from fitting more insulation which helps retain heat for longer, and from replacing older boilers with more efficient ones. A typical gas boiler from 20 years ago had an efficiency of 70%, meaning that 30% of the energy released in burning gas did not heat the home and was mostly being lost through the flue pipe. Modern condensing gas boilers can have efficiencies of 90% or more.

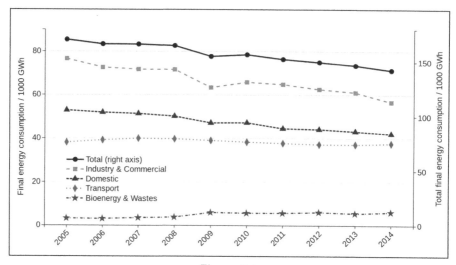

Figure 2.1

Final energy consumption by use 2005–2014.

Energy flows

Figure 2.2 gives an overview of how we move energy from its primary source to its end uses.

There's a lot going on in this chart. Start by looking at the large bar at the top called *Indigenous Productions and Imports*: a quarter of this is imported and the rest is energy from resources found within Scotland (indigenous). Most of this is primary oils (mostly crude oil) and natural gas, which together make up 84%, with coal and all other energy sources making up only 16%. (Note that this is nothing to do with the 84% and 16% going to the smaller circles – that's just a coincidence of numbers.)

The bottom-left bar labelled *Exports and losses* shows that the bulk of Scotland's energy resources – some 84% – is not used in Scotland, but leaves as exports. The majority of this is oil and gas extracted from the North Sea. About 12% of primary energy is lost. This is not due to absent-mindedness, but is inevitable in converting or distributing the energy (and the fundamental reason for it lies in the second law of thermodynamics).

It is clear from the level of exports that Scotland has much more in its energy resources than it uses itself. For example, only a minority of crude oil from the North Sea is processed at the Grangemouth refinery

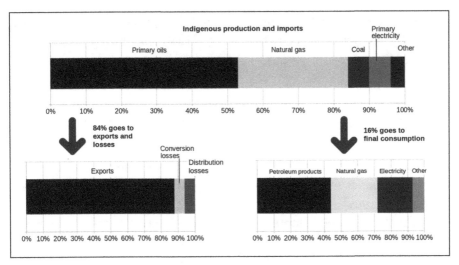

Figure 2.2
Flow chart from primary energy sources to end use 2014.

on the Firth of Forth to provide the majority of fuel supplies for Scotland's transport. But this does raise the question of why Scotland imports a quarter of primary energy. The answer is that certain types of fuel are not available within Scotland in the quantities needed or at viable cost. Coal was imported to fuel Longannet power (until its closure in 2016), and natural gas is piped to onshore processing plants from Danish and Norwegian North Sea facilities. A recent, controversial example is Grangemouth's processing of products from unconventional gas extraction, more often referred to as fracking. These must be imported because no fracking takes place in Scotland.

The bottom-right bar in the diagram breaks down the 16% of energy that stays in Scotland and goes into what is termed *Final consumption*. This is all the energy that is used in some way and not exported or lost. The bulk of consumption comes from burning petroleum (crude oil) products such as petrol and diesel, and natural gas. Electricity makes up just over a fifth of final consumption.

Fracking
Fracking, or hydraulic fracturing, is a process in which a hole is drilled into rock beneath the ground, and water and other chemicals are pumped in at high pressure. This fractures or cracks the rock and

releases oil or gas that is trapped within it. The process was discovered almost by accident by an engineer in the US in 1995.[3]

Opponents of fracking primarily point to local environmental concerns citing examples of fracking in the United States that are associated with groundwater contamination. There is also the wider concern that exploiting new sources of fossil fuel will impede initiatives to reduce greenhouse gas emissions that contribute to global warming.

Against this, advocates of fracking argue that it can create jobs and boost the economy especially in areas of the UK that were adversely affected by post-industrial decline. More recently, proponents of fracking have argued that its introduction in Scotland could help offset the loss of jobs in the North Sea oil and gas industry following the fall in the oil price (see Chapters 5 and 6), and provide a cheap, local source of gas for processing plants already operating at Grangemouth.

Explorative fracking tests were carried out in England in 2011 by the private company Cuadrilla, but they were suspended after being associated with a minor earthquake near Blackpool. No further activity took place until July 2017 but Cuadrilla's operations were hampered by protestors at the drilling site.

In October 2017, the Scottish Parliament voted to endorse the SNP Scottish government's effective ban on fracking by 91 votes to 28. The ban is described as 'effective' because it is not put into law by an Act of Parliament and as such could be reversed by a future Scottish government without any vote in parliament. Scottish ministers have said fracking 'cannot and will not take place in Scotland' and the Energy Minister Paul Wheelhouse said the ban was 'sufficiently robust' and that there was no need to take up parliament's time to pass a bill that would give the ban legal force.[4]

Processing of shale gas imported from fracking in the United States began in late 2016 at the Grangemouth facility run by petrochemical company Ineos.[5] Opponents of the ban have pointed to this inconsistency and argued that Scottish ministers had given too much weight to a public consultation that strongly opposed fracking and too little to expert evidence from engineers and academics. That said, in at least one academic expert's opinion, fracking in the British Isles is nonviable being some 55 million years too late.[6]

And there is also an historical footnote to this story in that Scotland pioneered the extraction and processing of shale oil in the mid-19th century through the work of James 'Paraffin' Young. This spawned a significant industry based around Broxburn and Addiewell in east, central Scotland. The industry collapsed just after the First World War due to a fall in the oil price caused by competition from foreign producers, an event that had eerie echoes in North Sea oil and gas a century later.[7]

2

Electricity – national grid

Of the three major uses of energy in Scotland, electricity has the smallest share. Just over half of all energy usage involves fuel burning for heating, a quarter involves fuel burning for transport and a little over a fifth is in the form of electricity.

Figure 2.3 shows electricity consumption measured by sales and split into domestic (ie household use) and non-domestic parts.

As we saw with all energies in Figure 2.1, a gradual decreasing trend is evident. The effect of the 2008 financial crisis is visible as a drop in non-domestic sales in 2009, although there is a slight increase in 2010 and a larger one in 2015. Over the ten years, domestic sales have fallen by 14% and non-domestic sales by 9%.

Tall, metal pylons supporting high voltage wires are a familiar sight on the landscape and they serve to integrate power stations and end users into a single network. This network is called the **national grid** and is currently operated by the company National Grid plc (the national grid also refers to the system of squares used in ordnance survey maps which has nothing to do with electricity.) The (electrical) national grid is often referred to as the GB grid as it spans most of mainland Britain.

Within such a single network it is not possible to identify the electricity used in your household with any particular power station. For example, if a company claims to source the electricity they supply to you from wind farms, then this is based in accounting with units of energy or money – the electricity in your wires will be the same as anyone else's.

This also means that there is no separation of the GB national grid into English, Scottish and Welsh ones: all three countries are integrated into the same GB grid (technically the north of Scotland has a separate grid, but it is also operated by National Grid plc).

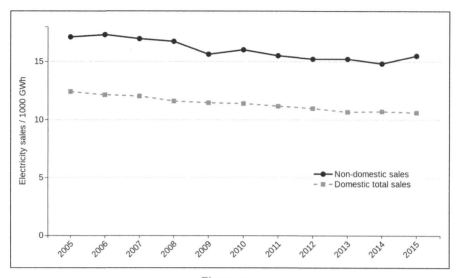

Figure 2.3

Electricity consumption measured by domestic and non-domestic sales 2005–2015.

With that in mind, we can still talk about electricity generated by power stations located within Scotland and also talk about how much is consumed by users located within Scotland. Excess electricity above what is needed in Scotland must be exported via the GB grid, although a small proportion can be stored, as we'll see later.

The GB grid can import or export electricity via cables called **inter-connectors**. The GB grid has four inter-connectors that run under the sea to France, the Netherlands, the Republic of Ireland, and Northern Ireland. The first two join the grid in England, and the last two in Wales and Scotland respectively. When we talk of Scotland exporting, this is mainly in an accounting sense within the GB grid, which may itself be exporting via its interconnectors.

Scotland is almost always exporting electricity because it generates more energy than it uses, but if generation does fall short of demand in Scotland that won't cause a problem because supply and demand are matched across the whole GB grid.

Renewable targets

The Scottish government has committed to a target of providing 30% of total energy consumption in Scotland from renewables by 2020. The latest version of the Energy in Scotland report published in 2017 states that 15.2% of total consumption came from renewables in 2014. Individual targets for electricity, heat and transport are shown in Table 2.2. Latest values for electricity and transport are for 2015, but the heat and overall values are for 2014.

	Electricity	Heat	Transport	All
Target	100%	11%	10%	30%
Latest	59.4%	3.8%	3.2%	15.2%

Table 2.2
Scottish government 2020 renewable targets.

Between 2005 and 2014, the share of renewables in all forms of energy has increased from 3.7% to 15.2%. Most of this increase can be attributed to generation of electricity from wind which has seen a rapid rise in capacity since 2001 (Figure 2.5). This is partly because Scotland's terrain is well suited to wind generation but also due to companies seeing an investable future in the business with policy support from successive Scottish governments.

In 2017 the Scottish government set a new target of meeting 50% of consumption from renewables by 2030, and to reduce greenhouse gas emissions by 66% by 2032. It also plans to create a public-owned energy company which will compete with private energy companies. The hope is that this new energy company can help in meeting these targets and also help keep prices low for households that struggle with energy costs.

Electricity generation

Table 2.3 shows the proportions of generated electricity by source in Scotland and the UK in 2015.

Scotland is currently much less reliant on fossil fuel electricity generation than the UK as a whole. Burning of fossil fuels is problematic because it releases the greenhouse gas carbon dioxide (CO_2) which contributes to global warming. Although the burning of biomass, which

	Nuclear	Renewables	Coal	Gas	Oil
Scotland	35%	42%	17%	3.7%	1.6%
UK	21%	25%	24%	30%	0.6%

Table 2.3
Electricity generation mix by source for Scotland and the UK 2015.

makes up a small but increasing amount of renewable generation, also produces carbon dioxide, it does not increase atmospheric levels because the biomass comes from sources such as trees that have spent recent decades extracting carbon dioxide from the atmosphere.

Power stations operate by releasing energy from a fuel and using it to heat water which produces steam that turns turbines to generate electricity. In this sense, even a nuclear power station is a type of steam engine. Overall, 38% of primary energy going into electricity generation is lost in the conversion process, with coal powered generation being responsible for the largest losses.

Figure 2.4 shows how the electricity generation mix in Scotland has changed over time.

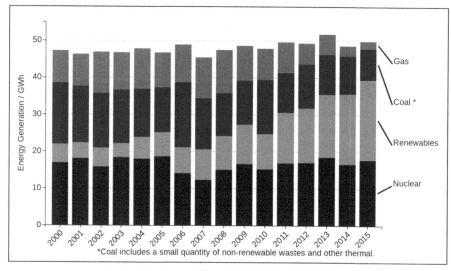

Figure 2.4
Electricity generation by fuel 2000–2014.

During 2015, a total of 50 GWh of electrical energy was generated, and of that 18 GWh was from nuclear power stations, 22 GWh was from renewables (mainly wind farms), 8 GWh was from coal and 2 GWh from gas power stations.

Generation from nuclear and renewables has increased in recent years whilst that from fossil fuels such as coal and gas have decreased. Bear in mind that this graph shows how much energy was actually generated rather than the generation capacity of each source, which we will look at below.

The mix of sources used for generation at any time will depend on the price offered for the electricity as well as the availability, for example some power stations may be offline due to maintenance or faults. The total amount generated has to be varied to match demand on the GB grid quite closely because there is relatively little capacity for storage, or for exporting outside the grid via inter-connectors.

The year 2010 is notable in Figure 2.4 because below-average rainfall meant hydroelectric reservoirs were depleted and there were also lower than average wind speeds in winter months. The result was that, despite renewable capacity increasing (see Figure 2.5 below), the amount generated from renewables dropped and coal generation had to be increased to meet demand in 2010. In addition, the end of 2010 saw unusually cold weather[8] which increased the demand for heating across all forms of energy which can be seen in the total sales data in Figure 2.3.

Table 2.4 lists all major electricity generating facilities in Scotland that were operational at the end of May 2015 and draws mainly on data from the Digest of UK Energy Statistics (DUKES) 2015.[9] Capacity is the maximum *rate* at which electricity can be generated and so we are not dealing with an amount of energy, but a power quoted in GW (see the example comparing speed and power earlier in this chapter).

The amounts in rows listed as 'Other' are the sum of many smaller power facilities. In fact, over 6 GW of the 13.6 GW total comes from around 200 of these facilities.

Company	Name	Fuel	Capacity / GW	Commissioned
Scottish Power	Longannet	Coal – closed 2016	2.260	1970
EDF	Torness	Nuclear	1.185	1988
SSE	Peterhead	Gas (CCGT)	1.180	1980
EDF	Hunterston B	Nuclear	0.965	1976
Scottish Power	Cruachan	Pumped storage	0.440	1966
Scottish Power	Whitelee	Wind	0.322	2007
SSE	Foyers	Hydro / pumped storage	0.300	1974
Scottish Power	Whitelee 2	Wind	0.217	2012
SSE	Griffin	Wind	0.189	2011
SSE	Sloy	Hydro	0.153	1950
Other		Wind	3.711	
Other		Hydro	1.157	
Other		Biomass	0.127	
Other		Diesel	0.138	
Other		Renewables (EIS report)	1.22	
Other total			6.38	
Grand total			**13.6**	

Table 2.4
Large electricity generation facilities.

Scotland's largest power station, coal burning Longannet, was capable of generating 2.26 GW, which is roughly equal to each of these:

- one million standard kettles boiling
- 300,000 cars driving at urban speeds
- 2.2 million 1 kW electric bar fires

- Raising *all* water in Loch Lomond at 30 cm per hour
- One flux capacitor from Back to the Future's time travelling Delorean

Longannet's closure in 2016 not only marked the end of coal-fired power generation in Scotland but was also significant enough to cause some speculation on whether it might have a measurable impact on Scotland's economy, not least because it employed several hundred workers.

Figure 2.5 shows the dramatic rise of renewable energy generation in Scotland at the start of the 21st century. When there's mention of capacities in what follows, it just means the total amount of electricity that can be generated by operating power stations, wind farms and other such facilities (it's nothing to do with flux capacitors!).

Capacity has grown from 1.4 GW in 2000, when 95% of it was hydroelectric, to 7.8 GW in 2015 by which time 72% was wind and only 20% was hydroelectric. Over this time, the amount of hydroelectric generation did slightly increase, but was dwarfed by the exponential rise in wind generation (and it is literally exponential in the mathematical sense). Various other forms of renewable generation – such as solar photovoltaic (PV), burning of landfill and sewage gas, and wave and tidal – have also seen significant increases over this time but still only make up a small amount of the total.

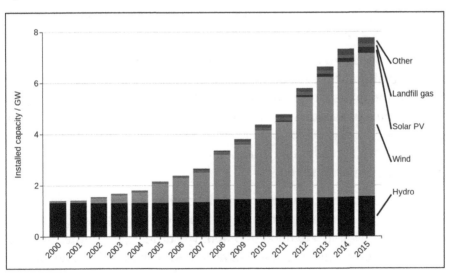

Figure 2.5
Renewable electricity generation capacity by source 2000–2015.

Source	Capacity / GW	De-rating factor	De-rated capacity / GW
Wind	5.20	29.4%	1.53
Coal	2.26	87.9%	1.99
Nuclear	2.15	82.3%	1.77
Hydro	1.50	85.0%	1.27
Gas	1.18	89.0%	1.05
Pumped storage	0.74	96.6%	0.72
Diesel	0.14	84.6%	0.12
Other renewable	0.53	87.9%	0.47
Total	**13.6**		**8.90**

Table 2.5
Electricity generation by source at full and de-rated capacities 2015.

The capacities as of May 2015 from all sources are shown in Table 2.5.

According to these figures, total energy generation capacity on the grid in Scotland in 2015 is 13.6 GW. Losses in the conversion to electricity are accounted for in the stated capacities, but not all of the capacity will be available for supply for a few reasons.

First, we need to account for the fact that generation at maximum capacity will not be possible because of issues such as routine maintenance and faults. To do this we can calculate the **de-rated capacity** by multiplying each capacity by de-rating factors provided by the National Grid.[10] The 29.4% value for wind in Table 2.5 is calculated from historical values and accounts for both mechanical issues with wind turbines and the variation in wind speed.

The de-rated capacity still does not tell us what is available to meet the electricity demand from consumers. Typically, only 85% of generated electricity is available to meet demand. The other 15% is either used by the power companies themselves or lost in transmission over power lines.

Figure 2.6 shows electricity supply available to meet demand. It's the result of taking the de-rated capacities from Table 2.5 and multiplying by 85%. Two scenarios are presented: actual figures for 2015 and an estimate for a scenario in 2023 with no generation from coal and reduced nuclear but more wind power.

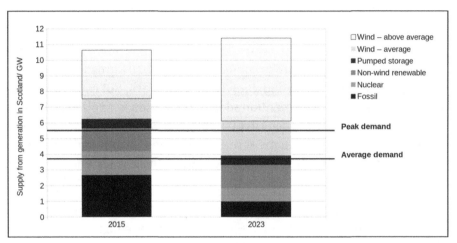

Figure 2.6
Electricity supply and demand for 2015 and a scenario for 2023.

The fact that generation from wind is highly variable is highlighted by its two sections on the graph. The bottom of the outlined box represents the *average* power supplied from wind based on historical data. The power supplied from wind at a given time can be anywhere from the top of the pumped storage segment (no wind) up to the top of the outlined box (optimum wind).

Let's consider the 2015 column first.

Average demand is 3.7 GW, and Figure 2.6 shows that an average of 7.4 GW was available to meet demand in 2015. This tells us that Scotland could export 7.4 – 3.7 = 3.7 GW on average. Exports in recent years have been about half of this because they are limited to what customers outside Scotland require and are willing to buy at the prices on offer.

Peak demand in a year usually occurs only for a short time at around 6pm on a cold winter's evening. Estimates from recent years put it at about 5.5 GW. Figure 2.6 makes it clear that peak demand in 2015 can be met easily even if there is no wind.

Electricity generation is dramatically changing in Scotland. Longannet, Scotland's largest power station, closed in 2016 and it is planned that Hunterston B nuclear power station will close also by 2023. Scotland's other nuclear power station, Torness was also to have been closed by this date but its operational life has been extended to 2030. These three stations together accounted for over 40% of de-rated capacity in 2015.

Against such losses there are expectations of a significant increase in renewable generation, for which the Scottish government has set a target[11] equal to 100% of gross consumption by 2020 ('gross' has nothing to do with energy from eating deep fried mars bars, but refers to generation before the above-mentioned 85% for losses is applied). There is 13.3 GW of renewable capacity in planning,[12] of which 95% is wind. About a third of this is enough to meet the renewables target, and this forms the basis for the wind power capacity used in the 2023 scenario.

So in this scenario, with all coal and about half of nuclear generation removed, and extra wind added, the supply available to meet demand is as shown in the 2023 column in Figure 2.6. Average supply available in Scotland will still be able to meet average demand, but, unlike 2015, it can fall short of peak demand in times of below average wind generation.

Once Longannet, Hunterston B and Torness are all closed, and assuming the renewables target is met, it is likely that Scotland will have to import electricity at times of high demand and low wind, but electricity will still be exported in more usual circumstances.

This 2023 scenario is intended as a thought experiment rather than a prediction. If Torness stays open past 2023 or the renewables target is missed or exceeded then the conclusions will change. And, as mentioned above, there is no problem meeting demand even if Scotland does become a net importer of electricity as long as there is sufficient capacity on the whole GB national grid.

But there are issues beyond simply having sufficient capacity to meet demand. For example, stabilising voltage and frequency has to be done regionally and is a job best suited to coal and gas power stations and the closure of Longannet has already made this more difficult.

Storage, supply and demand

Our demands must be met. When we plug an electrical device into a mains socket electrical energy is expected to flow immediately (well, at the speed of light if you're a physicist) and we trust that we will not open the freezer to find it full of ruined food. Given such expectations, and because storage and interconnectors are limited, the generated supply of electricity must be varied to match demand quite closely at any given time.

Figure 2.7 shows real data on electricity demand for the GB grid. Scotland would be similar, except demand would be about a tenth of the GB total. The data shown covers a seven day period starting at midnight on Monday 16 November 2015. You can view live feeds that also show the current generation mix.[13]

Notice the daily rhythm:

- a minimum occurring at 4am when most people are asleep
- a rapid increase from 4am until about 9am as people wake up
- little change until mid-afternoon
- another rapid increase from 3pm until 6pm: school home time until the evening meal
- a fall from the maximum to the next morning's minimum

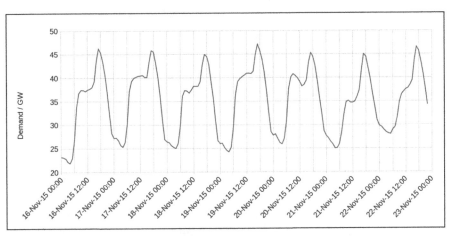

Figure 2.7
Example of GB daily demand variation for the week from
Monday 16 November 2015.

Notice also that demand varies from about 25 GW at night to 45 GW during the day (and these values depend on season). In an ideal world we would be able to store electricity overnight and use it during the day to lop off the peaks in the above graph so we can fill in the troughs. And this is done to an extent, but storage on the GB grid that can help match supply and demand can only provide 2.8 GW with reserves that would last about 9 hours.[14] Figure 2.7 shows that night-time troughs last only a mere 6 hours or so, even in winter, and demand can jump by over 10 GW in a few hours. As such, grid storage is nowhere near enough to balance day and night variations.

The bulk of this storage is **pumped storage** in which excess electricity at times of low demand, mostly at night, is used to pump water up into reservoirs. When demand is high during the day, pumped storage stations behave like hydroelectric stations by allowing the water to fall to turn their turbines and generate electricity. There are currently four large pumped storage facilities in the UK, all located in areas of mountainous terrain. Two are in Wales and two in Scotland. There are proposals for expansion of facilities on new and existing sites though they face public and political concerns on costs to the public purse and to the local environment.

Although pumped storage cannot itself ensure that supply meets demand, it has one unique feature: it can go from producing zero electricity to a GW or more in a matter of minutes. This is vital because, in addition to the daily variations in supply and demand, there can be sudden and irregular events, such as a major power station failure, or spikes in demand caused by popular events on TV. Following the kiss on the Buckingham Palace balcony after the 2011 royal wedding, the National Grid reported a surge of 2.4 GW – the equivalent of one million kettles being boiled. The largest surge of 2.8 GW occurred after England's penalty shootout in the 1990 World Cup.

The bulk of the job of tuning supply to match demand is performed by coal and gas power stations. These are not as rapidly variable as pumped storage but are the only alternatives as nuclear generation levels cannot easily be varied and wind generation depends on the weather. Coal is currently being phased out for environmental reasons across the GB grid, and elsewhere in the world too, leaving gas power stations to do the job, and causing what some describe as a 'dash for gas'.

If we are to rely more on wind power, the longer term solution is likely to come from innovations in distributed storage. Batteries in cars and homes could be charged overnight when the wind is blowing but demand is low, and there are already plans for attaching banks of battery storage to the GB grid. A necessary improvement here will be in producing storage devices that are low enough in price and that do not have the environmental manufacturing and disposal costs of current battery technology. One interesting idea relies in reusing old electric car batteries, which, after several years of use, will drop in capacity and limit the range of the car. At this point owners will want to replace them but rather than pay for costly disposal and recycling they could be sold to the owners of battery farms.

Water

Most of the water used in Scotland is drawn from lochs, reservoirs and rivers which are continually supplied by rainfall and it is rare that there is insufficient supply. Other parts of the world face a more difficult situation. California, for example, is experiencing drought and it relies more on underground aquifers which are replenished on much longer timescales. Water management in Scotland is relatively straightforward. It involves piping water to where it is needed, ensuring it is fit for human use and that waste water and sewage is transported away and responsibly returned to the environment.

Whereas England is served by a number of private water companies, and Wales has its water services provided by a not-for-profit company, Scotland and Northern Ireland both have their water service providers in public ownership.

Scottish Water[15] is 100% owned by the Scottish government and so its £1.1 billion revenue is considered to be part of the Government's accounts. This revenue comes from charges to its customers and is usually collected alongside council tax. Figure 2.8 shows how various water company charges compare across GB.

A couple of things should be borne in mind when comparing these water charges. Population density is much higher in England than in Scotland, and rainfall in much of England is considerably lower than Scotland.

Scottish Water makes a substantial surplus that is returned to the Scottish government. Since 2010 this annual surplus has been between

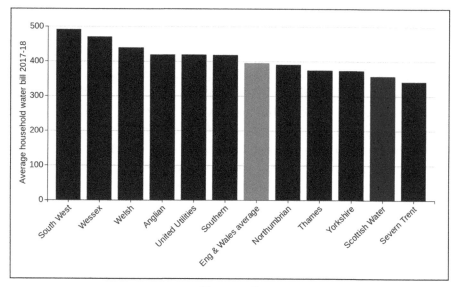

Figure 2.8
Comparison of water costs in GB 2017–18.

£85 million and £140 million. These figures are comparable, as a percentage of turnover, to the net profits of private English water companies.

Scottish Water provides 1.3 billion litres of drinking quality water per day to 2.5 million households and 150,000 non-domestic premises across Scotland. It also manages 850 million litres of waste water per day. The annual report also states that microbiology and chemical regulatory limits were met in over 99% of tests, rising from 99.36% in 2002 to 99.91% in 2016.

Public versus private

Even mention of the words 'nationalise' and 'privatise' can get political pulses the racing. First, let's be clear what these terms mean. When a company is owned by the government, it is said to be nationalised. Such companies are sometimes said to be in public ownership. Privatisation is where a government owned company or service is bought by private companies or individuals. Usually this involves splitting up one large organisation into a number of smaller, competing private companies. The distinction between nationalised and privatised is not always so clear-cut, as we will see.

In recent years there have been calls to nationalise both the railways and Scottish Water. But this is absurd for the latter because it is already publicly owned having been established by the Scottish government (or Executive as it was called at the time) in the Water Services etc (Scotland) Act 2005. And few people appreciate the extent to which railways across the UK have been nationalised over the last decade or so. As with many things, the current situation and its historical backdrop are far from straightforward and merit careful scrutiny.

From 2006 to 2015, Scottish Water's wholly-owned subsidiary, Business Stream, has provided water services to Scottish public sector facilities, such as schools and hospitals. In 2015, this contract was awarded by the Scottish government to the English private water company Anglian Water[16] and is worth about £350 million over four years. For context, Scottish Water's annual revenue is £1,000 million. Much of the £350 million paid by the Scottish government to Anglian Water will in turn be paid to Scottish Water who will continue to maintain the infrastructure of piping and processing.

So Scottish Water is owned by the Scottish government but must, under EU rules, compete with private companies for government contracts. But, things are more complicated still. In 2016 Business Stream bought Southern Water's non-domestic water business which serves the south of England, giving Business Stream a 10% market share and making it the third largest non-domestic water supplier in the UK.[17] But, as a subsidiary of Scottish Water, any profits made will either be reinvested in the company or contribute to public revenues as there are no shareholders to pay.

The situation with ScotRail is even more intricate and requires a little historical background to appreciate. Originally, railways across Britain were created by private companies. This grew in fits and starts through the 19th century with bubbles and busts aplenty. By the early 20th century the network was extensive and sprawling but the infrastructure and rolling stock badly needed investment. Calls to address this problem by nationalising the railways were resisted following the First World War and instead the government decided to group the myriad of small railway companies into four large ones. But as road transport began to grow, both investment and attention went elsewhere. Following the Second World War the dilapidated state of the railways again became an acute concern. This time the government chose to nationalise the railways to form what became British Rail.

By the 1990s, the issue of inadequate investment in the railways arose yet again and the UK government decided on privatisation, and asked companies to bid to run services as franchises on various parts of the network. The job of track and infrastructure maintenance was given to a single private company created for the purpose called Railtrack. Although services did seem to improve as a result, that was thrown into sharp relief by several railway incidents, most notably the Hatfield derailment in 2000, which killed four people and injured many more. This tragedy prompted an investigation which uncovered serious flaws in track inspection and maintenance that had developed in the years since privatisation. The extent to which this was caused by privatisation and to which it was a problem Railtrack inherited can be debated, but elements of both are true. To prevent many potential repeats of Hatfield an extensive programme of investment in rail infrastructure was instigated which disrupted train travel across the network for several years. Railtrack ran up high debts and by 2002 was no longer financially viable so the government handed its responsibilities to the new publicly owned company Network Rail.

Network Rail currently manages infrastructure, such as the track, signals and overhead wires across Great Britain (England, Scotland and Wales but not Northern Ireland). Although Network Rail is not a private, shareholder-owned company like its predecessor, its status remained ambiguous until 2013 when the Office for National Statistics ruled that it was a government body in the public sector.[18] As a result its debts of £34 billion were added to the UK's public debt.

The train services that run on Network Rail's infrastructure are operated by private companies. They procure and maintain rolling stock, manage staffing and are responsible for many train stations. Trains in Scotland are run by the ScotRail franchise which is awarded to private companies in a competitive tendering process. National Express won the first contract in 1997, and was followed by FirstGroup in 2007 and most recently Abellio was awarded a ten year contract starting on 1 April 2015.

Abellio is owned by the Dutch national railway company which is in turn publicly owned by the Netherlands. As such, Abellio is a bit like Scottish Water's Business Stream arm. Ultimately, any profits made by ScotRail whilst operated by Abellio will go towards Netherlands public revenue. However, in its first full year of operating the service, the flow of money was in the other direction with ScotRail needing investment from its operator.[19]

In summary, railways in Scotland, and across Britain, are currently partly nationalised in that the track and other infrastructure are managed by publicly owned Network Rail. The services that run on these tracks are run by private companies but they mostly struggle to make a profit even with above-inflation fare increases. These companies pay Network Rail for use of the infrastructure but this does not cover Network Rail's costs and so it must rely on public finances. Without such state subsidy no private company would be making a profit from the railways. The situation has some similarities with the road network in that car manufacturers would struggle to make a profit if they had to shoulder some or all of the cost of maintaining the roads. The history of the British railways shows that neither nationalisation nor privatisation alone has been able to solve a recurring problem of under-investment.

Transport

A pulse of energy can travel the length of Scotland in a 1000th of a second and an email can be sent anywhere in the world in a fraction of second. But despite such advances in our technology, it is still important for us humans to meet face to face and move our physical items around the country.

The majority of Scotland's population is concentrated in the central belt and along parts of the east coast. This is mainly because the land is relatively flat in those areas and so transport is easier and cheaper to provide. The challenges in providing access to more remote parts of Scotland, combined with Scotland's much lower population density compared to England, explains why 15% of the UK's public expenditure on transport is spent in Scotland. To put this another way, the cost of transport infrastructure per person in Scotland is almost double that for the whole UK.

Almost all transport infrastructure – roads, railways, stations, bridges and tunnels – are built and maintained using public funding. The vehicles and services that use this infrastructure are privately owned, either by individuals or companies. The main exception to this is Caledonian

MacBrayne which is owned by the Scottish government and operates ferries on the west coast to the islands.

The information in this section comes from Scottish Transport Statistics,[20] though some data on passenger and commuter journeys are sourced from the Scottish Household Survey.[21] Most comparisons are made with Great Britain or GB statistics because statistics for the whole UK are not always available.

Figure 2.9 shows the statistics on how people travel to work and school in Scotland. These are for passenger journeys and do not account for the distance travelled, which we'll look at later. For example, 11.2% of people say they usually take the bus to work.

The majority of people drive themselves to work, mostly with no passengers, and a quarter of people walk or take the bus. A much smaller number take the train or cycle. About half of journeys to school are on foot, with a quarter of them being by car, and a fifth by bus. Relatively few children take the train or cycle to school.

The number of pedal cycles on the road has risen by 15% in the five years to 2015–16. However numbers dropped by 7% between 2014–15 and 2015–16. Caution is required here as cycles make up less than 1% of road traffic and so the sample sizes are fairly small and statistical uncertainties relatively large.

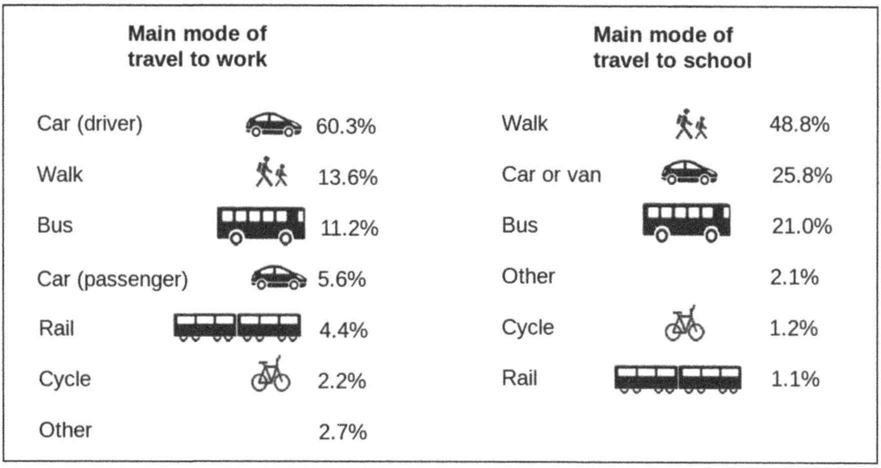

Main mode of travel to work			Main mode of travel to school		
Car (driver)		60.3%	Walk		48.8%
Walk		13.6%	Car or van		25.8%
Bus		11.2%	Bus		21.0%
Car (passenger)		5.6%	Other		2.1%
Rail		4.4%	Cycle		1.2%
Cycle		2.2%	Rail		1.1%
Other		2.7%			

Figure 2.9
Statistics on travelling to work and to school 2015.
Transport Scotland, Open Government License.

But travel in Scotland, as with many countries in the world, is dominated by road transport. Scotland has 7.9% of registered vehicles in GB whereas its total road length is 14.2% of GB's total. For comparison, 8.5% of GB's population is in Scotland. Between 1990 and 2014 the total length of roads in Scotland has increased by 8%, whereas the number of vehicles has increased by 58% from 1.8 to 2.8 million. If we take the average vehicle to be 5 m long, a little longer than most cars, but shorter than vans and lorries, then, ignoring lanes, all vehicles in Scotland in 2014 would fill 25% of its public road length. The figure for GB is even higher at 45%.

Figure 2.10 shows trends in travel within Scotland over the last decade. The data in this graph is indexed to make comparing trends easier. This means each value is divided by the value that the series had in 2005 and multiplied by 100. For example, there were 69 million journeys made by passengers on Scotrail in 2005, and 93 million in 2015. So, for example, to work out the index for 2015, you do this:

2015 Scotrail index = 93 divided by 69 = 135

Indexing is useful here because of the different scales involved, but caution is needed because indexing emphasises trends and conceals other aspects of the data: a glance at this graph may give the incorrect

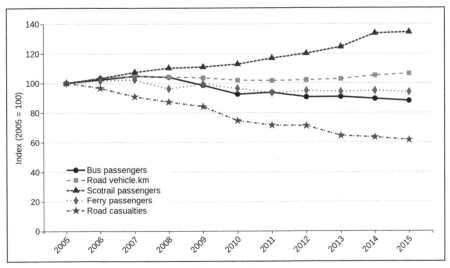

Figure 2.10
Indexed measures of passenger journeys, km driven by road
and road casualties 2005–2015.

impression that there were more rail journeys than any other. In actual fact, in 2015, there were 409 million passenger journeys by bus, but only 93 million on ScotRail and 7.8 million by ferry (all these journeys were within Scotland).

ScotRail's index is 135 in 2015 which means there has been a 35% increase since 2005. Bus and road transport rose by a few per cent between 2005 and 2008 but then fell in the following years to about 90% of its 2005 value. All forms of transports show effects that are likely due to the financial crisis, though for rail it merely slowed its growth for a couple of years.

The number of road casualties has fallen by 40% between 2005 and 2015 even though road vehicle use has risen by 6%. This suggests that road safety has benefited from improvements in technology and perhaps raised awareness of the dangers involved.

Figure 2.11 shows the number of terminal passengers for airports in Scotland and the UK. The numbers for the UK (right scale) are approximately ten times those for Scotland. Terminal passengers[22] are all those who board or leave an aircraft, including those transferring between aircraft at an airport.

There has been a dramatic increase in air passengers with both UK and Scotland numbers more than doubling since 1990. Although the UK's population is currently 12 times larger than Scotland's, the number of

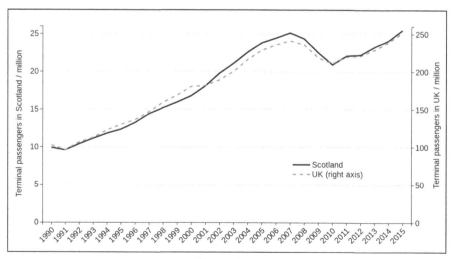

Figure 2.11
Numbers of air passengers for Scotland and the UK 1990–2015.

UK terminal passengers is, on average, 10 times that of Scotland. The obvious explanation for this is Scotland's relatively remote location from the population centres of Europe, including London.

The effect of the financial crisis is clear on this graph. The drop in passenger numbers between the peak year of 2007 and the low of 2010 was 17% for Scotland and 13% for the UK as a whole, and it was not until 2015 that the pre-crisis peak was exceeded.

Figure 2.12 shows the total tonnage of freight broken down into road, non-road and air. Note that the scale for air freight on the right is in *1,000s* of tonnes *carried* to and from Scottish airports, whereas road and non-road freight is stated in *millions* of tonnes of freight *lifted* within Scotland.

Data after 2012 for road and some non-road freight is not available. Also, the method of estimating road freight changed in 2004 and is probably the cause of the jump in values for that year.

Total freight shows no clear trend before 2007, after which it fell by 23% to its lowest point in 2010. Road freight makes up about 70% of all freight and so is responsible for many of the changes seen in total freight.

Air freight, which is negligible in terms of tonnage relative to all other methods, reached its maximum a year earlier in 2006 and dropped

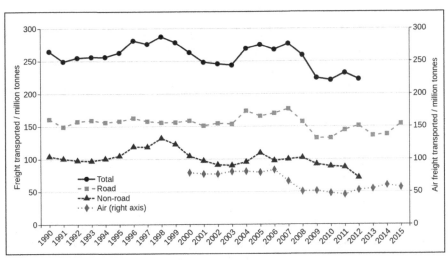

Figure 2.12
Tonnages for road, non-road transport, air and total freight 1990–2015.

sharply in both 2007 and 2008 eventually reaching its lowest point in 2011. Air freight is the only data set in this book that shows a fall in 2007 rather than 2008, a point which we'll return to later on.

Non-road freight in Figure 2.12 consists of

- pipeline – transport of crude oil products for 50 km or more over land
- coastwise shipping – freight lifted in Scotland destined for another UK port
- inland shipping – on lochs, rivers and canals
- rail – goods lifted within Scotland by freight trains

The decline in non-road freight in Figure 2.12 is mainly due to coastwise shipping which has halved since 1990. In contrast, rail freight tonnage nearly tripled from 1993 to 2005 but has since fallen to almost half its peak value. This fall is likely related to decreasing supplies to the large coal power stations of Cockenzie (closed 2013) and Longannet (closed 2016) which is also evidenced in Figure 2.4. Surprisingly, following the fall of coastwise shipping, pipelines are now the dominant form of non-road freight transportation in Scotland. The amount they carry has hardly changed since 1998 and Scotland makes up just over half of the GB total.

Internet

Internet usage in Scotland has been increasing steadily, as it has throughout the UK and in many other countries. Scottish Household Survey (SHS)[23] data shows that in 2005 just under 50% of households had access to the internet and this grew to 82% in 2016, and almost all of them – 98% – had broadband. Perhaps surprisingly, 86% of households in rural locations have access to the internet, though speeds are substantially slower than those available in urban centres. In areas classed as being in the bottom 20% of deprivation, 73% of households had internet access which compares to 85% in the rest of Scotland. According to the Office of National Statistics (ONS),[24] 89% of households in Great Britain had internet access in 2016.

Figure 2.13 shows the percentages of households with internet access in eight net income bands. Here net means after tax is deducted and benefits are added. Median household net income for 2016 in Scotland was £24,400 meaning that half of households have a higher income than this and half less (see Chapter 3).

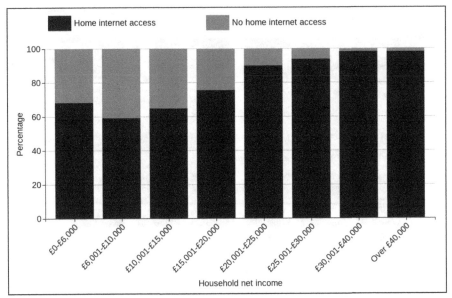

Figure 2.13

Household internet access percentages by net income 2016.

Internet access increases with income and is 98% in the top two income bands on this graph. The lowest income band includes students and that is the likely explanation of why its percentage is higher than the second lowest band. The gap between the lowest and highest income bands has dropped substantially from 67pp (percentage points) in 2007 to 30pp in 2016.

Levels of internet access can also be assessed according to SIMD – the Scottish Index of Multiple Deprivation.[25] SIMD splits Scotland up into 6,976 small areas, each with typically 800 people, and combines a number of measures of deprivation, such as income, health and education, to rank the area from 1 (least deprived) to 6,976 (most deprived). Household internet access is 73% in areas in the bottom 20% of deprivation, which compares to 85% in the rest of Scotland. We'll discuss SIMD further in Chapter 4.

In addition to a question on the household internet, the Scottish Household Survey (until 2015) also asked a randomly selected adult in the household about how often they used the internet. Figure 2.14 shows how frequently people of different ages use the internet. There was no significant difference in internet usage between males and females.

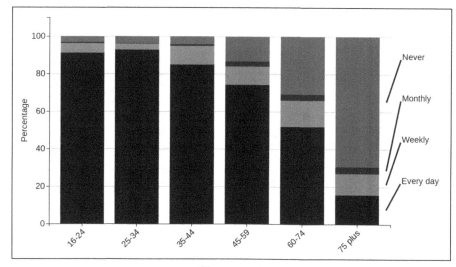

Figure 2.14
Usage frequency of the internet by age in 2015.

Over 95% of those under 45 use the internet, and this drops to 87% in the 45–59 bracket. About two thirds of those aged 60–74 and a third of those aged 75+ use the internet. The majority of internet users in any age group say they use it daily.

Some thoughts

The internet is the newest technology discussed in this chapter and so has seen the biggest changes in recent years. This so-called information revolution brings with it efficiencies that can benefit people's lives and the economy: meetings can be conducted online and information can be searched for and retrieved in a few clicks. These have particular benefits for Scotland given its peripheral geographic position in Europe and its low population density. It is without doubt easier to operate certain types of businesses from remote locations, such as the highlands and islands, than it was a decade or two ago.

There are, of course, some downsides, such as loss of in-person contact, and an increase in potential distractions. But when you look at the immense changes brought about by the industrial revolution over the last 200 years, it's clear that the full effect of a new technology, such as rail travel or electricity, can take decades to be realised in society. We are probably still in the early stages of the information revolution and its effects on a new generation are only just starting to manifest themselves.

The rise of wind power over the last decade is dramatic, but it is not the first time that renewable energy has been capitalised on Scotland's favourable geography. The previous such example was when Tom Johnston, journalist and later Labour MP, and Secretary of State for Scotland during the Second World War, created the North of Scotland Hydro-Electric Board and developed it in the post-war period. Its legacy continues today, providing a relatively small but stable renewable baseload (Figure 2.5). The name Scottish Hydro-Electric continues as a brand in Scotland within Scottish and Southern Energy plc. Although radical changes to the local landscape were not always welcome at the time, the reservoirs, dams and power stations are often appreciated by walkers and tourists today.

But both these mini-revolutions are dwarfed by the industrial revolution that was primarily driven by the unleashing of coal as an energy source. The technological advances of the 18th and 19th centuries that made this possible did not, for the most part, arise in traditional seats of learning such as universities, instead they came from the likes of Richard Trevithick in Cornwall, George Stephenson in the North East of England, Matthew Boulton in Birmingham and of course James Watt in Glasgow. What these pioneers had in common was that they worked in places where natural resources of coal and iron were plentiful, and they solved the engineering problems associated with mining and trans-porting these raw materials.

The industrial revolution shaped our cities and we still rely on much Victorian infrastructure and even value it aesthetically. The elegant, iron bulk of the Forth Bridge is a prime example and has been designated by UNESCO as a World Heritage Site. Its reassuringly solid appearance is no accident as it was built with the memory of the 1879 Tay Bridge collapse fresh in the public mind.

The coal and oil that fed factories, power stations and locomotives and created our modern way of life came from ancient life. Over millions of years flora and fauna died and their carbon-rich corpses became the rich seams of energy that the industrial revolution consumed. But burning these fuels involves combining their carbon with the oxygen in our atmosphere which produces the gas carbon dioxide. In the space of a 100 years or so we have taken carbon deposits that were built up over millions of years and exhausted them through chimneys into the atmosphere.

Not a word of the last paragraph is disputed (except perhaps by people who believe in a flat Earth, or believe that it was formed only a few thousand years ago, but they have their own books to read). The next step, to say that we have altered our climate by increasing levels of carbon dioxide and other greenhouse gases is challenged by some, so I feel it is important to explain why I believe there is good reason and evidence to take the matter seriously.

First, a simple argument on well-established principles of science shows that without the greenhouse effect the Earth would have an average global temperature well below the freezing point of water. Gases such as carbon dioxide, which together make up less than 1% of our atmosphere, punch far above their weight. Like the panes of glass of a greenhouse, such gases are transparent to the energy-laden sunlight that arrives at the Earth but opaque to infrared radiation emitted by the Earth's surface. This means that the greenhouse gases in effect form a blanket around the Earth keeping its surface and atmosphere at a temperature at which life on Earth, at least most life as we know it, can thrive.

The temperature of the Earth is very sensitive to changes in the small fraction of gas in the atmosphere that causes the greenhouse effect. The consensus of most scientists, many of whom have dedicated their working lives to understanding the climate (note, not simply proving global warming) is that global temperatures are rising and that this is caused by a rise in carbon dioxide levels. The most likely explanation for the carbon dioxide rise is that we humans have been burning fossil fuels for the last 200 years or so.

Now, it is possible that the scientific consensus is wrong, and there is historical precedent for scientists getting together *en masse* and collectively fooling themselves. A belief in the steady state theory of the universe in the mid-20th century being one example, and the initial rejection of Darwin's natural selection in the 19th century being another. Scientists are, after all, humans. But these cases are exceptions to the rule, and when a consensus did prove to be incorrect, it was eventually demolished by evidence carefully collected by a new generation of scientists. (Think-tanks with opaque funding from wealthy organisations with vested interests were not involved.)

My own view, that I took years to arrive at, is that the evidence for human-induced global warming is solid and that I am willing to trust the scientific consensus that has been well documented in many international reports written and reviewed by scientists.[26] I do not know with 100% certainty it is correct, but believe on balance it is more likely true than not. Even if you hold the opposite view, you must at least entertain an element of doubt. Given the consequences of global warming, most notably the rise in sea levels, perhaps even that doubt should be enough to prompt you to support action. Consider, for example, whether you would cross a road if the chance of survival was 95%. Most people, once they understand what that percentage means, would see that risk as too great.

In this context the move to renewables in Scotland is welcome, and even if its impact on the *global* issue of warming is small, it may serve as an example to follow. But it is not without problems. Part of the reason Scotland can contemplate a target of 100% of consumption being from renewables, and most of that from wind, is because it can depend on the GB grid during times when demand is high but the wind does not blow or the rain has not fallen in sufficient quantities to fill hydroelectric reservoirs. Such weather conditions are rare, but they can occur, and have mostly recently in 2010. In other words, Scotland still relies on non-renewable power stations elsewhere on the GB grid. This problem is likely transitional and can be solved in time with improved technology, particularly in storage.

The next expansion of wind generation looks likely to involve larger turbines (some with blade diameters similar to that of the London Eye), that are sited offshore. As offshore wind blows more consistently than onshore wind this, together with storage improvements is likely to make wind generation across the grid less sensitive to periods of low wind. Whereas Scotland has led on onshore wind generation, development of offshore wind has mainly taken place in other parts of Britain. This is in good part due to Scotland's more lively weather and rugged coastal geography, but such challenges can also be addressed with technological innovation.

Underlying the infrastructure for networks of energy, water, transport and, most recently, the internet, is human progress in technology. A look back at history doesn't suggest that this is directly under any one government's control. Far from it. Take the World Wide Web for example. Tim Berners-Lee, who created it, was a CERN employee, and CERN is a multi-government funded body concerned with experimental nuclear and particle physics. And the web relies on the internet which grew out of a project funded by US Government's Department of Defense. What history does tell us is that, as Tom Johnston did with hydroelectric power in the post-war period, governments can create large job-creating projects for the long-term public good, as well as providing a fertile environment for private companies to innovate and grow, as is currently happening, at least to an extent, with wind generation.

Questions to ponder:

- To what extent should we rely on a wider energy distribution network involving the GB national grid and interconnectors to overseas?
- Is it a problem if wind electricity generation continues its rapid rise with our baseload being provided by generation outside Scotland, possibly from non-renewable sources?
- How do we balance the economic and tax revenue rewards of fossil fuel extraction, be it North Sea or from fracking, against environmental concerns including that of global warming?
- Scotland's low population density (see Chapter 1) means that transport, energy and internet infrastructure spending per person will be higher than other countries, but to what extent should that be centrally funded, both within Scotland or the UK (see Chapter 5)?
- Given decades of rising car ownership, have we run out of capacity on the roads, and should we prioritise non-road methods of passenger and rail travel?
- Does the example of Scottish Water suggest we should bring other essential public utilities, such as electricity, rail travel or internet provision into public ownership?

Chapter 3
Poverty and inequality

3

Samuel Johnson once said 'a decent provision for the poor is the true test of civilization'. Johnson is most famous for his dictionary, but he is also remembered for his connections to Scotland, which extend beyond his portrayal by Robbie Coltrane in Blackadder. In 1773 he travelled to Scotland to visit his friend James Boswell who later wrote about their experiences in a book entitled *A Journey to the Western Islands of Scotland*. Johnson, who had rarely left London, had expected to find a primitive and perhaps unspoilt land, and although reality confirmed some of his preconceptions, he was also intrigued by the differences in the society he found, and was moved by the experience of visiting a unique college for the deaf and mute in Edinburgh. Then, as now, the differences in society between Scotland and London, particularly regarding poverty and inequality, are more nuanced than popular perceptions.

People from a wide spectrum of political and moral beliefs can approve of Johnson's statement about the poor according to how they interpret 'provision'. There is considerably less agreement on how such provision should be achieved nor on what levels of poverty and inequality are acceptable.

Poverty and inequality are of course related. No one wishes for a perfectly equal society where everyone is poor, but some might accept a very unequal society in which there is no poverty. Others might look at that same society and say that there is *relative* poverty and that it matters because it is unjust. In this way, the debate is necessarily moral.

An important technical point is to distinguish between inequalities of income and wealth. **Income** describes the rate at which a person (or household) earns assets in a given amount of time, usually a year, whereas **wealth** refers to the value of assets held at a particular point in time. In this sense you can regard wealth as the accumulation of many years of previous income.

For the majority of people income is money earned from being in employment. State benefits are not just given to the unemployed, but form a significant part of the income of the lowest paid in society. For the richest people, income from employment can be paid in both money and shares, and they'll likely receive income from their accrued wealth, and see it rise if values of shares or property increase. Inheritance is also a significant source of wealth, especially for children inheriting their parents' homes. At the very top end of the wealth distribution, income from work can be negligible next to the returns on wealth and what is inherited from previous generations.

Tax and benefits serve to redistribute income. A consequence of this is that, in order for the state to collect tax and decide who should receive benefits, it must collect information on each individual's income. For this reason we have relatively good data on how income is distributed. In contrast, there are fewer taxes on wealth, so data on it is much more uncertain. The wealthy are also able to optimise their taxation, legally or otherwise, often by taking advantage of differing tax regimes between countries.

The question of what kind of society we want, and how we wish to treat the poor, and what freedoms people ought to have to lead fulfilling lives, are moral ones. There can be no simple agreement on these matters, but political discourse can, and has, established compromises that are tolerable to most people, and produced solutions to the technical issues of setting tax rates and benefit levels. In this chapter I wish to present a picture of poverty and inequality and its recent history that will, I hope, help you judge the situation for yourself and decide what, if anything, ought to be done about it.

Income
The Scottish government publishes an annual report called Poverty and Income Inequality in Scotland[1] from which data here is taken. This draws on UK-wide data collected for the Housing Below Average Income (HBAI) report[2] published by the UK government's Department for Work and Pensions (DWP). Unless otherwise stated, we'll deal with income after tax is deducted and benefits are added, and work with financial years.

The average household income in Scotland in 2015–16 was £24,400 per year or £468 per week. The measure of average used here is the **median**. By definition, half the households have an income above the median, and the other half have an income below it.

You might wonder why the median is used rather than the more familiar average which professional statisticians call the **mean**. (In everyday usage, the word 'average' is often taken to mean 'mean', but I won't dwell on this potential confusion as that would be mean.) The mean would be calculated by adding up all household incomes and dividing by the number of households. The problem with the mean is that a few people in the population with very large incomes will tend to increase the mean and give us a misleadingly high value. For example, imagine a group of three people that earn £10,000, £20,000 and £1,000,000. The median of this group is £20,000 but the mean would be £343,333.

Rather than just divide the population into two halves as we do with a median, we can divide it up into ten groups, called deciles. The 10% of the population who have the lowest incomes are said to be in the first income decile, then the next 10% are in the second income decile and so on.

Figure 3.1 shows the income deciles for 2015–16.

Each block represents 10% of the Scottish population – about 540,000 people – but the income assigned to an individual is not simply their own income but is related to their household's income. If this wasn't done then, to give just one example, children would all have zero income and be in the first decile even if they lived in affluent households. We'll come back to how differing households are dealt with later on.

To appreciate what this chart is showing us, take a look at the lower bar which is for *Before housing costs*. The first decile, which is shown on the far left, represents the 10% of the population with the lowest incomes.

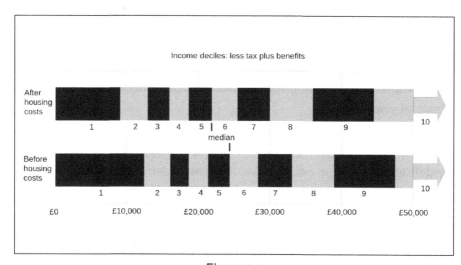

Figure 3.1
Income deciles for 2015–16.

To be in this group your income needs to be less than £12,500 a year after tax is deducted and state benefits are included. The upper bar is for *After housing costs* – this lowers the first decile's threshold to £9,100 a year.

The tenth decile, on the far right, represents the 10% of the population with the highest incomes. The arrow indicates that there is no upper limit to decile 10. In fact, if we kept the same scale and tried to represent the small number of individuals with the highest incomes in Scotland then we'd probably need a page 50 metres wide. If we extended it to the highest incomes in the world then the page might have to be more than a kilometre in width. But, in truth, it's very hard to discover what the incomes are for the super-wealthy, and they might not even know themselves.

Before housing costs, the upper limit of decile 5 is at £24,400. This is the median we mentioned above: half the population have incomes below this and the other half have higher incomes. After housing costs, as shown on the upper bar, the median falls to £21,900.

You might be wondering which decile you are in. But, you'll only get the right answer if you live with a partner and have no children. This is because the data is collected per household and then converted by a Dr Who-esque-sounding process called **equivalisation** to a standard of a household with a couple and no children. This allows for a more meaningful comparison of living standards between households. For example, a family of two adults and three children will require a higher income than a household with just one pensioner to sustain a similar standard in living.

To get a feeling for what equivalisation involves, take a look at the medians before housing costs for a few types of Scottish households shown in Table 3.1.

Guided by such information, equivalisation would not simply double a one adult's household income to make it equivalent to a two adult household, but would increase it by 50%, that is, multiply it by 1.5. Similarly, to equivalise a four person household consisting of a couple with two children their household income would be reduced by less than a factor of 2; with reference to the above table, it would be divided by 2.3 and multiplied by 1.5.

	Median annual income	Factor above one adult, no children
One adult, no children	£16,300	1.0
Couple, no children	**£24,400**	**1.5**
One adult, children aged 5 & 14	£29,300	1.8
Couple, children aged 5 & 14	£37,300	2.3

Table 3.1

Median income by household type for 2015–16.

The point highlighted by these figures is that sharing a household reduces living costs per person. There are several reasons for this, but most obviously, rent and mortgage costs do not depend on how many people live within a given house, and grocery shopping in bulk brings economies of scale.

If you want to know which decile you are in, then look at Tables 1 and 2 in Chapter 2 of the Scottish government's above-mentioned Poverty and Income Inequality report, or you can use an online tool provided by the Office of National Statistics[3] or the Institute for Fiscal Studies[4] to find your place in the whole UK.

Some caution is required. Households in the lower deciles are not necessarily poorer households. Even though equivalising adjusts for some factors that link income to a standard of living, there are others that it doesn't address. Compare, for instance, a household with a single young adult who has commuting costs and a mortgage to pay with a household with a retired pensioner who lives alone in a home owned without a mortgage. The pensioner will have lower outgoings and so for the same household income could well enjoy a substantially higher standard of living than the young adult.

To summarise income inequality we can divide the deciles into three groups: lowest incomes (1,2,3); the middle incomes (4,5,6,7); and richest (8,9,10). The history of percentages of total income going to these three groups in Scotland is shown in Figure 3.2, though the Poverty and Income Inequality in Scotland report does not include such data beyond 2013–14.

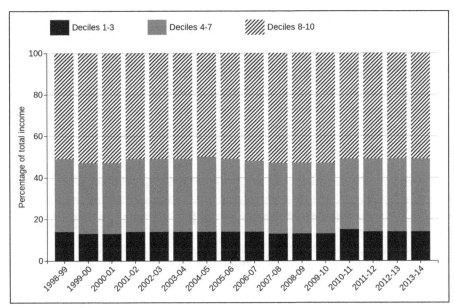

Figure 3.2

Percentage of total income by decile group for from 1998–99 to 2013–14.

What this tells us is that if we were to add up everyone's income (after tax and benefits), then, in 2013–14, the 30% of the population with the lowest incomes receive only 14% of this total, but the top 30% by income get 51% of it. The middle 40% get 35%. The inequality is obvious, but what's also remarkable is how little inequality appears to have changed over these years.

But, it turns out that expressing inequality in terms of percentages of total income provides a measure which is very insensitive to change (in fact, this can be shown mathematically). Worse still, it hides some important changes in people's incomes.

Perhaps for such reasons, the Poverty and Income Inequality report no longer offers data such as shown in Figure 3.2 but instead provides two alternative measures of inequality. The first is the **Palma ratio** which is used to monitor progress towards the Scottish government's enigmatically named Solidarity Purpose Target.[5] The Palma ratio is defined as the income of the top 10% divided by that of the bottom 40%. For example, the ratio for 2015–16 is 1.38 which means the top 10% earned 38% more than the bottom 40%.

The **Gini index** is better known but has a more intricate mathematical definition and so is harder to understand intuitively. It is zero for perfect equality in which all people earn the same, and 100 for complete inequality where one lucky person receives all the income. Countries in Africa and South America have the greatest inequality with Gini indices exceeding 60. Scandinavian and eastern European countries have the lowest inequality with Gini indices in the mid-20s.

Figure 3.3 shows the history of both measures in Scotland.

The two measures show similar changes: a ramping up of inequality in the years before 2008–09, and a sharp fall in inequality after the financial crisis. Both remained roughly constant for five years before they increased in 2015–16.

Scotland's Gini values are amongst the lowest in the world with the index remaining stable in the low 30s for the last couple of decades. The UK's Gini index is generally a little higher than Scotland's, most likely because of a minority of very high incomes in London, but shows much the same trends.[6]

Summarising inequality in one number is problematic. For example, we cannot tell what is behind the fall post-2008 or the rise in 2015–16. For the latter, did higher earners do well in 2015–16 or did low earners

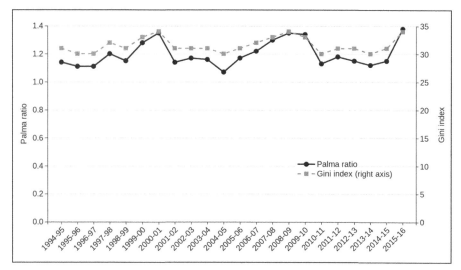

Figure 3.3
Palma and Gini measures of income inequality 1994–95 to 2015–16.

lose out? Although the Palma ratio has the clearer meaning, it would hide an increase where the bottom 40% and top 10% both saw the same proportionate change. If, for example, both groups saw their incomes increase by a quarter, the Palma ratio would remain unchanged. And this lack of change would also conceal the important fact that the gain for the higher earners would be much larger in absolute terms. A better approach is to look at decile boundaries.

Figure 3.4 shows the upper limits for the 3rd and 7th income deciles which are the two boundaries that divide the population into the three groups shown in Figure 3.2. It also shows the median – the upper limit of the 5th decile. The figures are *real* in that they are adjusted for inflation to be in 2015–16 prices.

Figure 3.4 shows us what the income shares in Figure 3.2 and the indices in Figure 3.3 conceal: that incomes rose steadily until the 2008 financial crisis and then fell with a slight recovery taking place thereafter.

Annual incomes for all these deciles over the last two decades have risen by more than £5,000. To be clear, this data *is corrected for inflation.*

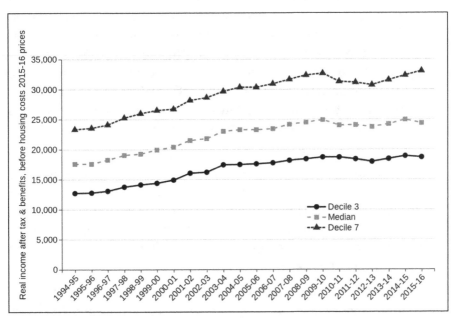

Figure 3.4
Decile boundaries of annual income from 1994–95 to 2015–16.

In other words, a typical household in any of these deciles in 2015–16 had over £5,000 extra in income compared to one in 1994–95 – an income growth of 40% or more. At the 3rd decile boundary, there was a 47% growth in income, and a 40% growth at the 7th decile boundary.

So although higher income groups did experience a larger rise than lower income groups in absolute terms – £9,700 for decile 7 against £6,000 for decile 3 – the lower incomes benefited the most in percentage terms – 47% against 40%. So depending on how you choose to measure inequality you can claim that inequality both increased and decreased slightly.

It's worth looking at the effect of the recession since 2008. Incomes peaked in 2009–10 and fell in following years, though the fall for the 3rd decile was the smallest in both absolute and percentage terms. The fall continued in all groups until a slight recovery began from the low of 2012–13 but only decile 7 saw this continue in 2015–16.

The reason that the recession reduced higher incomes the most is because a significant proportion of income in the first three deciles is from state benefits and these are not directly affected by the recession, unlike wages from employment. Government changes to the welfare system with the introduction of Universal Credit have not gone smoothly and this could be part of the reason why income in lower deciles fell in 2015–16, though it does not obviously explain the fall in median income. A more concerning problem is that from the start of 2016–17 benefits will be frozen and not rise with inflation. This did not seem problematic when CPI inflation was low, being only 0.3% in April 2016, but in 2017 inflation rose to about 3.0%. This will almost certainly cause incomes to fall for those in the lowest deciles that rely on benefits.

People on higher incomes tend to save a greater proportion of their income than those on lower incomes, and those on the lowest incomes are likely to save little or nothing, or, as we'll see shortly, end up in overall debt. As such, a fall in income may have a substantial impact on the standard of living afforded by people in the bottom deciles, whereas it might have no effect on people in upper deciles other than reducing the rate at which they save.

Despite post-crisis problems, it remains true that real incomes are substantially higher now than they were 20 years or more ago. But there are two crucial caveats to the apparently happy story of increasing income. The first and more important is that the plight of the very poorest is hidden inside the first decile. Remember each decile is 10% of the population, and so each one represents 540,000 people. To understand poverty we'll need to look more closely at those inside the first and also second deciles, which we'll do in the next section.

The second caveat is similar, in that there is a class of very rich people at the top of the tenth decile. For the top 1%, and particularly the top 0.1%, we can expect some of their incomes to be missing from the kind of data we are looking at here for reasons mentioned at the start of this chapter. In fact, to understand such incomes it's necessary to look beyond any one country. If you're interested in understanding more about this then I recommend reading *Capital in the Twenty-First Century* by Thomas Piketty.[7]

Perception of change

Some people express scepticism that almost everyone has seen their income rise in real terms over the last 20 years, even despite the recent recession. But the evidence for it is clear, and can be expressed in one short statement: real median household income after taxes are deducted and benefits are added has increased by just over 40% in the last two decades.

If this still surprises you, possibly because it jars with public perception expressed in traditional and online media, then there is an explanation. Our intuition fails in appreciating the effect of slow growth over long time periods. An annual growth rate of 1.7% may seem fairly modest, but over 20 years this would lead to an increase of 40% (1.017 raised to the power 20). In fact, economic growth in GDP has exceeded 1.7% per year, but not all gains in GDP go to household income and also the number of households has grown too.

The psychology associated with gains and losses is complex. On the one hand, people tend to judge how they are faring against their peers. This means that the steady rise in incomes was probably under-appreciated *because* almost everyone benefited from it. Also, people tend to feel greater displeasure at a loss than they would feel pleasure from an equal gain. For this reason, and because it was more rapid, the post-2008 income drop was felt more acutely than the overall gain in real incomes over the last 20 years or more.

Poverty

There are two main measures used to track poverty in Scotland and throughout the UK and both are based on income. One is called **relative poverty** and the other is **absolute poverty**. In both cases, an individual is deemed to be in poverty if their household income is below a certain amount, often referred to as the threshold.

The relative poverty threshold is, as the name suggests, set relative to the rest of the population that year, and so it can change every year. In contrast, absolute poverty is defined using a threshold that does not change each year, but is revised every five years or so. Unfortunately, 'absolute' is a bit of a misnomer because absolute poverty is still set relative to a threshold; 'real-terms relative poverty' would be a better name.

It may help to draw an analogy. Imagine ten competitors in a race on a running track. You could define a runner's performance as poor if they finish in eighth, ninth or tenth place. This is like relative poverty. But, you could instead define a runner's performance as poor if they failed to beat the time of whoever came seventh in last year's race. This is like absolute poverty.

The precise definitions are as follows. An individual is living in **relative poverty** if they live in a household with an equivalised income of less than 60% of the median income for that year. An individual is classed as being in **absolute poverty** if their household has an equivalised income less than 60% of the inflation-adjusted median for 2010–11. Both measures are stated *before* and *after* housing costs – **BHC** and **AHC**.

Table 3.2 shows the thresholds below which households are classed as being in poverty according to these measures. The poverty rate is the percentage of the population below the relevant threshold.

As before, the threshold is equivalised to be for a household with two adults and no children. According to these measures one in five people in Scotland is classed as living in some kind of poverty. Poverty numbers are higher for AHC measures suggesting that housing costs are a significant factor in poverty.

The reason that the relative poverty thresholds are slightly larger than the absolute ones is that median incomes have risen faster than inflation since 2010–11. But the fact that the relative poverty rates are

Measure	Threshold	Number of people	rate (% of population)
Relative BHC	£15,000	880,000	17%
Relative AHC	£12,900	1,050,000	20%
Absolute BHC	£14,500	780,000	15%
Absolute AHC	£12,400	960,000	18%

Table 3.2
Poverty statistics for 2015–16.

higher than absolute poverty rates tell us that incomes of lower deciles have failed to do so. A check of the underlying data confirms this: in real terms, incomes in the first decile have fallen by 3.2% since 2010–11 whereas median income has increased by 1.5%.

Table 3.3 tells us about relative poverty in three broad age groups for 2015–16. Working age adults are all those who are 18 years old or over but below the state pension age, which is 65 for men and was 60 for women up until April 2010. After that the female state pension age rose to 63 and by November 2018 it will be 65.

Bear in mind that an individual is classed as being in poverty if their household is in poverty, so, for example, the first row of the table says that 19% of children live in a household classed as being in relative poverty before housing costs.

Relative poverty rates *before* housing costs are the same for working age adults and pensioners at 16% but slightly higher for children at 19%.

In relative poverty	Before housing costs	After housing costs	Gap
% of children (under 18)	19%	26%	7pp
% of working age adults	16%	20%	4pp
% of pensioners	16%	13%	-3pp
% of population	17%	20%	3pp

Table 3.3
Poverty rates by broad age group 2015–16.

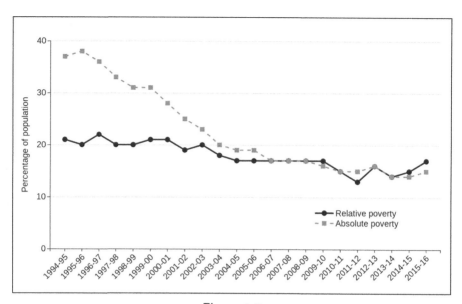

Figure 3.5
Relative and absolute poverty after housing costs
(AHC) 1994–95 to 2015–16.

However, *after* housing costs, the pensioner poverty percentage drops to 13% and is significantly smaller than that for working age adults, and is half the percentage for children. Pensioners are more likely to have reduced housing costs either because they own their home without a mortgage, or they have downsized.

Figure 3.5 shows the percentages of the population in relative and absolute poverty after housing costs during the last 20 years.

The absolute poverty percentage halves in the first ten years. This is telling us people were moving out of poverty because incomes increased faster than inflation.

Relative poverty shows a more gradual drop over the two decades, which tells us that people on lower incomes were slowly moving closer to the median. This means that income inequality was lessening, at least for those in the bottom half of the income distribution.

Figure 3.6 shows how the difference in poverty rates for before and after housing costs has varied. The stepped appearance of these graphs is because poverty rates are published rounded to the nearest per cent

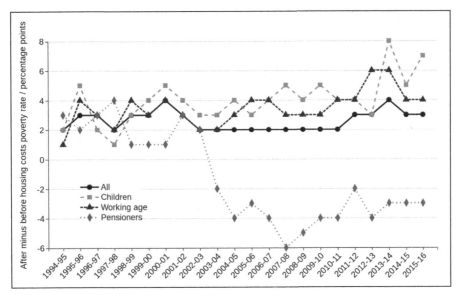

Figure 3.6
After housing costs minus before housing costs relative poverty
rates 1994–95 to 2015–16.

which is reasonable because the statistical uncertainty on them is typically 3 or 4 percentage points (pp).

The relative poverty rate after housing costs is generally a few percentage points (pp) higher than that for before housing costs and the difference has mostly remained stable over the last 20 years. The rise in recent years is worth noting but may be due to statistical fluctuations. The evident change for pensioners that started in the early 2000s is statistically significant, however (see above). They are the only group to show a negative gap. The AHC-BHC gap for absolute poverty rates show much the same patterns for all age groups.

If an individual, child or adult, is living in a household that is in relative poverty, and at least one adult is working, then the individual is said to be in **in-work poverty**. Of working age adults that are in relative poverty in 2015–16, 62% of them are also in in-work poverty. Of children, this figure is 66%. The AHC percentages are a little higher at 64% and 70% respectively. Since 1998–99, the adult figure did not change significantly until 2013–14 but has risen in recent years. The percentage for children has increased by about 20pp. The situation with in-work poverty is worth bearing in mind when looking at recent employment rates, which are discussed in chapter 6.

Figure 3.7 shows the relative in-work poverty rate after housing costs for working age adults and children. Remember that these percentages are not of all households, but of households classed as being in relative poverty after housing costs.

From 2013–14 there was a pronounced increase for both *Children* and *Working age* in-work poverty, though there was a much slower rising trend beforehand that is somewhat obscured by the expected statistical fluctuations. Since 1998–99, in-work poverty has risen by 15pp for working age adults and by 25pp for children. This, taken together with less dramatic increases in overall poverty rates, suggests that there is a generational divide opening up, with the incomes of younger households with children failing to keep pace with those of older households, especially those of pensioners.

Figure 3.8 shows data from the Institute of Fiscal Studies[8] which compares rates of absolute poverty before housing costs amongst UK nations and regions around the time of the 2008 financial crisis. Figure 3.9 shows the same data but for after housing costs.

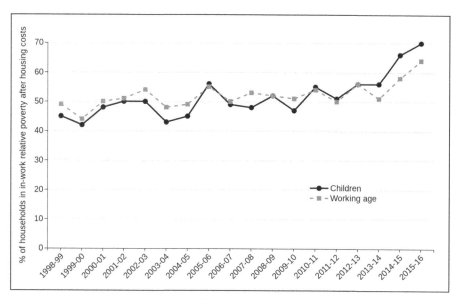

Figure 3.7
In-work relative poverty rates 1998–99 to 2015–16.

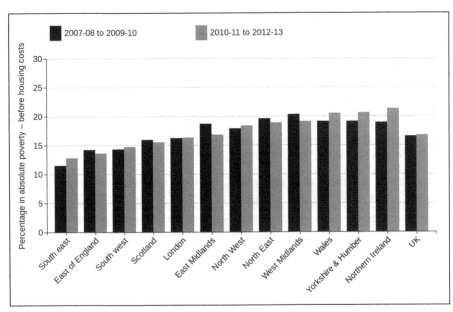

Figure 3.8
Changes in absolute poverty rates across the UK following
the financial crisis – before housing costs (BHC).

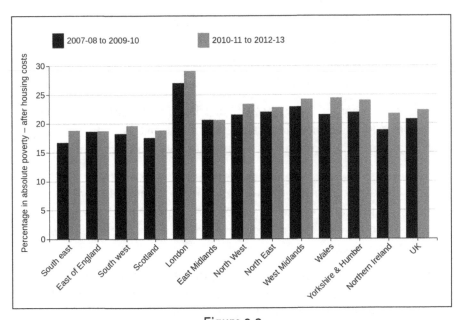

Figure 3.9
Changes in absolute poverty rates across the UK following
the financial crisis – after housing costs (AHC).

These graphs show that Scotland has one of the lowest rates of absolute poverty before housing costs. After housing costs, its poverty rate is, within statistical uncertainties, the same as those for the southern regions of England, including the South east.

Rates for AHC poverty are typically several percentage points higher than those for BHC. Northern Ireland is notable as it shows the smallest difference between the two. London shows by far the highest rates of absolute poverty AHC, even though it is similar to Scotland in BHC.

The change in absolute poverty BHC between the two time ranges has no particular pattern throughout the UK. The whole UK showed a small 0.2pp increase in poverty whereas Scotland showed a larger decrease in poverty of 0.4pp, though neither is likely to be statistically significant. In contrast, AHC poverty increased in every nation and region, with Scotland's increase of 1.4pp being similar to that of the whole UK's 1.6pp.

International poverty

Poverty where families starve, have no shelter or access to medical care or education is all but consigned to history in Scotland, and throughout the UK. Of course, this is not true of every country in the world. Items such as a toothbrush or a bicycle, regarded as unremarkable and every day in Scotland, would be transformative to some families living in the poorest countries.

The United Nations 1995 definition of **absolute poverty** is:

> A condition characterised by severe deprivation of basic human needs, including food, safe drinking water, sanitation facilities, health, shelter, education and information. It depends not only on income but also on access to services.

This is obviously a much more severe form of poverty that the UK's definition of the same name. It is often associated with the World Bank's income-based definition[9] of **extreme poverty**: an adult living on less than $1.90 per day.

This amount is not in US dollars but in **purchasing power parity dollars (PPP)** that are stated in 2011 prices. The PPP system accounts for the fact that prices of common goods and services in a richer country tend to be higher than those in a poorer country. For example, a loaf of bread that costs $1 in the USA may cost the equivalent of $0.50 in Rupees in India.

Using PPP conversion factors from the World Bank[10] and the CPI inflation measure[11] as used in the UK's definition of absolute poverty, this can be equated to about £2.70 per day in 2015–16 UK prices. The threshold for Scotland's absolute poverty in 2015–16, before housing costs, is £14,400, which divided by 365 gives £40 per day. This is for a household of two adults, so according to Table 3.1 we need to divide by 1.5 to obtain the amount per person amount, giving us £25.

So, in summary, the international definition of extreme poverty is equivalent to £2.70 per day in the UK, and the UK's definition of absolute poverty is £25 per day, about *nine times* higher.

Scotland, and the whole of the UK, is very much richer than countries with high levels of extreme poverty, such as those in sub-Saharan Africa. For example, the UK's gross national income per person[12] is about 15 times that of Cameroon (in 2011 PPP dollars) where a third of the population lives in extreme poverty.

Poorer countries where many individuals have to live on low incomes are also likely to lack provision of healthcare, education and justice. For this reason, it's important to remember that poverty cannot be reduced to a simple numerical comparison, but must be defined in terms of access to vital services as is done in the above UN definition.

Wealth

The Wealth and Assets Survey in Scotland[13] provides data on the wealth of households between 2006 and 2014. This data is drawn from the GB-wide survey conducted by the Office for National Statistics (ONS). Scotland's islands were not included in the survey's sample, nor is the area north of the Caledonian Canal.

Figure 3.10 shows how broad categories of wealth have changed in recent years. The data is split into four two-year periods: July 2006 to June 2008; July 2008 to June 2010; July 2010 to June 2012; July 2012 to June 2014. The figures are adjusted for inflation to be in 2015 prices using the CPIH index.

The four components of wealth are defined as:

- *Private pension wealth* is that in occupational pension schemes with employee contributions.
- *Physical wealth* is the value of cars, household goods, electronic devices, jewellery and other material possessions.

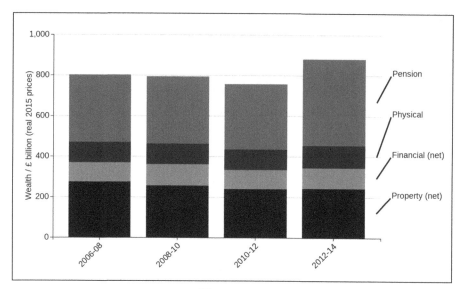

Figure 3.10
Changes in wealth by broad type 2006–14.

- *Financial wealth (net)* is the total of financial assets less the value of non-property related debt.
- *Property wealth (net)* is the value of property less debt secured on property, typically mortgages.

Notice that financial and property wealth are both defined as differences and so are described as 'net'. This means that these can be negative due to debt. In the case where a mortgage exceeds the value of the property this is referred to as negative equity.

Over this whole time range, total wealth increased by 10% in real terms and this was mainly driven by a 29% increase in *Private pension wealth*. *Physical wealth* and *Financial wealth (net)* both saw increases of just under 10%, but *Property wealth (net)* fell by 12%.

Almost all the increase in wealth took place between 2010–12 and 2012–14 and is likely related to the UK's central bank (The Bank of England) creating £375 billion in its Quantitative Easing programme during 2008 to 2012.[14] This had the effect of increasing the value of assets such as government bonds and company shares that are held in wealth funds, particularly private pension funds.

In 2012–14, the median net wealth of Scottish households was £186,500 (half of households have more, the other half less). Due to property prices being higher in London and the Southeast of England, the GB median is somewhat higher at £225,000.

Figure 3.11 shows the household wealth owned by the ten deciles for each two-year period. Each decile represents 10% of the population (about 540,000 people). Bear in mind, as explained previously for income, that measuring inequality using shares of wealth can hide some important trends.

The inequality in wealth is clear: the first decile owns near zero wealth whereas the tenth decile owns more than double that of any other decile. In 2006–08 the top decile owned 48% of the wealth but this has dropped to 43% in 2012–14. Wealth inequality for the whole of GB shows a similar pattern.

Household wealth shows much greater inequality than household income. For income in 2013–14, shown in Figure 3.2, the top 30% received 51% of the total, and the bottom 30% received 14%. For wealth shown in Figure 3.11 for 2012–14, the top 30% (deciles 8 to 10) own 75% of the wealth, and the bottom 30% (deciles 1 to 3) about 2%.

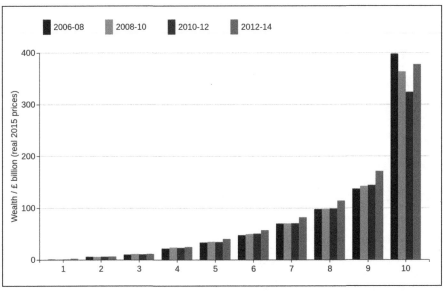

Figure 3.11
Changes in household wealth held by deciles 2006–14.

It's important to realise that the deciles for wealth and income are distinct. For example, it is not the case that the 10% of the population in the top decile for income are also in the top decile for wealth. A pensioner living in a home for which the mortgage is paid off may be in a high decile for wealth, but a lower decile for income.

Figure 3.11 shows that the only decile to experience a significant drop in wealth is decile 10 which shows a 5% drop in real terms over the time period. This is plausible because the richest in society hold much of their wealth as assets such as shares and property and these saw significant falls because of the financial crisis.

Figure 3.12 shows the Gini index (see income section above for definition) for overall household wealth and also for each individual type of household wealth.

Overall, the index has dropped from 66 to 61 over this time and this fall seems mostly due to private pension wealth inequality dropping. This accords with figure 3.10 which shows that such pension wealth has become the increasingly dominant type of wealth.

Figure 3.13 shows the Palma ratio, which is the wealth owned by top decile divided by that of bottom four deciles for overall household wealth.

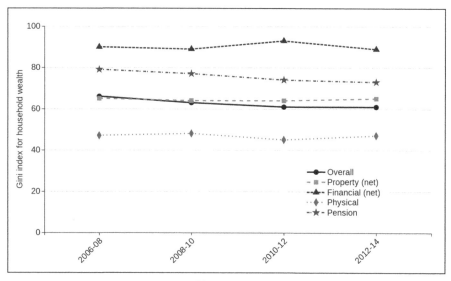

Figure 3.12
Gini index for household wealth 2006–08 to 2012–14.

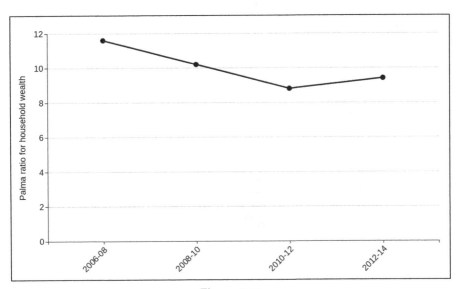

Figure 3.13
Palma ratio for household wealth 2006–08 to 2012–14.

The Palma index shows a similar trend of decreasing inequality, dropping from 11.6 to 9.4 over this time although, unlike the Gini index, it shows a rise in recent years. The difference is probably because Palma is, by its definition, more sensitive to changes in the top 10% and the bottom 40%, and although the shares of both groups have dropped, the bottom 40%'s share dropped by more. Notice that this also means that the share of middle 50% increased.

But compare these wealth inequality measures with those of income we saw earlier in Figure 3.3. In 2012–14, Gini for income was 34, but that for wealth was much higher at 61. And whereas the Palma ratio for income tells us the top 10% received 1.4 times the income of the bottom 40%, for wealth the figure is 9.4. Wealth inequality is clearly far greater and the obvious reason for this is that income is progressively taxed whereas wealth is very lightly taxed in comparison.

Unlike the Poverty and Income Inequality in Scotland report, the Wealth and Assets in Scotland report does not give detail on how decile boundaries of wealth have changed over time, not even for the median (decile 5). As argued above, this can give valuable insight in addition to knowing the shares of each decile. The report does, however, provide information on households that have moved up or down a decile or stayed

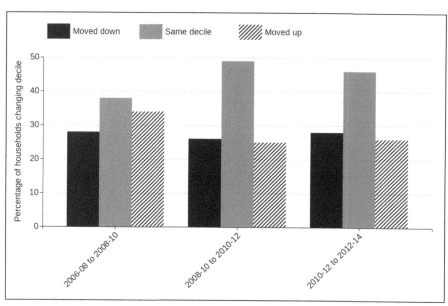

Figure 3.14

Movement of households across wealth deciles 2006–08 to 2012–14.

in the same decile. It does this by looking at responses from the same households that were included in all four two-year waves of the survey (2006–08 to 2012–14).

Figure 3.14 shows the percentage of households that moved across deciles each year.

In these terms, the wealth distribution appears to show little change. Although there was more movement upward in deciles in the first two-year period, there was more movement downward in more recent time periods. The majority of all the movements are by just one decile.

Debt

The four different types of wealth exhibit different levels of inequality, with physical wealth showing the least inequality, and financial wealth, shown in Figure 3.15, showing the greatest.

The first and second deciles have negative financial wealth which indicates that debts exceed assets. The debt of the first two deciles – the least wealthy 20% – is £3.2 billion (2015 prices), which equates to about £2900 per individual, and is similar to the wealth of the seventh decile.

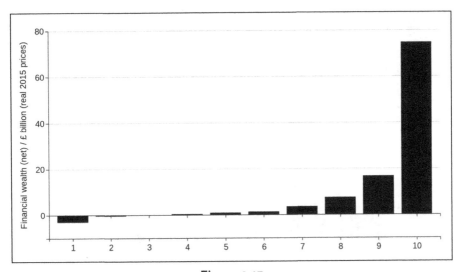

Figure 3.15
Financial wealth (net) held by deciles 2012–14

The debt of the lowest decile decreased slightly in 2012–14 having remained constant since 2006–08.

The median of financial wealth in 2012–14 was £3400, but the distribution is so lop-sided that the median is of limited use. Consider it together with the fact that the bottom half hold 1.9% of total financial wealth, whereas the wealthier half hold 98.1%.

Figure 3.16 shows the median amounts of outstanding debt for households in the bottom three deciles of wealth.

Student loans show the highest levels of outstanding debt and is the only type of debt to show consistent growth with it more than doubling between 2006–08 and 2010–12. Median values for Student loans were omitted from the 2012–14 report even though they are still referred to in the text.

Redistribution

Without the redistributive effects from tax and benefits, income inequality would be considerably higher than it would be otherwise. And income is taxed progressively, which has a precise definition in this context: a **progressive tax**, or change to taxation, is one where people on higher incomes pay proportionately more tax. In other words, higher earners are subject to higher tax rates. We can put some numbers to

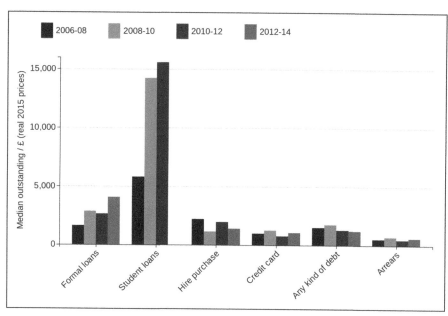

Figure 3.16
Median outstanding debt for household non-mortgage debt
in the least-wealthy 30% of the population 2006–08 to 2010–12.

this using information published for the whole UK by the Office for National Statistics.[15]

Figure 3.17 shows quintiles of the UK income distribution. Quintiles are like deciles except they divide the population into five groups instead of ten. The height of each bar is the income averaged over all households in that quintile.

There are three bars for each quintile:

- *Original income* is gross income before direct taxes are deducted or benefits are added. A direct tax is one levied directly on income, such as income tax or national insurance.
- *Disposable income* is income after direct taxes are deducted and benefits are added. This is what is available for all household outgoings, and is comparable with income before housing costs data used elsewhere in this chapter.
- *Final income* is disposable income with indirect taxes such as VAT and fuel duty deducted, and benefits in kind for services such as health and education added.

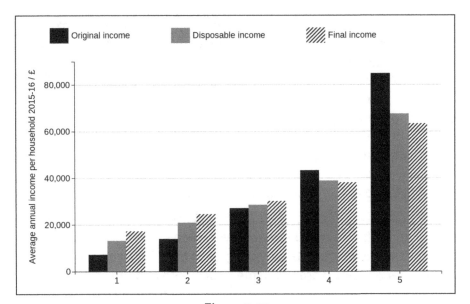

Figure 3.17
The redistributive effect of tax and benefits on the UK
income distribution 2015–16.

For original income, the average for quintile 5 is 12 times bigger than that for quintile 1, but for disposable income this drops to five times. From this alone, it is clear that tax and benefits have a profoundly redistributive effect on the income distribution.

Households in the first quintile – the bottom 20% or deciles 1 and 2 together – are mostly classed as being in some kind of poverty. Their average annual original income is £7,150, but with the addition of state benefits, and the deduction of very little tax, this becomes £13,140 of disposable income. Just under half of quintile 1's disposable income comes from benefits. Benefits also boost the incomes in quintiles 2 and 3 but to a lesser extent.

For quintiles 4 and 5, redistribution means that direct taxes reduce disposable incomes to be 10% and 20% less than their original incomes respectively. If these seem low to you given the basic rate of tax in 2015–16 was 20% and the higher rate was 40%, then bear in mind that the first £10,600 of *personal* income attracted no tax, and the higher band started at £31,786, and that households, especially better off ones, often have two people bringing in income.

The difference between final income and disposable income makes the most difference for the lowest two quintiles because the benefits in kind represent a larger fraction of their smaller incomes. Also, indirect taxes such as VAT are not progressive like income tax: you pay 20% VAT on most VAT-able items irrespective of how much you earn, and even greater percentages for duties on fuel, alcohol or tobacco. For households in the upper quintiles, benefits in kind are outweighed by VAT because they spend more money on goods and services that attract VAT. For disposable income, the average for quintile 5 is five times bigger than that for quintile 1, but for final income this drops to under four times.

These figures are for the UK, but the situation in Scotland would be similar with a few minor differences. Very high earners in London would tend to pull the top quintile average higher than Scotland's. In 2015–16, tax rates and bands were the same in Scotland and the rest of the UK, but this will change in subsequent years, though the differences are not expected to be large. In Scotland, people are entitled to free prescriptions and they do not have to pay tuition fees at university. By the definition given above, these measures are not progressive, but are called universal, meaning that they apply to everyone regardless of income. These differences would increase benefits in kind and slightly raise final income in all quintiles in Scotland relative to the rest of the UK.

Taxing wealth is fraught with problems, not the least of which is that those with the most wealth are adept at resisting attempts to tax it and the idea of a wealth tax still feels alien to our society. But let's leave such issues aside, and the moral questions about whether it should be done, and ask what a wealth tax of 1% per annum might look like. We will only consider household wealth because ultimately every company is owned by some individual through shareholding, and any declared shareholding owned by a resident in Scotland would attract our proposed wealth tax. Again, this issue is not so simple, but let's sidestep it so we can make progress.

Let's start with the 2006–08 value of total household wealth in Scotland which is £802 billion in 2015 prices. A tax of just 1% per annum would yield £8.0 billion a year. This is about one seventh of Scotland's total revenues in 2015 (see Chapter 5), and so a significant sum.

If, for simplicity, we suppose a stock of wealth does not change in real terms, that is it just grows with inflation, then an annual 1% tax deduction would reduce £802 billion in 2006–08 to £755 billion in 2012–14. Although this is much less than the actual total of £882 billion for 2012–14, it's comparable with the £756 billion for 2010–12, and that did not prompt howls of rage from the wealthy. That said, the noises people emit do differ depending on whether it is the perils of fortune or the tax man that is depleting their wealth.

If instead we suppose wealth grows in real terms at 1% per annum then the stock of wealth would not change, all gains would just go to tax. Historically, wealth has reliably attracted *average* annual returns of a few percent, with big annual variations. Even for the troubled financial period between 2006–08 and 2012–14, wealth managed average growth at 1.7% per annum. So even with a 1% wealth tax, and all else being equal, the wealthy would continue to become wealthier in real terms.

But how would wealth inequality be affected? Let's say, just for simplicity, that there's no attempt to make this tax progressive, that it's a 1% tax on any wealth, no matter how much wealth you own. If this was true of returns too, that is percentage returns were the same no matter how much wealth you own, then inequality would be unaffected. However, in reality, returns tend to increase with greater stocks of wealth, so the most wealthy will see their wealth grow faster, and this means that inequality will increase over time. For this reason, a progressive element to wealth taxation is required if the goal is reduce inequality.

But there are other goals for a wealth tax. You could, for example, make it redistributive so that people in debt receive money. This needs some care, and could be designed to target those on low incomes who are trapped in debt, and to avoid rescuing a failed tycoon from debts incurred in a risky business venture. Alternatively, you could tax certain kinds of wealth for purposes that benefit social or economic policy. A land tax could encourage landowners to sell unused land and invest their money in lower taxed assets, thus freeing it up for housing or some other productive use. Finally a wealth tax of even 0.1% could be introduced simply for the purposes of measuring wealth, and getting people used to the idea.

It is not my intention to advocate such ideas, merely to present them. They may be difficult to implement but they are not impossible. What they do require is sufficient public consensus so that politicians can propose them without fear of being punished at the ballot box, and that, at least at present, seems unlikely.

Other measures of inequality

Inequality can and should be assessed by a spectrum of methods. Income and wealth receive the most attention, perhaps because they have clear meanings and are easy to quantify, but there are other measures that are worth attention, some being proxies for inequality rather than direct measurements.

In Chapter 1 we briefly met the Single Index of Multiple Deprivation or SIMD which is constructed for local areas across Scotland. This is used in many Scottish government reports to assess inequality and deprivation. We'll take a closer look at its uses and misuses for education in Chapter 4.

We also saw in Chapter 1 that there were significant differences in home prices across Scotland with particular contrasts between Glasgow city and its wealthier suburbs. These are indirect measures of inequality in both wealth, through the value of a property, and income, which limits mortgages. Unlike other assets, an increase in the value of a home will not attract capital gains tax in most cases, and most home values sit well below inheritance tax thresholds.

A related proxy of inequality is in how people pay for their home. Broadly, you either own your home, possibly with a mortgage, or you rent it. Home ownership increased from 61% in 1999 to 66% in 2009 with a corresponding fall in rental. But this growth in home ownership reversed after the financial crisis, and the figure has returned to 61% in 2016. To understand what has happened we need to look at ownership and rental in more detail. Figure 3.18 shows percentages for four types of household tenure from the Scottish Household Survey.

The breakdown into sub-classes explains how inequality is involved in this story. As mortgages are paid off, the number of properties owned outright increases. And following the 2008 financial crisis, ownership with a mortgage declined significantly, though the decrease began from 2004 at a gentler pace. The net result is that although overall home ownership is 61% in 2016, as it was 1999, its make up is very different: homes owned outright increased from 22% to 32%, and ownership with a mortgage or loan dropped from 39% to 29%. The decline in mortgage ownership is in part because first time buyers find it increasingly difficult to afford their first home because of rising house prices, but

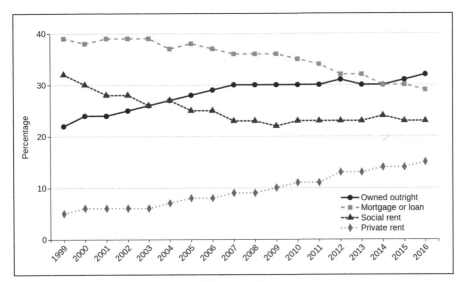

Figure 3.18
Classes of home tenure from 1999 to 2016.

also conditions of mortgage lending were significantly tightened following the 2008 financial crisis.

There has also been a significant shift in the make-up of rented housing, with social rental dropping from 32% to 23% and private rental increasing from 5% to 15%. The increase of private rental means that some people who have invested their wealth in property will have seen a growth in their income. Because this income is drawn from tenants who are probably less wealthy, this shift from social to private rental is likely to have driven growth in income inequality.

Social rental is provided by councils or housing associations on a not-for-profit basis with special provision for people with disabilities or who are otherwise disadvantaged. Through the 1970s an increasing number of social rental properties were bought by their tenants, which no doubt encouraged the UK parliament to pass the Housing Act 1980 which gave such tenants the 'right to buy' their home. The result was a growth in home ownership but a reduced stock of properties available for social rental. 'Right to buy' was significantly revised in the Scottish parliament's Housing (Scotland) Act 2001 and the Housing (Scotland) Act 2014 closed the scheme to new applicants from August 2016. Wales also abolished 'Right to buy' in December 2017 but it continues in England and Northern Ireland.

Some thoughts

Inequality can be a vague term. It is important to be clear on whether it refers to income or wealth because the former tells us about the present situation, and the latter about the historical accumulation. Also, inequality in wealth is much greater than for income. Measured by the Palma ratio, wealth inequality in Scotland is seven times greater than income inequality after taxes are deducted and benefits are added. And the reason is simple enough. Income is taxed much more progressively than wealth. It is also more comprehensively taxed with people and businesses compelled to report incomes by law so we know much more about its distribution.

Housing and debt are two pressing concerns on society, and they are most acutely felt by those on lowest incomes. Increasing house prices have meant that an increasing share of income is needed to fund a household. Renting is, overall, more expensive than owning, yet people who begin their adult life without wealth are finding it harder to find the deposit needed to buy even a modest home. Connected to this is that these same people are having to rely more and more on credit, and so are running up debt to sustain a standard of living that they have seen their parents enjoy.

Poverty requires careful definition, and some prefer the word 'deprivation' because it emphasises that more is involved than a lack of money. At one extreme we have the international definition of poverty which includes people who are unable to feed themselves or their children, but also those who cannot access basic services of health and education. Even in wealthier countries, being poor, or being a child of parents who are poor, will limit your opportunities in life and that creates an inter-generational poverty trap.

This book's purpose is to look at Scotland, and although that offers an easy excuse to dodge some tough questions concerning global issues, it's still important to be aware of geographical myopia. Consider, for example, focusing attention on the city of Glasgow. You would find that poverty rates were higher than for Scotland as a whole, but you would also find that inequality is lower. If you expanded your boundary to greater Glasgow, taking in some of the wealthy suburbs, then you will find that inequality jumps up. (The survey-based data on income and wealth presented in this chapter is too sparse to be of use for this purpose, but we can use home prices and SIMD.) When expanding from Scotland to the whole of the UK, inequality measures will increase because London is included. As your geographical boundary grows, it is almost inevitable that inequality will too.

Questions to ponder:

- Are poverty rates in Scotland too high?
- If poverty rates are brought down to acceptable levels, does it also matter that a very few people have so much wealth?
- Would you reduce poverty in rural areas by redirecting funds from wealthy areas of the central belt?
- And would you redirect funds from parts of the UK with the lowest poverty, such as Scotland or the South east of England, to reduce poverty in Wales or Yorkshire (see Figure 3.8)?
- How much of those funds should be in welfare to alleviate hardship, and how much should be invested in infrastructure or education to boost the local economy?
- How much money should go abroad to tackle extreme poverty that meets the UN or World Bank definitions?
- Is a growth of income and wealth inequality within a wealthy country such as Scotland tolerable if it is determined that this is due to global inequality improving, say, because manufacturing jobs have transferred to the far east?

Chapter 4
Supporting society

4

Our society is underpinned by public provision of education, healthcare and justice through schools, colleges, universities, hospitals, courts, police and fire stations and the various associated professions. This book is, by intention, mainly concerned with what can be summarised in numbers and then understood in a wider context with many more words. Unlike previous chapters, the essence of society involves aspects that cannot be quantified easily, or at all, such as education, art, culture, religion and community. Nevertheless, with such limitations in mind, numbers can help us assess the state of our society and the stability of the base upon which we make our lives.

Education

Education is fundamental. Without it, our society would have no nurses or doctors for its hospitals, no lawyers or judges for its courts, and no way to train and nurture the next generation of teachers and lecturers. Changes to the education system are therefore compounding and only apparent over a generational timescale beyond the four or five years of the electoral cycle.

Schools

Children's development is most strongly influenced by parents, schooling and, increasingly as they grow older, by their peers. The school a child attends will be determined by where their parent or parents have chosen to live, or, in many cases, where they can afford to live.

Education is compulsory in Scotland from the age of 5, as is the case in England and Wales. Schooling in Northern Ireland starts at 4. Cyprus and Malta also have a school start age of 5 but it is 6 in most of Europe[1] with several countries having a school start age of 7. Pupils can leave school at age 16[2] in Scotland, but, unlike England, there is no requirement to continue in education or some form of training or apprenticeship until the age of 18. Most pupils will spend 7 years in primary school followed by 5 or 6 years at a secondary school.

Most of the information in this section is taken from the Scottish government report Summary Statistics for schools in Scotland[3] which is based on a census of all publicly funded schools in Scotland in September of each year.

At the start of the 2017 school year, there were 2,514 publicly funded schools in Scotland,[4] of which 2019 were primary, 360 were secondary and 135 were special schools. Special schools cater for children who have physical or mental disabilities that mainstream schools are not equipped to deal with. There were also 2,532 Early Learning and Childcare or ELC centres for pre-school children. Most publicly funded schools are not oriented to any particular religion. Of those that are, 366 are Catholic, three are Episcopalian and one Jewish.

Information on schools that are not publicly funded, known as independent or private schools, are not regularly published by the Scottish government, but as of 2013 there were about 102 independent schools[5] and they educate about 4% of all Scottish pupils.[6] Independent schools are funded by fees paid by parents and also donations from former pupils and other fundraising activities.

The Scottish government publish historical data on numbers of schools, pupils and teachers that extend back to 1966.[7] The data in the next six graphs are all drawn from this source.

Figure 4.1 shows the number of schools. Note that there are about five primary schools for every secondary school and so the primary school numbers use the scale on the left axis.

Since 1998, primary school numbers have decreased by 12%, secondaries by 8% and special schools by 27%. Much of the decline in special school numbers took place in 2010.

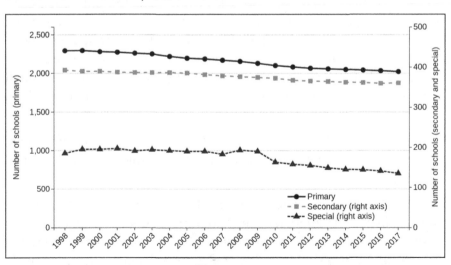

Figure 4.1
Numbers of state primary, secondary and special schools 1998 to 2017.

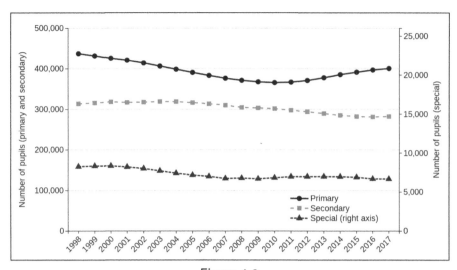

Figure 4.2
Numbers of pupils at state primary, secondary and special schools
1998 to 2017.

Figure 4.2 shows the change in the number of pupils in each type of school. On this graph the number of special school pupils is much smaller and so uses the scale on the right axis.

Primary pupil numbers show a decrease from 1998 to 2010, followed by a rise. Secondary pupil numbers show little change until 2004 after which there is a sustained decline which came to an end in 2017 as the rise in primary numbers began to feed through to secondary schools. Numbers of pupils at special schools declined until 2007 but have shown a slight rise since then. From 1998 to 2017, primary pupil numbers have declined by 8%, secondary by 10% and special school pupils by 19%.

Figure 4.3 shows the number of teachers in each type of school. Again, special teacher numbers are lower and so use the scale on the right-hand axis.

All types of teachers show a rising trend until peak numbers are reached in 2007. Primary teacher numbers fell until 2012 and rose past their 2007 peak in 2016. Secondary teacher numbers continued to fall until 2016, but rose slightly in 2017, but were well below their 2007 peak. Numbers of special teachers have fallen in recent years and in 2017 reached their lowest level since the 1990s. From 1998 to 2017, secondary

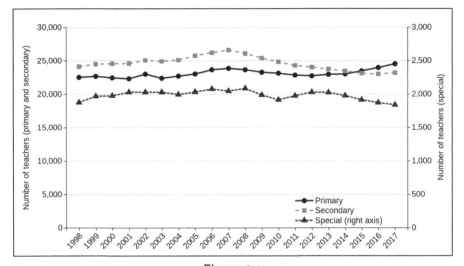

Figure 4.3

Numbers of teachers at state primary, secondary and special schools
1998 to 2017.

teacher numbers fell by 4% and special teacher numbers by 2% but primary teacher numbers have increased by 8%.

The following three graphs show two ratios: pupils per school and pupils per teacher. Before looking at them it's worth considering what these figures can tell us.

The pupil to teacher ratio should be as low as possible so that each pupil can gain more individual attention from their teacher. This is especially true for special schools where the ratio is lowest (3.5). But against this are pressures on education budgets and local demographics. It may seem surprising that the ratio for primary schools is higher than that for secondary schools – 16.4 compared to 12.2 in 2017 – but teachers specialise by subject in secondary school much more than is the case in primary school and so more teachers are needed to cover the range of subjects offered.

The effect of the pupil to school ratio on education quality is a little harder to interpret. On the one hand a large ratio may be because there are large schools that can offer a wider range of facilities and curriculum choices for pupils with a spectrum of abilities. This is particularly true for secondary and special schools. However, a large pupil to school ratio could also indicate that some schools are operating at capacity,

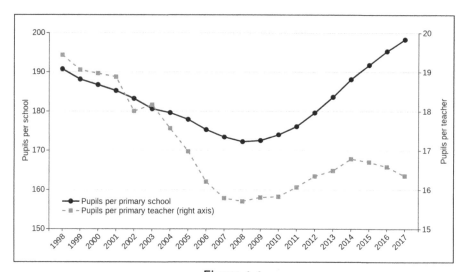

Figure 4.4
Pupil to primary school and teacher ratios 1998–2017.

placing strains on facilities and staff. For primary schools, a lower pupil to school ratio is desirable so that young children do not have to travel too far each day. In fact, this is why primary schools are both more numerous and smaller than secondary schools.

Figure 4.4 shows the pupil to school, and pupil to teacher ratios for primary schools.

The graph shows roughly U-shaped profiles – both ratios decrease until 2008 after which both start rising. This is because the number of pupils started rising but the number of schools and teachers continued to decrease after 2008. From 2014, the number of teachers began to increase rapidly enough to cause the ratio to fall again. The numbers of primary pupils were about the same in 2004 and 2017 but there were 198 more primary schools in 2004. The implication of this is that some children in 2017 will have further to travel than in 2004.

Figure 4.5 shows the pupil to school, and pupil to teacher ratios for secondary schools.

This graph also shows a U-shaped profile for the pupil to teacher ratio, though the variation is smaller than for primaries (note the scale of this graph) with the ratio remaining roughly constant since 2011. The pupil to school ratio increases until 2003 because the number of secondary

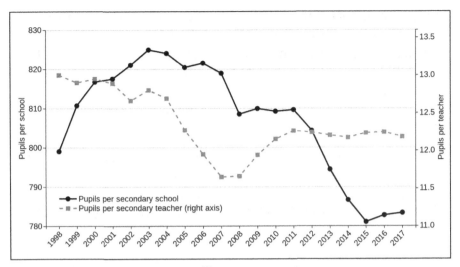

Figure 4.5
Pupil to secondary school and teacher ratios 1998–2017.

pupils didn't vary much whilst the number of schools fell slightly. After that, the number of pupils decreased faster than the number of schools causing the ratio to drop.

Figure 4.6 shows the ratios for special schools.

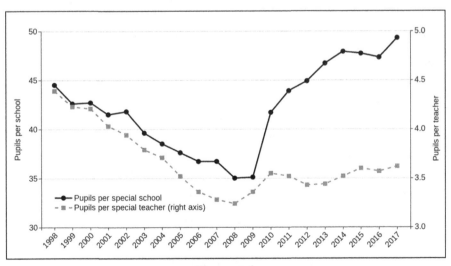

Figure 4.6
Pupil to special school and teacher ratios 1998–2017.

The obvious feature of this graph is that the number of pupils per school increased rapidly from a low of 35 in 2008 and 2009 to 49 in 2017. This suggests that pupils are now having to travel further to reach their school, but they may also be benefiting from larger schools that are each able to cater for a greater range of needs. Since 2010, the pupil to teacher ratio has stayed about the same, though it fell significantly from 1998 to 2008.

Table 4.1 gives a summary of how totals across primary, secondary and special schools have changed from 1998 to 2017.

Change	1998 to 2007	2007 to 2017	1998 to 2017
Schools	-4.8%	-7.9%	-12.3%
Pupils	-8.7%	-0.5%	-9.2%
Teachers	8.2%	-5.7%	2.1%

Table 4.1
Changes in numbers of state schools, pupils and teachers 1998 to 2017.

From 1998 to 2007, the number of pupils fell, as did the number of schools, but the number of teachers increased. From 2007, the decline in the number of pupils halted but the number of teachers and schools both fell. Overall, the number of teachers in 2017 is slightly up on 1998 whereas the numbers of pupils and schools are about 10% lower.

Population projections from the National Records of Scotland shown in Chapter 1 tell us that the rise in primary school pupil numbers will continue but slow in the next few years with numbers levelling off in the next decade or two. The rise in primary numbers is just starting to feed through to secondary school pupil numbers which will rise through the next decade then also level off. These projections should be viewed with some caution because it is difficult to anticipate the effects that leaving the EU will have on migration in and out of Scotland.

Measuring standards of school education

From 2011, the Scottish government has conducted the Scottish Survey of Literacy and Numeracy[8] or SSLN to assess the performance of pupils in primary years P4 and P7 and secondary year S2. The intention was that this information would guide future educational policy. Numeracy and literacy are assessed in alternate years and results are available for 2011, 2013 and 2015 for numeracy, and 2012, 2014 and 2016 for literacy.

Figures 4.7, 4.8 and 4.9 show percentages of those who were classed as doing well or better in reading, writing and numeracy. Statistical uncertainties are considered at the 95% confidence level. In other words, if a change is deemed to be statistically significant, there is only a 5% chance that it could have occurred by chance.

The fall in standards in reading between 2012 and 2016 is slight and only considered statistically significant for P4 and P7. For writing, the falls are statistically significant for P7 and also for S2 which shows the largest fall in all of these charts at 15 percentage points. The falls in numeracy percentages between 2011 and 2015 for P4 and P7 numeracy are statistically significant whereas the slight fall for S2 is not.

Results are further divided into three broad categories according to the Scottish Index of Multiple Deprivation or SIMD for each school's local area: the most deprived 30%, the middle 40% and least deprived 30%. We'll take a closer look at SIMD later on. For P4 numeracy in 2015, the

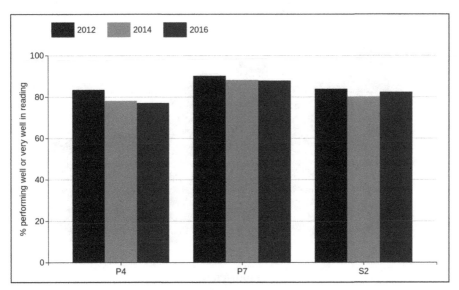

Figure 4.7
Reading results from the Scottish Survey of Literacy
and Numeracy 2012 to 2016.

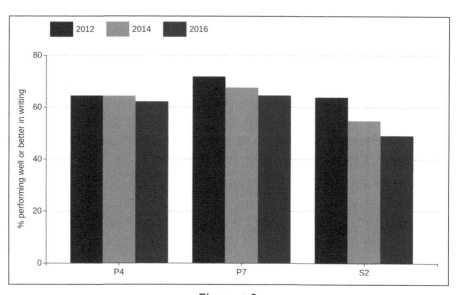

Figure 4.8
Writing results from the Scottish Survey of Literacy
and Numeracy 2012 to 2016.

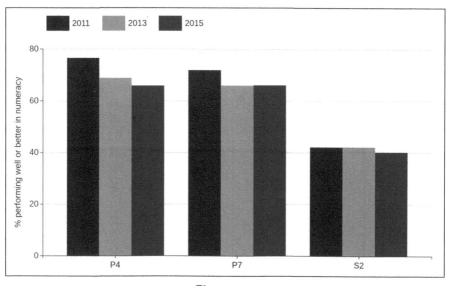

Figure 4.9
Numeracy results from the Scottish Survey of Literacy
and Numeracy 2011 to 2015.

least deprived category had 76% scoring well or better, and 55% scoring well or better in the most deprived category, giving a gap of 21%. But in 2011, this gap was 13%, which means the gap grew by 8 percentage points between 2011 and 2015. Table 4.2 shows the differences between the most and least deprived categories between 2011 and 2015 for numeracy, and 2012 and 2016 for reading.

Numeracy	2011–15 change	Significant?	Reading	2012–16 change	Significant?
P4	8	Yes	P4	1	No
P7	7	No	P7	–1	No
S2	0	No	S2	0	No

Table 4.2

Changes in the least deprived minus the most deprived area's score in the Scottish Survey of Literacy and Numeracy 2011–16.

A positive change indicates a widening gap in performing well or very well between the least and most deprived areas, and so a negative change is desirable. The 8pp growth in the gap for P4 Numeracy is the only statistically significant change across all areas and all stages over the entire time span covered by SSLN.

In 2017, the Scottish government decided to end SSLN with no firm plans for replacing it. Even if it is replaced, the results of any future surveys will almost certainly not be comparable with the SSLN results. It will be many years before progress in standards can again be tracked by a survey that is specifically designed for the Scottish school education system.

International benchmarks of Scottish education have been measured with tests on 15 year olds conducted as part of the Programme of International Student Assessment (PISA).[9] Figures 4.10, 4.11 and 4.12 show the results for reading, maths and science. PISA is run by the Organisation for Economic Co-operation and Development or OECD which is made up of 34 wealthy countries. The average OECD score is shown for comparison.

The results are not shown before 2006 for science and 2003 for maths because aspects of the test changed so that scores are not comparable. Scotland's scores used to exceed the OECD average in all three subjects by a statistically significant margin, but by 2015 the scores had fallen to the OECD average.

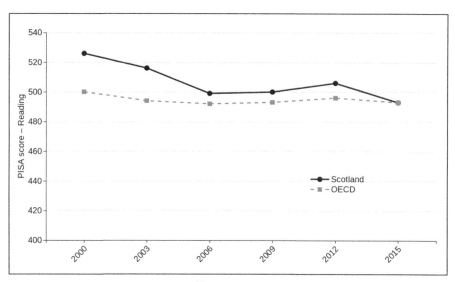

Figure 4.10
Reading scores from PISA 2000 to 2015.

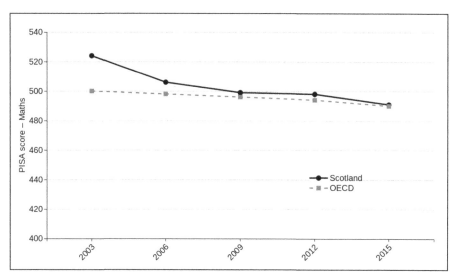

Figure 4.11
Maths scores from PISA 2003 to 2015.

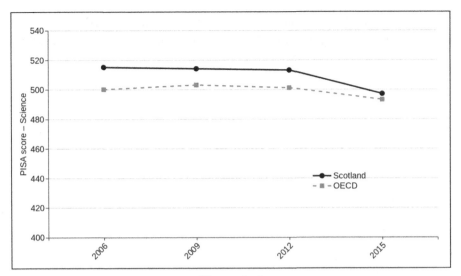

Figure 4.12
Science scores from PISA 2006 to 2015.

Levels of study

The structure of school education into primary and secondary is familiar to most people, but the structures of tertiary (third tier) education are more complicated and less well known. The Scottish Credit and Qualification Framework (SCQF)[10] defines a series of levels that allow comparison of qualifications offered by different types of educational institutions. Table 4.3 lists the 12 defined levels with examples given under three headings.

The Scottish Qualifications Agency (SQA) administers the qualifications obtained at schools and colleges from levels 1 to 7, though Level 7 straddles colleges and schools. Levels 8 and above relate to diplomas and degrees and are mostly obtained at universities.

Most Higher National Certificate (HNC) and Higher National Diploma (HND) study is done at colleges. Scottish Vocational Qualifications (SVQs) are studied at colleges and are geared towards learning skills for a particular career. The lower levels concentrate on specific skills, such as hairdressing or common IT tasks, whereas the higher levels relate to management.

Tertiary education is split into two broad groups: **Further Education or FE** refers to levels up to and including SCQF 6, and **Higher Education or HE** refers to SCQF level 7 and above. Unlike primary and secondary education, tertiary education is not compulsory and is mostly aimed at adults.

SCQF levels	SQA National Units, courses and group awards	Higher Education (HE) qualifications	Scottish Vocational Qualifications
12		Doctorate	Professional apprenticeship
11		Masters	SVQ 5 Professional apprenticeship
10		Honours degree	Professional apprenticeship
9		Ordinary degree	SVQ 4 Technical apprenticeship
8	HND	Diploma of HE	Technical apprenticeship
7	Advanced Higher / HNC	Certificate of HE	SVQ 3 Modern apprenticeship
6	Higher		SVQ 3
5	National 5 (Intermediate 2, Credit S Grade)		SVQ 2
4	National 4 (Intermediate 1, General S Grade)	National Certificate	SVQ 1
3	National 3 (Access 3, Foundation S Grade)		
2	National 2 (Access 2)		
1	National 1 (Access 1)		

Table 4.3
Levels of awards and qualifications.

Further education and colleges

There were 20 colleges in Scotland in 2015–16. This is down from 37 in 2011–12 due to a programme of reform involving mergers and closures. Scottish government funding for colleges fell in real terms between financial years 2009–10 and 2014–15, and the number of college staff fell following the mergers until 2013–14. Since then both have seen slight increases but not to previous levels. In this section, unless otherwise stated, 2015–16 does not refer to the financial year as it does elsewhere, but to the college year which begins on 1 August.

In 2015–16, 73% of college funding came from the Scottish government via the Scottish Funding Council (SFC). In real terms, between 2012–13 and 2015–16, total incomes to colleges fell by £25 million, or 4%, and funding from SFC fell by £15 million. The bulk of college spending is on staff costs. This information and further detail on colleges and funding can be found in Audit Scotland's colleges report published in June 2017.[11]

Figure 4.13 shows three different measures of student participation in colleges from the document College Statistics 2015–16[12] published in January 2017.

The number of students attending a college in a year is the **headcount**, which is less than **enrolments** because each student typically studies, or enrols, on more than one course. The Full Time Equivalent or **FTE** measure counts a full time student as 1.0 but a part time student as a number less than one; for example, a half-time student would count as 0.5.

The fact that headcount and enrolments have both fallen substantially – by over 35% – whilst the **FTE** count of students has remained relatively

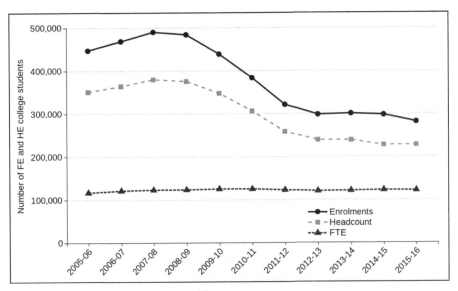

Figure 4.13
Numbers of students attending colleges 2005–06 to 2015–16.

constant tells us that there has been a significant decrease in part-time student numbers.

The proportion of female students is 51% and roughly the same as the population overall, though there remain significant variations by subject: 85% of engineering students and 92% of transport students are male, whereas for health and social work 78% and 87% are female.

Around 6% of college students are from an ethnic minority background and this has remained constant since 2011–12. The number of students from the most deprived areas, as defined by the lowest 15% of areas in the Scottish Index of Multiple Deprivation or SIMD, has increased from 21% in 2011–12 to 22% in 2015–16. We'll take a closer look at SIMD and its limitations later in this chapter.

The majority of college students are in further education and three-quarters of them are studying towards HNCs or HNDs, with most of the rest studying towards a sub-degree level award. A minority of students at University are classed as being in FE, that is studying towards HNCs, HNDs or awards other than university degrees.

Tuition fees and student loans

Changes made to how students are required to pay for their higher education are arguably the biggest divergence of devolved government policy within the UK to date. Tuition fees for higher education students were introduced across the UK by the Teaching and Higher Education Act 1998. From 2001, tuition fees were abolished in Scotland for EU and Scottish students in full-time higher education, and replaced by the graduate endowment, which differed in two respects. Firstly, tuition fees were paid upfront each year, but the graduate endowment was paid on graduation. Secondly, whereas tuition fee income goes to fund universities, income from graduate endowments was to be ring-fenced for bursaries for students who might not have otherwise decided to study in higher education.

On introduction, tuition fees were set at £1,000 *per year*, but this rose with inflation to £1,225 for the 2007–08 academic year. The *one-off* graduate endowment fee started at £2,000 and rose to £2,289 for graduates that had started their studies in 2006–07. Students were exempt from paying the graduate endowment if they were mature students aged over 25, training to be a teacher or in receipt of grants for being a lone parent or disabled.

Graduate endowments were abolished by the Scottish government in 2008 which meant that students graduating from 1 April 2007 would not have to pay anything. Students domiciled elsewhere in the UK studying in Scotland still have to pay tuition fees, though EU domiciled students do not. Also, tuition fees are payable by Scottish domiciled students attending university in other parts of the UK. In 2010, the Westminster parliament voted, albeit with a substantial rebellion of MPs from government benches, to raise the tuition fee cap to £9,000 per year, which later rose with inflation to £9,250 per year.

Proponents of tuition fees argue that tuition has to be paid for in some way, and that abolition of tuition fees means that it is paid for through public spending and that may divert it away from other priorities, such as health, and increase pressure to raise taxes in the future. Also, through the introduction of student loans, tuition fees need not be paid for up front, but only when a former student's income rises above a certain threshold, which is currently £21,000 per year in England.

Viewed in this way, the tuition fee debate is really about whether tuition is paid for only by students who achieve sufficient incomes or by society as a whole through government spending. But this debate is clouded because the way student loans are handled in the country's finances is far from intuitive, involving 'fiscal illusions' and misunderstandings of how public spending is funded and the nature of public debt.[13] We will return to these wider issues in Chapters 5 and 6.

One argument against student loans is that it unfairly saddles students with debt from the start of their career. More fundamentally, some argue that there is a moral right to free higher education just as there is for primary and secondary education.

Although many students in Scotland do not have to pay tuition fees, they may still need to take out loans or rely on grants to pay for accommodation and living expenses whilst they study. To help students on low incomes, there is a means-tested grant called the Young Student Bursary. This was frozen in cash terms from 2010 to 2012 and then cut in 2013, with total Scottish government spending on maintenance grants falling by about a third. From 2015, some of these cuts were reversed. The overall result is that students from less well-off backgrounds have to rely increasingly on loans rather than grants to fund living costs whereas students from more affluent backgrounds will borrow nothing at all.[14] Although cause and effect are hard to establish, and comparisons must be made with care, there is evidence that the proportion of students from deprived areas going to university in Scotland is significantly lower than it is in England.[15]

Higher education and universities

Scotland has 19 **Higher Education Institutions or HEIs** that are funded by the Scottish government through the Scottish Funding Council or SFC. Fourteen of these are traditional campus universities, and the other five are: Scotland's Rural College (SRUC), the Royal Conservatoire of Scotland (for music and performing arts), the Open University in Scotland, the University of the Highlands and Islands and the Glasgow School of Art.

Of the 285,450 students in higher education in 2015–16, 82.5% were studying at an HEI and 17.5% at colleges. Figure 4.14 shows the total number of students at HEIs broken down by level of study.

All study at and above degree level shows an increase, with research postgraduate increasing by 38%, taught postgraduate by 2% and first degree by 18.5% over the time range shown. In contrast, HNC/HND increased by only 5% (though this apparent increase seems to be due to re-classifications when SRUC was formed as an HEI in 2012) and Other,

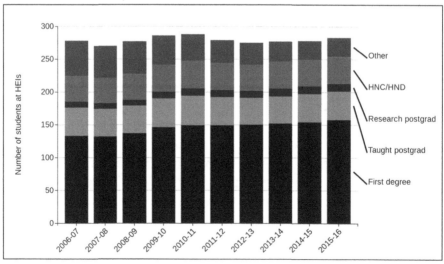

Figure 4.14
Students in higher education by type of qualification 2006–07 to 2015–16.

which is all for sub-degree level awards, fell by 45%. Overall, student numbers have increased by 2% over this time, though there has been a slight decrease since 2010–11.

Figure 4.15 shows the percentage of entrants to HE from deprived areas in Scotland going to different kinds of institutions. Here deprived is defined as from areas in the bottom 20% as ranked by the Scottish Index of Multiple Deprivation or SIMD. Institutions classified as *ancient* are the universities of Aberdeen, Edinburgh, Glasgow and St Andrews; those as *newer* are Dundee, Heriot-Watt, Stirling and Strathclyde; *post-92* universities are Abertay, Napier, Caledonian, Highlands & Islands, Queen Margaret, Robert Gordon and West of Scotland.

As you might expect, roughly 20% of Scotland's population comes from its 20% most deprived areas (actually, the percentage is a little lower, closer to 19%), so this graph shows that there is substantial under-representation of students from such areas. This is most pronounced for the ancient class of universities. In contrast, those from deprived areas are in fact slightly *over-represented* in college-based HE.

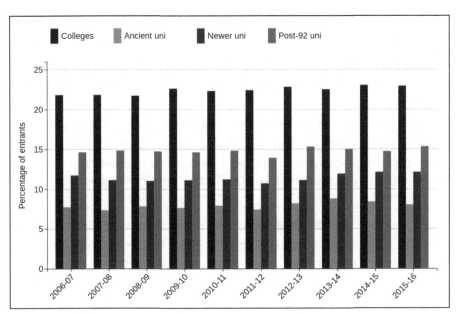

Figure 4.15
Percentages of entrants in Higher Education from the 20 per cent most deprived SIMD areas for Scottish colleges and campus universities 2006–07 to 2015–16.

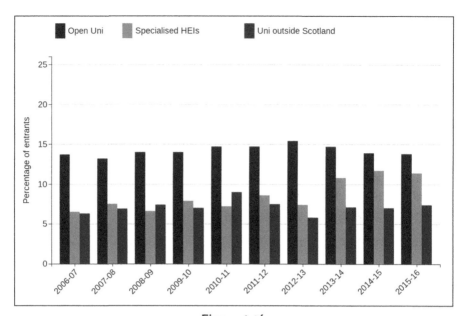

Figure 4.16

Percentages of entrants in Higher Education from the 20% most deprived SIMD areas for other institutions 2006–07 to 2015–16.

Figure 4.16 shows similar data but for other types of HEI. Specialised HEIs are those that concentrate on specific areas such as art, music and rural studies (see above). The scale is identical to Figure 4.15 to ease comparisons.

All of these show under-representation from deprived areas with the Open University coming close to that of the post-92 universities. Students from deprived areas are slightly less likely to go to universities outside Scotland than attend one of Scotland's ancient universities.

There has been a slight increase in the overall percentage of HE students coming from deprived areas, rising from 15.0% in 2006–07 to 16.1% in 2015–16. Amongst the types of HEI, this slightly rising trend is also evident. The jump for the specialised HEIs in 2012–13 is due to the creation of SRUC (see above).

Figure 4.17 shows where HE students studying in HEIs in Scotland have come from, or in the jargon, are domiciled.

Student numbers show no dramatic variations over this time, though a decline in Scottish domiciled students and an increase in numbers from

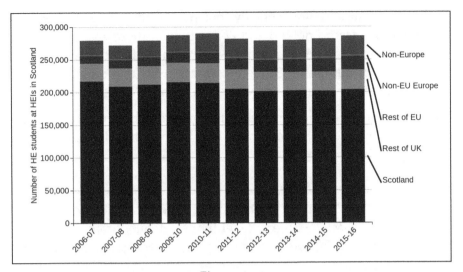

Figure 4.17
Numbers of students in Higher Education at Scottish HEIs
by domicile 2006–07 to 2015–16.

outside Scotland is evident. Table 4.4 summarises the changes between 2006–07 and 2015–16 and the current make-up of the Scottish HE student population.

In 2015–16, just over two-thirds of students were from Scotland with 10% domiciled elsewhere in the UK, another 10% from outside Europe, 7% from the EU and 0.8% from non-EU Europe

Total student numbers increased by 2% between 2006–07 and 2015–16. Numbers from Scotland have declined by 6% in this time, though the graph shows that numbers have been roughly constant in recent years. The trend for students from the rest of the UK is the opposite having

	Scot	Eng	Wales	NI	EU	Non-EU	Non-European	All
Change since 2006–07	-6%	17%	17%	-17%	74%	84%	31%	2%
% in 2015–16	71%	8.6%	0.2%	1.5%	7.4%	0.8%	10%	100%

Table 4.4
Change in HE student numbers at Scottish HEIs between 2006–07
and 2015–16, and percentages by domicile for 2015–16.

grown overall by 10% (not explicitly shown in the table) mainly driven by 17% increases from England and Wales though there was a 17% drop from Northern Ireland (the common 17% figure being due only to a coincidence of numbers). Students from the EU and outside Europe both show large increases, growing by 74% and 31% respectively.

Whereas the gender balance at colleges was similar to that of Scotland's population, the proportion of female HE students at HEIs in Scotland is significantly higher at 57%.

Deprived of deprivation

According to the Scottish government the Scottish Index of Multiple Deprivation or SIMD[16] is the 'official tool to identify areas of multiple deprivation in Scotland'. As its name suggests, SIMD goes beyond simply looking at deprivation in terms of money and uses 38 indicators of deprivation, such as on employment, health and education, to form a single number – the index – for each area or data zone.

There are 6,976 SIMD areas in Scotland with about 760 people living in each one. These areas are geographically smaller in urban areas such as Glasgow, and much larger in rural areas such as the Highlands where the population density is lower.

SIMD is useful if properly understood but it is essential to remember that not everyone in a deprived area is deprived. Two out of three people who are classed as income deprived do not live in the most deprived areas, and just under one in three people in a deprived area are classed as income deprived. Here, income deprived is defined as being in the bottom 15% of people in terms of income (actually households, see Chapter 3) and a deprived area means living in an area ranked in the bottom 15% according to SIMD.

The distinction between an individual being deprived as opposed to coming from a deprived area has important practical implications. For example, consider a school that is struggling by some measure such as exam results, university attendance or employment prospects. And suppose that its intake is equally drawn from two areas where one has a much lower SIMD ranking than the other. If you are unfamiliar with the school's locality and are deprived of further information, perhaps because you are a busy government minister who lives 200 miles away, it may seem sensible to concentrate extra resources on pupils from the more deprived area. But if, say, parental income is a crucial factor, then this could lead to as many as two thirds of pupils who need help missing out on it. Teachers at the school and local councillors would be much better placed to decide on which pupils should receive help.

While this example may be extreme, the risk of misapplication of resources from misunderstanding SIMD is nevertheless real and is not just present in school education but also in higher education where evidence of the problem has been studied.[17] SIMD can help alert us to a problem, for example that ancient universities have a low intake of students from deprived areas (Figure 4.15), but more information will be needed to craft a solution.

Health

A revolution in healthcare took place after World War II with the creation of the UK's **National Health Service**. The NHS is founded on three principles:

- that it meet the needs of everyone
- that it be free at the point of delivery
- that it be based on clinical need, not ability to pay

The system that preceded the NHS is now fading from living memory, but if you ask our elder citizens they may surprise or even shock you with their stories. In my family, for example, there is the story of a doctor's fee being paid with a valuable oriental vase.

The NHS in Scotland is divided into 14 regional boards with overall control and funding being fully devolved to the Scottish government. The boards pass on a minor portion of their funding and deploy staff to councils to support social health programmes.

As of October 2017, there were 274 NHS hospitals in Scotland.[18] These range from large city hospital complexes, such as Glasgow's new Queen Elizabeth University Hospital (formerly the Southern General, but now also known as the Death Star in Glaswegian banter, because of its size and shape) to smaller rural facilities such as Belford Hospital in Fort William or the Gilbert Bain Hospital in Lerwick, Shetland. This total also includes a number of specialist and outpatient facilities, such as those dealing with dental and eye care, but doesn't include community health centres that house GP practices and local clinics.

The NHS is the single biggest employer in Scotland as it is throughout the UK. About 1 in 20 people or 5% of everyone who is employed in Scotland works for the NHS. Staffing of the NHS has been growing faster than the population: staff numbers grew by 12% between 2005 and 2015, whereas the population only grew by 5%. We'll come back to the reason for this later. Nurses and midwives make up the single largest group of staff within the NHS, varying between 40% and 45% of the total during the last decade.

Information and statistics on Scotland's NHS is published by the **Information Services Division** or **ISD**. Data on patient stays at hospitals are shown in Figure 4.18 and are sourced from the ISD's annual release of Inpatient and Day Case Activity.[19] Elective inpatient stays are those that are arranged in advance, for example, for a planned surgical procedure. Day cases are similar except no overnight stay is planned. Some emergency inpatients are admitted through Accident and Emergency (A&E) departments though others are referred as emergency cases by GPs. The figures shown here are CIS (Continuous Inpatient Stays) which attempt to remove the effect of transfers within the hospital system. Numbers for 2016–7 are provisional.

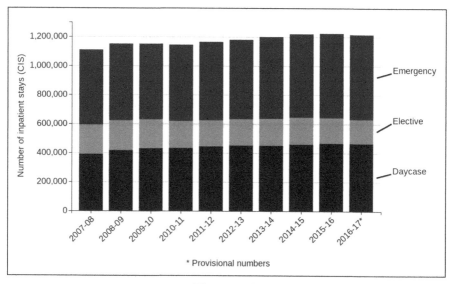

Figure 4.18
Numbers of inpatient stays by type of hospital admission
2007–08 to 2016–17.

The growth in hospital stays between 2007–08 and 2016–17 is 10% with the largest growth being in emergency inpatients at 19%. Elective stays decreased by 18%. For comparison, total NHS staffing levels grew by 6% over this time and nursing and midwifery grew at 4%.

Table 4.5 shows the average *annual* growth rates of staff numbers, patient stays and the population of Scotland. The time range is split into two groups because data on patient stays are only available back to 2007–08. Note also that patient stays are quoted for financial years and staff numbers are for September of each year, which is the middle of the financial year.

Annual growth rates	2002–2007	2007–16
All NHS staff	3.1%	0.6%
Medical staff	3.9%	2.4%
Emergency medical staff	3.2%	6.0%
Nursing and midwifery	1.5%	0.4%
All inpatient stays	-	1.1%
Emergency inpatient stays	-	1.5%
Population	0.4%	0.5%
Aged 75 and over	1.2%	1.6%

Table 4.5
Average annual growth rates of NHS staff, patients and population 2002–2016.

Inpatient stays are growing significantly faster (1.1%) than the number of people in Scotland in 2007–16 (0.5%), and the largest growth is for hospital stays admitted as emergencies (1.5%). This tells us that the need for hospital treatment per member of the population is growing. Further, the fact that the number of emergency inpatient stays is growing at a similar rate to those aged 75 and over in the population may not be a simple coincidence. In 2015–16, 27% of emergency admissions were for people aged 75 and over, whereas that age group only makes up 8% of the population. This is predicted to rise to 14% by 2039 (see Chapter 1).

Average annual growth in NHS staff (0.6%) was below that of hospital stays (1.1%) since 2007 with nursing and midwifery staff numbers growing most slowly (0.4%). Medical staff numbers (mainly doctors) have shown significant growth (2.4%). All categories of NHS staff grew significantly more in 2002–07 than in 2007–16, with the exception of emergency medical staff (6.0%).

Waiting times for healthcare have become a matter of public concern in recent years. Figure 4.19 shows the percentage of patients who waited 18 weeks or less from initial referral to receiving treatment (RTT). This graph is taken from the NHS waiting times – 18 Weeks RTT report[20] published in August 2017. The Scottish government's standard (or target) for RTT is 90%. Note also that, following the example of the official report, the scale on this graph starts at 65% rather zero; this helps to reveal smaller, seasonal variations.

The 90% target was consistently exceeded through 2012 and 2013, but a downward trend of RTT percentages is evident and since mid-2014 the target has not been met in any month. A seasonal pattern is visible on top of this trend in which the percentage peaks in the summer months and dips in the winter

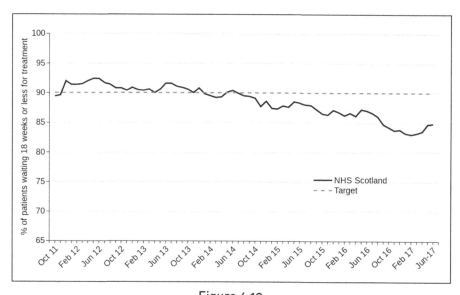

Figure 4.19
Percentages of patients waiting 18 weeks or less from initial referral to treatment (RTT) 2011–2017.

For Accident and Emergency there is currently a waiting time standard that no more than 95% of patients wait longer than four hours between arrival and being admitted, transferred or discharged. The 95% target was met or exceeded in every month from when the standard was introduced in 2007 until the end of 2010 when it was first missed. In every winter since then there has been one or more months in which it was missed. More elderly patients are brought to A&E in winter months and they often have more complex health issues which take more time to assess and treat. That said, attendance at A&E is often least in winter months, often being lowest in February, but highest in summer months, with the annual peak occurring in May. The early summer peak is explicable by the improving weather resulting in more outdoor activities including adult mishaps, some involving barbecues, trampolines and alcohol consumption.

Care outside hospitals is mainly handled by General Practitioners or GPs. In October 2017, there were 5019 GPs, excluding locums, working at 955 practices in Scotland.[21] Since 2015, the number of GPs have increased slightly from 5,002, but the number of practices have decreased from 981. Practice sizes range from small island ones, with a few hundred registered patients, to urban practices with tens of thousands of patients. The median number of patients per practice is 5,593, up from 5,247 in 2015.

The need for healthcare is growing faster than the population, and this is almost certainly because the population is ageing. To maintain current levels of care it's inevitable that more staff and more funding will be required. If we stay true to the founding principles of the NHS, funding should not be judged by its percentage of GDP, nor against inflation-adjusted historical trends, but by whether it meets the needs of the population.

Targeting failure

A target conjures up a mental image of coloured concentric rings with a clearly defined central circle. The targets that are applied in education, health, justice and other areas of society are far less clear-cut and are prone to three inter-related types of problem: quantifying an activity where a target is needed; deciding on the target; and the effect on non-targeted activities.

Quantifying an activity varies in difficulty. In health, the waiting time between a patient entering the system, at their GP or at an accident and emergency department, and receiving treatment is an obvious choice. In education, however, the matter is more complex, and the Scottish Survey of Literacy and Numeracy has to devise tests which are carefully calibrated against those of the previous years. Even for health, there are cases that are not clear which have the potential to be 'gamed'. Real examples of this exist where pressure to meet accident and emergency waiting time targets in England have resulted in patients' discharge times being distorted, and even of treatment taking place in an ambulance to delay the time of admission.[22] In Scotland, researchers at Aberdeen University found that the number of children admitted to hospital as emergencies increased by 50% but not because more children were becoming ill. Instead, changes to the out of hours GP service and the introduction of the four hour waiting time target were identified as likely causes.[23]

Once quantified, and with rules in place to avoid gaming, there is still the issue of setting the target. Although the instruction to set a target comes from on high, either from senior management or the government itself, a realistic target needs to be informed by the staff that must strive to achieve it. The four hour waiting time for Accident and Emergency introduced by the Scottish government initially stipulated that it was to be met in 98% of attendances. However, this target was only met in the summer months of 2008 and 2009 and not at all after that, so it was relaxed to a more realistic interim target of 95% in 2013 with 98% becoming a longer term ambition. Even this lower target has proved difficult to meet.

Arguably the biggest problem with setting a target in one area is that it may have unintended consequences for other areas. If, for example, it becomes known to the public that there is a target on accident and emergency, and resources are being directed at it to keep waiting times low, they may choose to attend A&E rather than wait for a GP appointment. The increased reliance on A&E evident in Table 4.5 may be an indication of this. Also, A&E is not only a costly and inefficient way to deal with minor ailments, it can result in unnecessary and disruptive upheaval for elderly people whose needs might be better served by care at home.

None of this is to say that services should not be summarised and quantified in numbers such as waiting time percentages or exam results. As noted earlier for the Scottish Index of Multiple Deprivation (SIMD), such measurements are useful for identifying a problem but they can easily misdirect a well-intentioned attempt at a solution.

Scots law and courts

The law in Scotland is formed from a historical mixture of sources. Laws passed in acts of the Scottish, UK or European parliaments are probably the most discussed and are referred to as legislative. A small number of current laws date back to the original Scottish parliament prior to the formation of the UK in 1707.

Less well understood is the important role of Scots common law which is distinct from its English equivalent. Common law is built up by the history of court rulings by judges on specific cases. For example, if a person is in court accused of murder, the defence may argue against it on the basis that a similar case in the past did not rule it as murder. If no sufficiently similar case exists and the judge rules that the present crime is murder, then this sets a precedent for any similar case in the future. Scots criminal law relies more heavily on precedent than English or Welsh law.

The law can also be divided into two broad categories: criminal and civil. Criminal law involves matters where an individual acts in a way considered unacceptable by society, whereas civil law deals with disputes between people and organisations. Murder, rape and robbery are examples of criminal law. Bankruptcy, divorce and property cases are examples of civil law.

The Scottish court system reflects these divisions as illustrated in Figure 4.20.

Cases that are less serious or complex will generally be dealt with by courts at the bottom of this diagram. For example, a Justice of the Peace or JP court (formerly known as a district court) deals with more minor crimes and cannot impose a sentence of more than 60 days imprisonment or a fine of £2,500. A sheriff court sitting with only a sheriff (a judge) but no jury can set sentences of up to 12 months and fines of up to £10,000. With a jury sentences of up to five years are possible and there is no limit on fines.

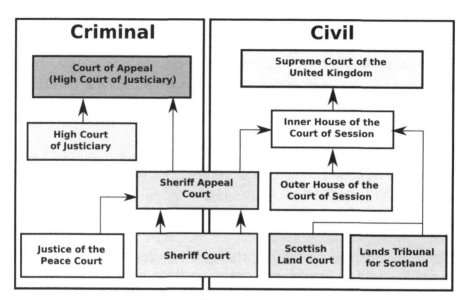

Figure 4.20
Hierarchy and appeal paths of Scottish courts.

The hierarchy also determines where appeals will be heard. If there is dispute on the ruling in a Justice of the Peace or Sheriff Court then this will be appealed at the Sheriff Appeal Court (created in 2015). Further appeals for criminal cases go to the Court of Appeal, and for civil cases to the Inner House of the Court of Session. Until 2009, an appeal from the Inner Court Of Session was escalated to the UK House of Lords, but it is now heard in the Supreme Court of the United Kingdom. This Supreme Court is also where legal issues concerning devolution will be heard such as the validity of Acts passed by the Scottish Parliament and powers of the Scottish government. The Supreme Court is subject to decisions made by the European Court of Justice in European Union Law.

The courts have been reformed in recent years with a programme of closures and refurbishments and installation of new communication technology with the aim of improving efficiency. From 2010 to 2017, 17 sheriff and JP courts have closed, 7 JP courts have been discontinued with 10 court buildings being re-purposed, sold or demolished. Currently there are 39 sheriff and JP courts, three high courts in Glasgow, Aberdeen and Edinburgh as well as the Court of Session.[24]

Legal aid ensures that people who are less wealthy can access advice from solicitors and be represented by lawyers in court. It is means-tested on provision of evidence to a Legal Aid registered solicitor who will then receive payment for their work from the Scottish Legal Aid Board, who are in turn funded by the Scottish government. In real terms, using 2016–17 prices, the legal aid funding in the Scottish budget (see Chapter 5) has fallen from £172 million in 2013–14 to £138 million in 2016–17, and the draft budget for 2017–18 sees a further fall to £135 million.[25] While some of this decrease can be explained by increases in efficiency, the Law Society of Scotland, the professional body overseeing standards for practising solicitors, are now concerned that access to justice is being eroded for poorer people, especially those in rural areas.[26]

Policing and crime

The Scottish government collects and publishes high-level trends on policing, justice and fire.[27] The data quoted in this section and the next on fire was published in October 2017.

Figure 4.21 shows the number of Full Time Equivalent or FTE police officers (two half-time officers counts as one FTE). Also shown is the number of residents in Scotland per police officer, that is, the population of Scotland divided by the FTE number of officers.

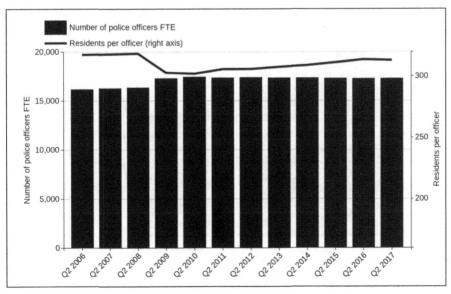

Figure 4.21
Numbers of police officers and residents per officer 2006–2017.

Since 2006 there has been a 6.7% growth in police officer numbers, though most of this increase occurred during 2008 with officer numbers rising from around 16,300 to 17,300. Since then, the number of officers has hardly changed, but the residents per officer has increased because the population of Scotland has grown.

The Scottish government proposed a bill to merge the eight regional police forces and fire and rescue services into single agencies covering the whole of Scotland. This bill was passed in the Scottish Parliament and became the Police and Fire Reform (Scotland) Act 2012. It took effect from 1 April 2013 and created Police Scotland and the Scottish Fire and Rescue Service. This change is not evident in the numbers of police officers in Figure 4.21 but consequences of this merger can be seen in fire and rescue service staff numbers which we'll come to shortly and also in Scotland's budget which we'll examine in Chapter 5.

Figure 4.22 shows the number of crimes recorded by the police.

Recorded crime has dropped by 38%, decreasing from 385,509 in 2007–08 to 238,651 in 2016–17 and is the lowest it has been for 43 years. Significant falls in crime levels have been recorded elsewhere in the UK, and in the USA and in many other countries.

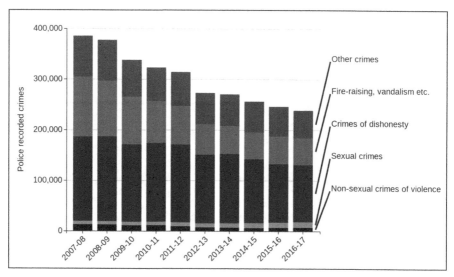

Figure 4.22
Numbers of recorded crimes by type 2007–08 to 2016–17.

Crimes of dishonesty, such as housebreaking, theft, shoplifting and fraud make up almost half of all recorded crime. *Fire and vandalism* was the second largest crime group in 2007–08 but has since seen the largest percentage decrease at 56%. *Other crimes*, which is mostly made up of drug and weapon offences, has also decreased, but more slowly and so it has now become the second biggest crime group.

Sexual crimes make up 4.5% of all recorded crimes, and non-sexual crimes of violence make up 3.0%. If these percentages seem low, that might be because such crimes are more newsworthy and so we hear about them more often. Sexual crimes was the only group to see an increase over the last decade, though this may be due to the Sexual Offences (Scotland) Act affecting how such crimes have been recorded since December 2010.

The total number of people sentenced, that is, convicted by a court, has dropped by 26% over the last decade. Most of this decrease has come from the reduction in the use of financial penalties, which is the most common type of sentence, making up half of all convictions. It's interesting that this reduction is less than the 38% reduction in recorded crime mentioned above as it implies that an increased proportion of crimes now result in a conviction.

Figure 4.23 shows how the prison population has changed over time. The number shown is the average daily prison population which is calculated by adding up the number of people in prison on each day of the year and dividing by the number of days in that year. The small number of prisoners from court martial in the military are excluded, as are civil prisoners such as people who have not paid fines.

The prison population in 2016–17 is 7,552 having increased by 25% from 6,056 in 1997–98. The population peaked at 8,179 in 2011–12 and has steadily fallen since then. A minority of prisoners are held on remand, that is, in custody awaiting court proceedings.

In 1997–98, 12 out of every 10,000 people in Scotland were in prison, rising to 15 in 2011–12, but falling to 14 in 2016–17. Although this is a small percentage, the 25% growth of prisoner numbers over this time is significantly larger than the 6.3% growth of the population. Also, it contrasts with the fact that both recorded crime and convictions have fallen significantly in the last decade, as we saw above.

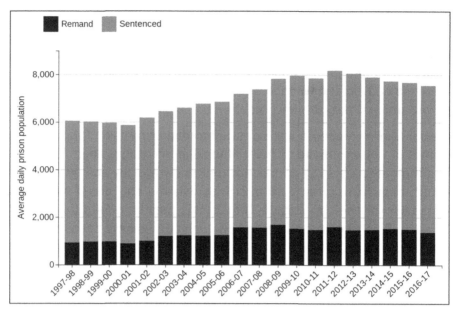

Figure 4.23
Prison population in prison 1997–98 and 2016–17.

Fire and rescue

Figure 4.24 shows the number of incidents attended by the fire and rescue service, drawn from the Scottish government report mentioned in the previous section. Primary fires are defined[28] as those involving inhabited or used buildings and property, and secondary fires involve burning of rubbish, derelict buildings, abandoned vehicles as well as some burning on farmland and other open ground. Numbers for 2016–17 are provisional.

The number of attended fires shows a fall across all types with the total decreasing by 38% between 2004–05 and 2016–17. In recent years, numbers have levelled off and there has been a slight rise in secondary fires since 2014–15.

Figure 4.25 shows the number of staff in the fire and rescue service on March 31 of each year from 2010 to 2017. It includes front-line staff, control and support staff as well as volunteers who make up about 10% of the total.

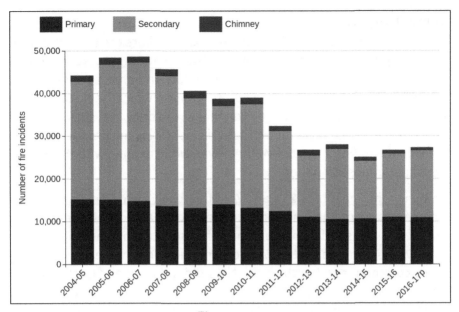

Figure 4.24

Number of attendances at fires by type of incident 2004–05 to 2016–17.

The number of staff dropped by 1,323 or 16% between 2010 and 2017. The fall from 2010 to the merger of regional fire services on 1 April 2013 was 3%, but the fall from then to 2017 was much larger at 12%.

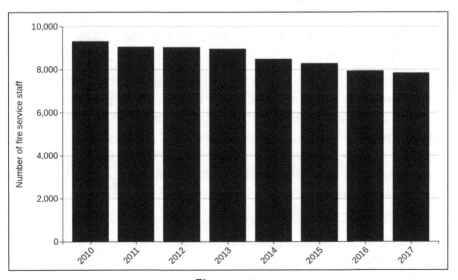

Figure 4.25

Number of fire and rescue service staff including volunteers 2010 to 2017.

Some thoughts

At the start of this chapter I mentioned that numbers are limited in what they can tell us about society, but I made no attempt to define what I meant by society. Some feel it is their duty to serve society loyally, whereas others devote their lives to causes which seek to change society radically, and there are even those who deny that society exists. The sense in which I use the word is this: society is the product of many individuals finding ways to live their lives while dealing with the limitations that imposes on them.

Imagine what chapters 2, 3 and 4 of this book would be like if it was written 100 years ago. To pick examples from each chapter: electricity in 1917 was in a smaller percentage of households than broadband was in 2017; the benefits system was embryonic and so poverty was much more common, and harsher; the NHS did not exist and healthcare as we know it today existed only for the wealthy. It is impossible to deny that there has been substantial progress in these and many other areas even if there were losses to society, such as the loss of community when old tenements were demolished and residents rehoused in the grey schemes of the mid-twentieth century. But the gains are clear, and many of them are driven by technology. That technology is in turn driven by human endeavour in many disciplines, including but not limited to engineering, mathematics, science, accounting and computing. All of these disciplines involve skillful processing of numbers. So although I argue that numbers are of somewhat limited use in describing our society, they have never been more intrinsic to how our society functions.

To round out this chapter, here is one of the best articulations of what society means in relation to science, art and patriotism. It was given by scientist Dr Robert R. Wilson, the first director of the FermiLab in the United States. The FermiLab was founded in 1967 to pursue experimental research in particle physics and in April 1969 Wilson testified before a committee to justify the value of his lab's work. He was pressed by US Senator John Pastore about its relevance to the military:[29]

SENATOR PASTORE. It has no value in that respect?

DR. WILSON. It only has to do with the respect with which we regard one another, the dignity of men, our love of culture. It has to do with those things.

It has nothing to do with the military. I am sorry.

SENATOR PASTORE. Don't be sorry for it.

DR. WILSON. I am not, but I cannot in honesty say it has any such application.

SENATOR PASTORE. Is there anything here that projects (sic) us in a position of being competitive with the Russians, with regard to this race?

DR. WILSON. Only from a long-range point of view, of a developing technology. Otherwise, it has to do with: Are we good painters, good sculptors, great poets? I mean all the things that we really venerate and honor in our country and are patriotic about.

In that sense, this new knowledge has all to do with honor and country but it has nothing to do directly with defending our country except to help make it worth defending.

There is a twist to this, however. Elsewhere in the hearing transcript there are clear indications that Senator Pastore supported the work of the FermiLab and that the above line of questioning was part of political manoeuvring ahead of selling the project to doubting fellow senators. What this illustrates is that no human endeavour, be it art or science, exists outside society and its politics.

Questions to ponder:

- Has education provision been adjusted for the recent rise in the number of school pupils?
- How can Scotland's universities, especially its older ones, attract more students from low income and other disadvantaged backgrounds?
- And related to that, are student loans for living costs problematic even though there are no tuition fees for Scottish and non-rUK EU-domiciled students?
- Why has the crime rate fallen while the prison population has grown?
- Has the drive to reduce public spending on legal aid affected the availability of legal representation, especially for those on lower incomes?
- Should we move away from a target-driven culture in the public sector towards a monitor and learn approach, and might that be relevant to private sector companies?

Chapter 5

Public spending and revenue

5

Modern society in a wealthy economy relies on public spending. Ample evidence of this can be found in previous chapters. What use would your car be without a road to drive it on? What levels of poverty and income inequality would you expect without a welfare system? How would you cope if attacked and injured without the NHS, police and courts? What would the future hold for society without adequate education?

There are three levels of government that control public spending. The councils handle local services such as schools, care services, refuse collection and local roads. The Scottish government has ultimate responsibility for Scotland-wide services, such as the NHS, the court system, water services, and, since April 2013, the police and fire and rescue services. The Westminster government controls what are called 'reserved' matters such as defence, international affairs and some of welfare (pensions and benefits).

Public spending is a flow of money out of the public sector into the private sector. The private sector is comprised of all residents and businesses in Scotland. There is also a flow of money from the private sector into the public sector which is known as public revenue. This is mostly from taxation but a not insignificant amount comes from fees, which includes everything from fines for late library books and parking up to licenses for farming salmon and drilling for oil.

Public revenue is collected at all three levels of government, but the revenue at each level does not match the spending. In fact, spending almost always exceeds revenue. In other words, the public sector is normally in deficit. Each level of government is mostly funded from the level above it. So the councils receive most of their funding from the Scottish government which in turn receives most of its funding from the UK government.

The details of how funding meets spending is intricate and confusing at the council level, and with the new revenue raising powers from the Scotland Act 2016, it will become fiendishly complicated in the Scottish government's budgets from 2018–19 onwards. But most of the deficit of public spending over revenues is handled at the UK level where matters go from confusing to perplexing and surreal, unless, as we'll see, you are willing to let go of everyday notions of debt, borrowing and money. The fiscal side of this much misunderstood issue is described in this chapter and I urge you to put your preconceptions aside, particularly if you believe that either deficits are always a problem or else that deficits do not matter. In Chapter 6 we'll explore the economic side of debt and deficit, and how it relates to sectoral balances, that is the flows between the public, private and foreign sectors.

Note that the word **fiscal** is generally used to distinguish government policy concerning tax and spending from **monetary** policy which relates to currency and interest rates. The term fiscal also has a completely separate use in Scotland in referring to the *procurator fiscal* who is a public prosecutor in law courts. The historical origin of this use comes from judges or sheriffs who also had significant financial responsibilities.

Public spending

The General Expenditure and Revenue Scotland report (GERS)[1] is published by the Scottish government each year and, as the name suggests, gives figures on what is spent in Scotland and also for the revenue generated in Scotland summed up over all three levels of government. The latest GERS available at the time of writing was published in August 2017 and covered financial years 1998–99 to 2016–17. GERS figures are given in **nominal** (or cash) terms whereas the figures given here are, unless said otherwise, corrected for inflation to be in **real terms** using standard deflators from HM Treasury September 2017 edition.[2] HM Treasury is the department of the UK government responsible for fiscal matters.

Figure 5.1 shows the spending per person in Scotland and also the UK expressed in real terms. Public spending is measured by **Total Managed Expenditure** or **TME** which we'll discuss in more depth later on.

For both Scotland and the whole UK, real spending per person rose to reach a peak in 2010–11 and then decreased. The growth in these figures between 1998–99 and 2016–17 is 45% for Scotland and 43% for the UK, with the fall since the peak being 4.4% for Scotland and 6.1% for the UK. Most of this fall is due to a population increase rather than a drop in TME (see Figure 5.5).

Public spending per person has been higher for Scotland in every year. For 2016–17, Scotland's public spending was 12% higher than the UK's.

Public spending presented as an amount per person offers an intuitive interpretation: in addition to the amount each individual spends themselves to support their lifestyle, the government spends an amount to

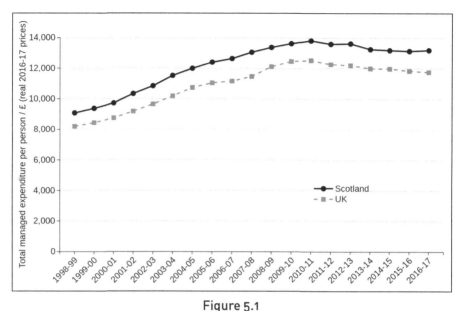

Figure 5.1

Real Total Managed Expenditure per person in Scotland 1998–88 to 2016–17.

support public facilities and services. This public spending covers health, roads, rubbish collection, education, state pensions, state benefits and much more. In contrast to private spending, public spending is of course mostly on areas of common use, including many that are essential to modern life. So, for example, an individual might spend money on buying a car, but the government makes this worthwhile because they spend money on behalf of all citizens to build and maintain roads.

In Chapter 3, we saw that the median income after taxes are deducted and benefits are added was £24,400 for a two adult household in 2015–16. The government spent £12,800 for each Scottish resident in 2015–16 prices, so we can say that the government spent £25,600 for a typical household. Not only is this slightly more than what the household can spend itself, but it is considerably more than such a household pays in taxes.

Figure 5.2 shows the top eight areas of Total Managed Expenditure or TME for 2016–17 with the remainder shown as *Everything else*. Note that here we compare Scotland to the rest of the UK or **rUK** rather than the whole UK because we'll go on to examine how Scotland's 'extra' spending per head is distributed over these areas. Although Scotland's TME per

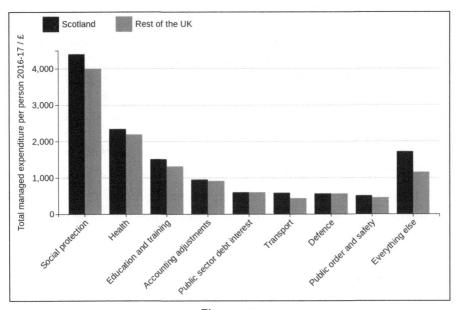

Figure 5.2

Top eight areas of Total Managed Expenditure in Scotland and rUK in 2016–17.

person is 13% higher than the rUK's, the UK's is only 1% above the rUK's because its population is so much larger than that of Scotland.

Scotland's public spending per person exceeds that of rUK in every area except for *Public sector debt interest* and *Defence* because these are apportioned to Scotland in GERS using the population share. *Social protection* is by far the largest area of expenditure and includes pensions, benefits and other welfare spending. The top three areas together – *Social protection*, *Health* and *Education and training* – make up 63% of Scotland's public spending and 65% of the rUK's.

The fourth largest area is *Accounting adjustments* at £5.1 billion, which is explained in Annex A of GERS.[3] It represents flows of money that should be counted in Total Managed Expenditure but do not belong in any particular area, or are included so that they balance an amount included by convention on the revenue side. With this being the case, both the expenditure figures here and the revenue figures given later are in fact overestimates and so caution is required in making comparisons with other countries. This does not appreciably affect trends over time, comparisons between Scotland and rUK, nor estimates of the deficit in which these adjustments cancel out.

Total public spending per person in Scotland in 2016–17 was £13,200 and for the rest of the UK it was £11,600. That is, around £1600 more is spent per resident of Scotland than for residents elsewhere in the UK. Multiplying this by the population of Scotland gives the total extra expenditure for Scotland as £8.5 billion. In other words, if the whole UK's TME was allocated to Scotland as a straightforward population share, then Scotland's TME would have been £8.5 billion lower in 2016–17. Figure 5.3 shows how this extra spending is distributed. The percentages sum to 100% to within rounding errors.

The three largest areas of spending – *Social protection*, *Health* and *Education and training* – together take 50% of this extra spending, and *Transport* takes 9% of it.

Scotland's Total Managed Expenditure for 2016–17 was £71.2 billion and, as shown below in Figure 5.5, has seen a slight real terms rise in the last couple of years even though it has fallen per person due to faster population growth. The top 3 areas of public spending together made up £44.6 billion or 63% of it. Figure 5.4 shows how these changed over time in real terms, that is, adjusted for inflation to be in 2016–17 prices.

Social protection shows a strong increasing trend until a fall in 2013–14 after which there was a slight rise. Health also showed strong growth

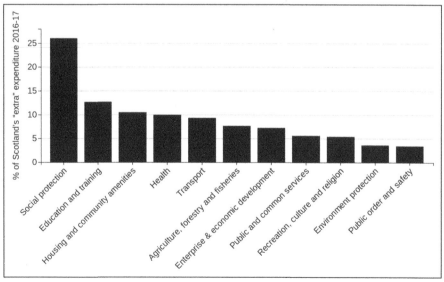

Figure 5.3
Where Scotland's extra public expenditure is spent 2016–17.

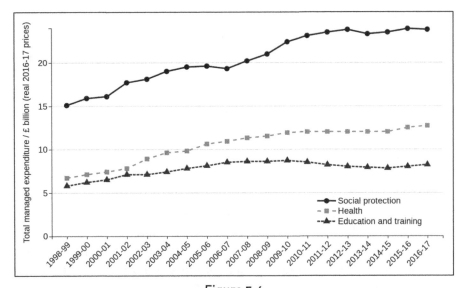

Figure 5.4

Top 3 areas of real Total Managed Expenditure in Scotland 1998–99 to 2016–17.

but then remained constant from 2010–11 with a rise in the last couple of years.

The situation for Education and training is quite different. Its rising trend ended in 2007–08 and then it fell from a high of £8.7 billion to a low of £7.8 billion 2013–14 – a real terms fall of 9%. To give this some context, most of this spending is on schools and although pupil numbers fell over this time, they did so by only 0.7%. Pupil numbers are now rising (see Chapter 4) and although education spending has also started rising in recent years, it still sits 6% below its peak value in real terms.

As with household incomes in Chapter 3, it's important not to lose sight of the significant real terms growth that has taken place in past decades, although most of it was before the financial crash of 2008. From 1998–99 to 2016–17, public spending has increased by 55% in real terms, whereas Scotland's population has only increased by 6.5%.

Of the major expenditure areas shown in Figure 5.2, *Public sector debt interest* is the only one that has decreased since 1998–99. In real terms, between 1998–99 and 2016–17, it decreased by 5% even though the UK's public debt has more than tripled. We'll discuss the reason for this in Chapter 6.

Public revenue

Figure 5.5 shows the revenue attributed to Scotland by GERS with figures adjusted for inflation to be in 2016–17 prices. Onshore revenue refers to that from individuals and businesses located in Scotland, and shown separately is the amount from the North Sea oil and gas industry which is a geographical share attributed to Scotland, discussed in more detail below. Total Managed Expenditure is shown for reference.

Total revenue including the North Sea grew somewhat unevenly from £42.7 billion in 1998–99 to reach a peak of £61.7 billion in 2007–08. It dropped by £6.2 billion or 10% over the following two years and although there was then a recovery, it suffered another drop in 2012–13 of £3.5 billion or 6% due to a sharp fall in North Sea revenue. Revenue decreased further as North Sea revenues dwindled to almost nothing but 2016–17 saw a large step up in onshore revenue, which we'll examine shortly. Total revenue for that year was £58.0 billion which is still short of the 2007–08 or 2011–12 peaks.

Onshore revenue shows a similar trend to total revenue up until the financial crisis. Onshore revenue in 1998–99 was £40.5 billion and it

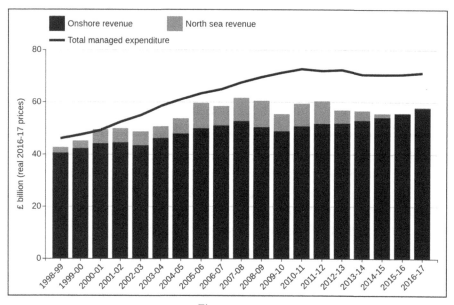

Figure 5.5
Onshore revenue, North Sea revenue and Total Managed Expenditure
1998–9 to 2016–17.

increased to a peak of £52.8 billion in 2007–08. It then dropped over the next two years but, unlike total revenue, it then grew steadily to reach a new high of £57.7 billion in 2016–17, well above the 2007–08 peak.

Public spending was larger than revenue in every year shown in the graph except in 2000–01 when revenues were £0.3 billion higher than expenditure. The gap between the two has grown larger since the financial crisis of 2008.

From 1998–99 to 2007–08, spending and total revenue both grew by about 5% each year in real terms. Onshore revenue growth grew too but more slowly at 3.4%. From 2007–08 to 2016–17, average annual spending growth was slower at 3.0% but outpaced the growth of total revenue at 2.0%, and onshore revenue at 2.4%. Total real terms growth between 1998–99 and 2016–17 was 55% for spending, 36% for total revenue and 43% for onshore revenue.

Figure 5.6 shows the revenue per person for Scotland and the UK in real terms.

When North Sea revenues are included, Scotland's revenue per person is higher than the UK's in every year shown except for the last three. If North Sea revenues are excluded then Scotland's revenue per person is lower than the UK's in every year.

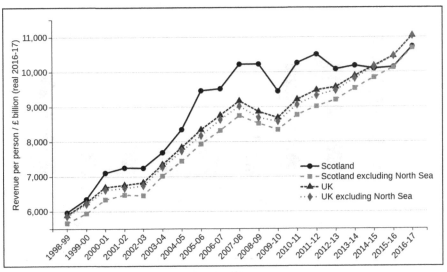

Figure 5.6
Revenue per person for Scotland and the UK 1998–99 to 2016–17.

Notice that the difference between including and excluding North Sea revenues is very significant for Scotland, but only makes a slight difference for the UK. This emphasises that revenues from the North Sea make up a much greater proportion of Scotland's revenue, and that the North Sea is the reason why Scotland's revenue per head exceeded that of the UK until 2013–14.

Figure 5.7 shows the top areas of revenue for the UK and Scotland.

Income tax, *National Insurance* (NI) and *Value Added Tax* (VAT) together make up 58% of the revenue total for both Scotland and the whole UK. *Income tax* and *National Insurance* are taken from each individual's income, though some additional NI is paid by the employer, and VAT is taken from purchases. Along with other taxes, such as council tax, stamp duty, alcohol and tobacco duties, at least two-thirds of public revenue is drawn from taxes on individuals.

Of the top eight areas, only two are exclusively drawn from private businesses – corporation tax and non-domestic rates – and together they make up 11.5% of the total for both Scotland and the UK.

The fourth largest revenue area in 2016–17 was *Gross operating surplus* which makes up 7.5% of Scotland's revenue and 6.6% of the UK's. This

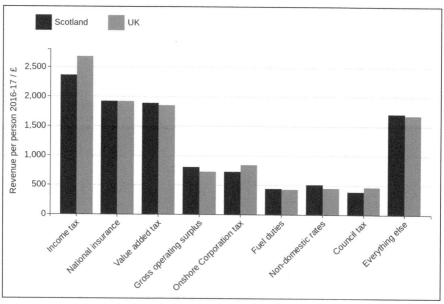

Figure 5.7
Top eight sources of public revenue in 2016–17.

is composed of two main parts. The first part is not actual revenue in that no money was received by the state, but is included to balance items in public spending's *Accounting adjustments* mentioned above. The second part of *Gross operating surplus* is the surplus made by publicly owned corporations. It is similar to the profits of a private company except that it is returned to the government as revenue rather than distributed amongst shareholders. Scotland's *Gross operating surplus* exceeds that of the UK mainly because Scottish Water is in public ownership and it returns a sizeable surplus; water companies in England are privately owned (see Chapter 2).

Taxes on wealth, as opposed to income, are included under *Everything else* and include interest and dividends tax, capital gains tax, inheritance tax, stamp duty and its Scottish replacement Land & Building Transaction Tax (LBTT). Together they make up only a few percent of total public revenue. In contrast income tax and NI together make up 40% of that total. The so-called 'sin taxes' on tobacco, alcohol and betting are also in *Everything else* and total 3.7%, which is notably higher than the UK's 2.7%.

Figure 5.8 plots the four largest sources of tax revenue in real terms at 2016–17 prices.

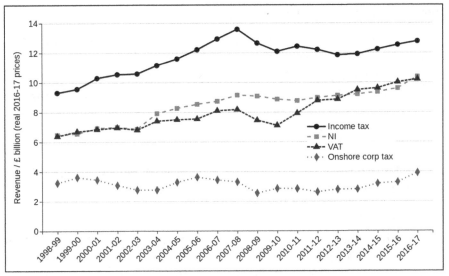

Figure 5.8
Scotland's largest revenue sources 1998–98 to 2016–17.

Income tax, *VAT* and *NI* all show a similar trend: growth until 2007–08 followed by a fall and some recovery. *Onshore corporation tax* is different because it does not show consistent growth before 2008, but has increased in recent years to achieve a new high in 2016–17. *VAT* and *NI* have also exceeded their pre-crisis peaks, but *Income tax* is still well below its 2007–08 peak.

Income tax is a more progressive tax than NI which means that a greater share of it is collected from people with higher incomes. The fact that income tax fell by more than NI tells us that higher incomes fell by a larger amount than lower incomes in absolute terms, and, as was also seen in Chapter 3, they also fell by more in percentage terms.

The step up in total revenue in 2016–17, which was mentioned above, is mainly due to the pronounced rises in NI and Corporation Tax evident in this graph, and both are in fact UK-wide. A change was made to the NI system – in effect, a tax rise – in April 2016 as announced in a previous UK government budget.[4] The rise in Corporation Tax is harder to explain but is in part due to tightening of rules on corporation tax payments, especially on larger companies and banks. Also, profits, on which Corporation Tax is taxed as a percentage, saw a sharp increase in 2016–17. This may not be a sign of corporate health, but could just be because companies are holding back money from investment and wage rises as they wait to see how Brexit unfolds.

For most revenue sources, Scotland's share of the UK total is a percentage point or two away from its 8.2% population share. In 2016–17, the percentages are: NI 8.2%, VAT 8.4%, income tax 7.3%, onshore corporation tax 7.1%. Exceptions to this on the high side are the sin taxes on tobacco and alcohol products at 13% and 9%, and also non-domestic rates (paid by businesses) at 9%. On the low side are capital gains tax at only 4% (paid when an asset that has increased in value is sold, eg shares), inheritance tax at 5.7%, and LBTT and stamp duty on land and properties at 5%.

North Sea revenue

Unlike other sources of revenue which don't deviate far from Scotland's 8.2% population share, about 80% of total UK North Sea revenue is typically attributed to Scotland. This is referred to as a 'geographical share' because most oil and gas fields are below the seabed off the coast of Scotland. The precise percentage varies from year to year depending on production and also due to revisions of how the geographical share is assigned.[5] This has been further complicated in recent years because there have been tax rebates which have made some revenues negative.

From 2000–01 to 2013–14, the North Sea provided more revenue than all of Scotland's onshore corporation tax. In the North Sea's best year, 2011–12, its revenues were four times larger than onshore corporation tax, and it was 17% of Scotland's total revenue. For most of the last 20 years this percentage has been above 10%; in 2016–17 it was 0.4%.

Most of Scotland's North Sea industry is concerned with oil extraction rather than gas. Figure 5.9 plots the oil price[6] and the UK's total North Sea revenue. Unlike most other graphs in this book, neither are adjusted for inflation. The name 'Brent' has come to be used to describe North Sea oil because Brent was one of the first major oil fields to be discovered.

It's clear that North Sea revenue is correlated with oil price: both increased until they peaked in 2008–09, and then both fell and rose to another peak in 2011–12, then they fell together dramatically in recent years. But differences are also clear. Only North Sea revenue peaked in

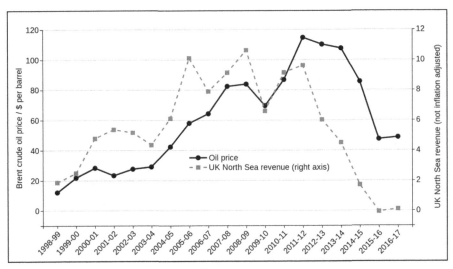

Figure 5.9
Brent crude oil price and UK North Sea revenue (nominal)
1998–99 to 2016–17.

2005–06 and the steep fall in revenue began two years before the oil price's sharp decline from 2013–14.

North Sea revenues are, in common with other forms of corporation tax, mostly levied as a percentage of profits. An oil company's annual profit is, roughly speaking, the volume of oil it sells multiplied by the oil price less its costs during that year. So if the volume produced or the costs do not vary too much from year to year then North Sea revenues will move with the oil price. Conversely, if the oil price is steady then revenues will go up with rising production or falling costs.

Figure 5.10 shows how UK crude oil production and North Sea company expenditure has varied. Expenditure is made up of two components. Operating expenditure, often called OPEX, is concerned with the ongoing running of oil platforms and associated services. Capital expenditure, or CAPEX, is spent on building or upgrading infrastructure, such as an oil rig or pipeline, and also on exploring for new oil and gas sources. You can think of CAPEX as being an investment that will bring returns in future oil production.

This graph together with the oil price in Figure 5.9 explains most of the variation seen the North Sea revenues. Production was in steady decline until 2012–13 and despite a gradual rise in expenditure from 2004–05,

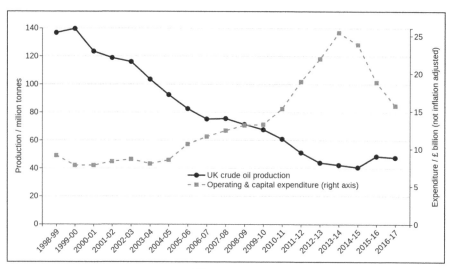

Figure 5.10
UK crude oil production and expenditure 1998–99 to 2016–17.

the oil price was rising fast enough so that revenues rose until the first peak of 2009–10.

After that the story changes as the oil price falls abruptly then climbs back up to a high in 2011–12 where it stays for several years. During that time, oil companies decided to bet that the oil price would remain high and ramped up investment with the intention of arresting and reversing the decline in oil production. Figure 5.10 shows this clearly as expenditure rising rapidly in the years of the high oil price while production levels out. This also explains why North Sea revenues fell from 2011–12 to 2014–15 while the oil price remained high – expenditure shot up, reducing profits. After that however, it was the dramatic fall in oil price that reduced profits, taking North Sea revenues to slightly negative values. From 2014–15 it became clear that the oil price had left its lofty values for the foreseeable future, and so companies reduced expenditure, especially on CAPEX. This has important implications for Scotland's onshore economy which we'll return to in Chapter 6.

The act of balancing

Matters relating to public spending and taxation are often referred to as **fiscal**. Public revenue minus public spending gives a figure called the **net fiscal balance**. Figure 5.11 shows this for the UK and Scotland as a percentage of Gross Domestic Product or GDP which is a measure of the size of the economy (see Chapter 6). Also shown is the balance for Scotland excluding North Sea revenues. This is not done for the UK because its balance is hardly changed which you can confirm by looking at Figure 5.6.

The net fiscal balance has been negative for Scotland in all years shown except for a very slight positive balance in 2000–01, and it has been negative for the UK since 2001–02. The balance decreased markedly following the 2008 financial crisis, mainly due to revenues dropping as the economy slowed, but also because public expenditure increased as benefit claims rose with unemployment.

A negative net fiscal balance is often referred to as the budget deficit or fiscal deficit or sometimes just as the **deficit**. Scotland's largest deficit was in 2009–10 when it reached 10% of GDP, though without North Sea revenues it would have been 16%. The UK's budget deficit also peaked at 10% of GDP that year. In 2016–17 the UK's deficit was 2.4% and Scotland's was 8.4%.

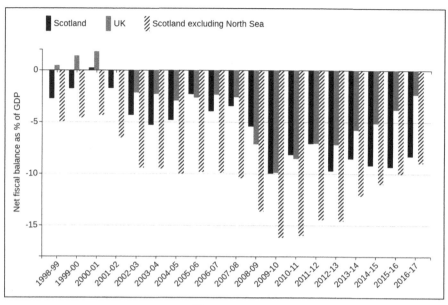

Figure 5.11

The net fiscal balance for Scotland and the UK 1998–99 to 2016–17.

Political deficits

Scotland's deficit does not appear in the Scottish government's budget, nor its national accounts, nor those of the UK. The UK government does not require or even ask the Scottish government to address it, and although the EU requires member states to have deficits of less than 3% of GDP, it does not insist on this for parts of member states. As such, Scotland's deficit is notional.

But this notional deficit is of political significance because if the Yes vote had carried in the 2014 referendum and Scotland had become independent in 2016 as planned, then it would have almost certainly faced a deficit of between 5% and 10% of GDP in its first year. Although GERS does not tell us about Scotland's fiscal situation in the medium to long term after independence, it does give us a reasonable idea for the short term of a few years. While it is true that running deficits is the norm for modern developed economies, running such a large deficit is not. In fact, on its debut as Europe's newest independent state, Scotland would likely have held the dubious distinction of having the largest deficit in 2016, with the next largest being Spain at 4.5% of GDP.[7]

Countries with control over their own currency, trusted government bonds (shares of government debt) and no dominant trade partner have considerable fiscal flexibility. For these reasons, the UK was able to deal with its 10% deficit. However, according to the plans of the Scottish government's Scotland's Future white paper,[8] a newly independent Scotland in 2016 would have remained in monetary union with the rest of the UK and not had its own currency. If Scotland were also still a member of the EU, or wishing to join the EU, it would be pressured to reduce its deficit to the EU's 3% limit. Economic growth of 4% to 5% in real terms for a decade could close Scotland's deficit, but no developed country has achieved such growth for a sustained period. The EU would very likely require of Scotland what it required of Ireland post–2008, which was a mixture of spending cuts and tax rises.

Such fiscal and technical concerns, important though they are, are not driving the political debate. They are products of it. Vocal advocates of staying in the UK are unlikely to change their minds if Scotland's fiscal situation were stronger, and those who yearn for a separate Scottish state are not fazed by fiscal obstacles. For the former, the deficit is emphasised as a problem, and for the latter it is often too readily rejected or dismissed. In reality, the deficit would be likely to cause short to medium term problems following Scottish independence with the severity depending on choices made on currency and public borrowing. In the longer term, no one can make any fiscal or economic prediction with any confidence, and if you accept that fact, then you must also admit that the debate of whether to remain in the UK or leave it must ultimately be driven by other, non-fiscal concerns.

Leading politicians have displayed deficits of understanding and candour on fiscal matters in recent years. First Minister Alex Salmond refused to acknowledge that volatile oil prices could have placed a newly independent Scotland in a precarious fiscal position. Prime Minister David Cameron refused to heed advice from economists that the UK's fiscal budget was unlike that of a household and that cutting spending following a recession would hamper economic recovery and thus thwart his own government's attempts to eliminate the deficit by 2015. This was proved correct, and eliminating the deficit was postponed to 2018, then to 2020, and attempts to set a date for it were then abandoned altogether.

For reasons we will explore further later in this chapter and the next, a government cannot control its deficit any more than it can control the confidence of its citizens and businesses. It can, at most, play mood music to them. What a government can do fiscally is invest and create a stable base for the long term benefit of society. How large that investment should be, and where and when it should be made are crucial questions in politics involving an inescapable mix of moral, psychological and technical aspects.

Scottish budget

The Scottish government sets out plans for spending and taxation in its annual budget. The key document is the **draft budget** which is published several months before the financial year it covers. It is then scrutinised by the Scottish Parliament's finance committee[9] which releases a report prior to it being debated by Members of the Scottish Parliament (MSPs) who may suggest amendments. The Act is then passed by a vote of MSPs just before the start of the new financial year.

For example, the draft budget for the 2017-18 financial year was released in December 2016, and passed as the Budget (Scotland) Act 2017[10] by a vote in the Scottish Parliament in February 2017. This process means there are three sets of figures: one in the draft budget, another in the budget that is passed and the outturn which is the amount that is actually spent. Usually they do not differ significantly.

The draft budget document starts with a high-level overview and then has a chapter devoted to each of the main areas of spending, known as portfolios, such as health, finance, education and justice. There are also some Annexes at the end which give more detail and some background information, including comparisons with earlier years.

We'll draw on data from the 2018–19 draft budget document[11] and quote figures in 2017–18 prices in what follows unless otherwise stated. The 2018–19 draft budget uses 2017–18 prices because no data was available on 2018–19 when it is written. The Scottish Parliament information Centre or SPICe publish visualisations and analysis on the budget including spreadsheets of data.[12]

There are three important totals for public spending: TME, DEL and AME.[13] This same structure is also used at the UK government level. The **Total Managed Expenditure (TME)** is the grand total of all spending and the TME specified in the Budget Act becomes a legal limit that cannot be exceeded unless the Act is amended by the Scottish Parliament.

TME is split into two components, DEL and AME:

TME = DEL + AME

The larger of the two is the **Departmental Expenditure Limit (DEL)**. This is the limit on spending allocated to government departments that can, to some degree, be planned in advance. For example, the DEL amount would cover the building of hospitals and also paying of hospital staff. The DEL amounts are set during spending reviews that occur every few years, though these amounts are not bound by law and they are often altered from year to year.

The other, smaller component of TME is **Annually Managed Expenditure (AME)**. This is money that is demand-led in that it cannot be reliably planned for in advance, but, by law, must be paid in response to whatever need arises. For example, AME increased after the 2008 financial crisis when people lost their jobs and started claiming unemployment benefits in greater numbers. AME covers other welfare payments and also pensions for retired public sector employees. Other, smaller areas of spending that do not relate to specific government departments are usually also included with AME under the heading 'AME & other'.

Figure 5.12 shows the TME split into DEL and AME for draft budgets for a number of years. Also shown are the **outturn** figures – the actual amount spent in previous years.

In real terms, inflation adjusted to 2016–17 prices, draft budget TME on this graph has varied between its low of £35.6 billion in 2008–09 and high of £39.4 billion in 2018–19, but shows no obvious increasing or decreasing trend.

Notice that the TME shown here is much less than that shown for the GERS figures in Figure 5.5. This is because the GERS figures include all spending by local and UK governments, whereas the figures in Figure 5.12 are only for funds under the Scottish government's control, though this includes the substantial funding it gives to councils. We'll examine how TME is spread across levels of government later in this chapter.

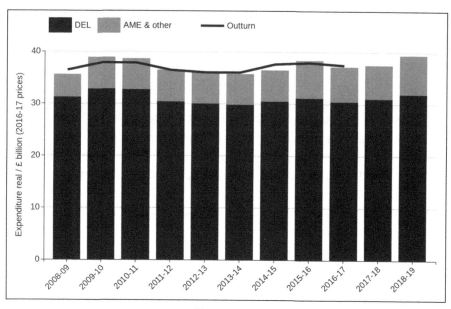

Figure 5.12

Total Managed Expenditure (TME) split into DEL and AME together
with the outturn TME spent for past years 2008–09 to 2018–19.

The outturn figures show that there is less variation in the actual amount
spent than draft budget figures would suggest. The year 2014–15 is
particularly interesting because the draft budget gave TME as £35.4
billion but the outturn was £1.1 billion higher at £36.5 billion (in prices
of that year). The TME set in the legislation is a legal limit and cannot be
exceeded, but if there's an exceptional need to do so, then the law must
be changed. For this reason, the Scottish Parliament passed amendments to the Budget (Scotland) Act 2014 in October 2014 and raised the
limit on TME to £36.7 billion.[14] The bulk of this increase was due to £0.9
billion transferred from the UK government to cover an AME increase
for NHS and teacher's pensions.[15]

Figure 5.13 shows how DEL and AME have varied in the draft budgets as
a percentage of TME.

The graph has a symmetric appearance because the two percentages
have to add to give 100%. The trend is clear: AME's percentage of TME
is rising and DEL's is falling. This suggests that the government is having
to react to events more than it expects, with spending on needs-driven
AME spending becoming more significant.

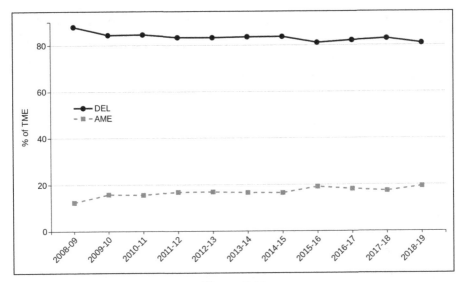

Figure 5.13

Draft budget DEL and AME as a percentage of TME 2008–09 to 2018–19.

Spending is further subdivided into resource and capital. Resource spending is the larger of the two being for everyday activities such as a paying a teacher or a doctor, whereas capital spending is mainly for infrastructure such as building a school or upgrading a hospital. The important distinction is that resource spending is one-off in that when you pay a teacher for a month of work, you just expect that one month of work. Capital spending however sees repeated use of the money spent, for example, £1 million might be spent to build a school during a year, but the benefits of that school in providing education for the community can last for 20 years or more.

Resource spending has fiscal and non-cash elements. Fiscal spending refers to conventional spending, such as the payment of a teacher's salary. The non-cash elements, which make up only a few percent of the total, are there for accounting purposes and, for example, represent the depreciation of a school building. Similarly, capital spending is split into a fiscal amount which would include building a school, and also the so-called financial transactions or FTs. Financial Transactions can only be used for specific purposes and will have to be paid back to HM Treasury though the terms and timescales are not clear at present. In the 2018–19 budget there was an unexpectedly large amount of FTs via the Barnett formula arising from the Help to Buy scheme implemented elsewhere in the UK. The Scottish government plans to put this to different uses in Scotland including £340 million for establishing a Scottish national investment bank.[16] Further details on these different types of spending can be found in the Scottish government's budget document.[17]

Since 2010–11, the UK government has pursued an austerity policy which involved attempts to cut public spending, and such cuts mainly applied to DEL as it is more within government control than AME. This can be seen in the drop that took place in 2011–12 when DEL dropped from £32.7 to £30.4 billion whereas AME increased slightly from £6.0 to £6.1 billion. Most of AME in the Scottish Budget is for pensions and, as with the UK as a whole, the rising number of people of pensionable age means that AME is likely to continue to rise for the foreseeable future.

Figure 5.14 shows how the TME outturns breaks down into different areas. Before 2013–14, police and fire were managed regionally and so included in Local government. From 2013–14, *Local government* expenditures are shown including and excluding police and fire.

The areas shown make up about 87% of TME with the remainder spread across many smaller areas. *Health* and *Local government* together make up about two-thirds of TME each year.

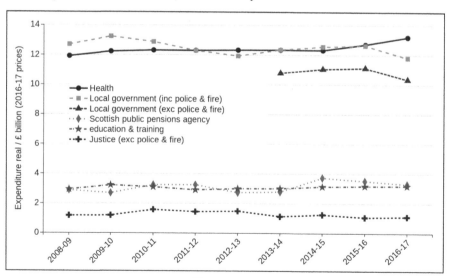

Figure 5.14
Scottish government TME broken down by area of spending
2008–09 to 2016–17.

Health spending increased by £1.3 billion in real terms between 2008–09 and 2016–17 whereas *Local government (inc police and fire)* spending fell by £0.9 with most of the decrease occurring in 2016–17. The draft budget for 2018–19 shows *Health* remaining at its 2016–17 outturn of £13.2 billion whereas *Local government* is budgeted to fall further to £11.5 billion.

Education and training in the Scottish budget is mostly made up of funding for further and higher education and this has varied around £3.0 billion since 2008–09. The fact that this shows little change means that the fall in total education spending in Scotland shown in Figure 5.4 must have mostly involved schools which are managed by councils. This is consistent with the fall in *Local Government* spending in the Scottish Budget.

Table 5.1 shows some statistics on how outturns in these areas of spending have changed. Because picking any pair of years may give misleading results, I have shown the changes for the whole time range of 2008–09 to 2016–17 but also for 2009–10 to 2015–16.

Total TME shows a modest rise in both time ranges. The largest fall in absolute terms is *Local government* which declined by several percent across both time ranges. The largest rise in percentage terms is for pensions which increased significantly in 2014–15.

Spending in real terms, 2016–17 prices	2008–09 to 2016–17 £bn	%	2009–10 to 2015–16 £bn	%
Health	1.29	10.8%	0.49	4.0%
Local government (including police & fire)	-0.89	-7.0%	-0.59	-4.5%
Scottish Public Pensions Agency	0.42	14.6%	0.83	31.0%
Education & training	0.25	8.6%	-0.04	-1.3%
Justice (excluding police & fire)	-0.06	-5.1%	-0.12	-9.8%
TME	**0.99**	**3.2%**	**0.57**	**1.8%**

Table 5.1
Spending changes in the Scottish government budget 2008–09 to 2016–17.

Scottish government funding

The majority of the funding for the Scottish budget, around 85% of it, comes from the UK government as a **block grant**.

The block grant only relates to Departmental Expenditure Limit or DEL spending. The UK government provides separate funding for demand-led AME spending, most of which is for pensions and benefits.

The key document for issues and details surrounding the block grant is HM Treasury's Statement of Funding Policy,[18] and much of the detail given here is sourced from it. The most recent edition at time of writing was November 2015.

The block grant is an amount of money that is given to the Scottish government by HM Treasury and the main purpose of the Scottish budget has been to decide how it is spent. The *change* in the size of the block grant from the previous year is determined by the **Barnett formula**. This formula works by using the planned change in spending for England (though it may be widened to England & Wales or further if appropriate) to calculate what the change for Scotland should be. The changes for all the various devolved areas (health, education, transport etc) are then added up to give the block grant total.

The formula itself is fairly simple – you multiply three numbers together.

Change in block grant = Change in England × population fraction × comparability factor

The population fraction is Scotland's population divided by England's and the comparability factor is a measure of devolution: the fraction of the spending in that area that is controlled by the Scottish government.

It's easiest to demonstrate with a couple of examples.

First, let's consider that the UK Government Department for Education has its Departmental Expenditure Limit (DEL) increased for the year ahead by £100 million. Education is completely devolved to the Scottish government, so the comparability fraction is 1.0 or 100%.

Next, we need to look up the population factor. These estimates are based on mid-year estimates provided by the Office for National Statistics and the National Records of Scotland (see Chapter 1). The populations of Scotland and England for mid-2014 are 5,347,600 and 54,316,600 respectively. The population fraction is Scotland's population divided by England's:

population fraction = 5,347,600 ÷ 54,316,600 = 0.0985 = 9.85%

So, if the Department for Education decides to spend an extra £100 million in England, this means that the change in Scotland's block grant will be:

Change in block grant = £100,000,000 × 0.0985 × 1.0 = £9,850,000

This means that the Scottish government will have another £9.85 million to spend on whatever it sees fit. Although the rise in block grant was caused by a rise in spending on education in England, the Scottish government could, if it wishes, spend the extra £9.85 million on building a hospital or a new road bridge.

Next, as a second example, let's imagine that the UK Department for Culture, Media & Sport has its Departmental Expenditure Limit (DEL) cut by £100 million. Its comparability factor is 0.769 or 76.9% which means it is mostly devolved. The change in the block grant is as follows:

Change in block grant = -£100,000,000 × 0.0985 × 0.769 = -£7,570,000

So the block grant to Scotland will be cut by £7.57 million, and again, there is no requirement to cut any specific area by this amount.

Table 5.2 lists comparability factors for major UK Government departments. These figures come from appendices of HM Treasury's Statement of Funding Policy document.

This table also serves to give a summary of how much of a major department's spending is devolved to Scotland. The way each factor is calculated is interesting. For example, take the Department of Health. Its spending is split into 22 sub-areas so that each one is either completely devolved or not devolved at all. The comparability factor is then the total of spending on all devolved sub-areas divided by the total over all sub-areas. For health, only 2 of the 22 sub-areas are not devolved (European aspects and medicine regulation) and these make up only 0.6% of total Department of Health spending, hence the 99.4% factor in the table.

It's important to remember that the Barnett formula only calculates *changes* to the block grant. The total size of the block grant for a given year is equal to the sum of all changes that have been made since Barnett was first introduced in 1978 plus the size of the block grant in that first year.

Department	Factor
Education	100.0%
Justice	100.0%
Environment, Food & Rural Affairs	99.8%
Health	99.4%
Home Office	91.7%
Transport	91.0%
Culture, Media & Sport	76.9%
Business, Innovation & Skills	66.4%
Energy & Climate Change	1.8%
Work & Pensions	1.4%

Table 5.2

Comparability factors for devolved spending.

As a consequence, although up-to-date population fractions have been used to calculate the change each year, the total amount of the block grant is still affected by historical population share from 1978. Since the population share has fallen from 12% to 8% since then, the Barnett formula results in more funding per person in Scotland than elsewhere in the UK. This is the main reason why Scottish expenditure per person is substantially higher than that for the UK as a whole, as seen in Figure 5.1. Although an argument can be made that Scotland has particular circumstances that require more spending per person, such as its low population density, this is not explicitly built into the Barnett formula. In fact, the formula was introduced as pragmatic measure in 1978 with the intention of being replaced after a couple years with a more equitable solution.

Changes in Scottish Devolution

The powers of the Scottish Parliament were originally set out in the Scotland Act 1998, then extended by the Scotland Act 2012 following the findings of the Calman Commission. The Smith Commission recommended further powers following the 2014 independence referendum and these came in the Scotland Act 2016.

A summary of how much of public revenue and expenditure is devolved is given in GERS and is shown in Figure 5.15. These figures are typical of recent years and although they will vary, the changes are no more than a few percentage points.

Since devolution began in 1998, about 60% of spending in Scotland has been controlled by the Scottish and local governments. No new spending powers came with the Scotland Act 2012 but the Scotland Act 2016 devolved some aspects of Universal Credit. Spending powers reserved to the UK are mainly for welfare and defence.

Revenue raising powers amounted to less than 10% initially. The main power in the Scotland Act 1998 being to raise or lower the income tax rate by up to 3p in the pound (or 3 percentage points) from the UK rate. This power was never used.

The Scotland Act 2012 went further and introduced the Scottish Rate of Income Tax (SRIT) as of 1 April 2016. In this, the rate of income tax was reduced by 10p (or 10 percentage points) in Scotland, and the Scottish Parliament tasked with setting its own rate to replace it. The decision for 2016–17 was to set it at 10p to match existing rates in the rest of the UK. This arrangement was only in place for a year before being replaced by more extensive taxation powers set out in the Scotland Act 2016.

Table 5.3 lists the taxes that have been devolved following the two recent Scotland Acts.[19] In 2015, a new Scottish government department called

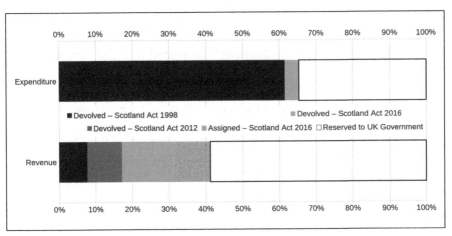

Figure 5.15
Changes in devolution.

Revenue Scotland was set up to collect devolved taxes. The first two such taxes – Land and Buildings Transaction Tax (LBTT) and Scottish Landfill Tax (SLfT) – came into effect from 1 April 2015 as a consequence of the Scotland Act 2012. LBTT replaces Stamp Duty on land and property purchases but remains similar to the Stamp Duty levied elsewhere in the UK (now called SDLT) except that it has higher rates for more expensive purchases.

Name of tax	Devolved from	Devolved?	Revenue in 2016–17	Collected by
LBTT	2015–16	Fully	£0.47 billion	Revenue Scotland
Landfill	2015–16	Fully	£0.15 billion	Revenue Scotland
Income tax	2017–18	Partial	£11.31 billion	HMRC
Air passenger duty	2018–19	Fully	£0.26 billion	Revenue Scotland
VAT	2019–20	Assigned	£5.10 billion	HMRC
Aggregates levy	TBD	Fully	£0.60 billion	Revenue Scotland

Table 5.3
Devolution of taxes from 2015–16 onwards.

The Scotland Act 2016 gave the Scottish Parliament control over all rates and thresholds for income tax (for non-savings and non-dividend income or NSND). Although it cannot reduce the personal allowance below which an individual pays no tax, it can effectively increase it by creating a zero rate band. The Scotland Act 2016 also assigned the first 10 percentage points of VAT raised in Scotland as Scottish revenue. With the VAT rate at 20%, this represents half of all VAT raised in Scotland. The word 'assigned' is used here rather than 'devolved' because European Union rules prevent VAT rates from varying within a member state such as the UK.

Table 5.4 shows UK-wide income tax bands and rates that also applied in Scotland in 2016–17.[20] In addition, there is a £100,000 limit such that the personal allowance is reduced by £1 for every £2 of income above that limit.

The scheme is best illustrated with a few examples.

Income	Name	Rate
Up to £11,000	Personal allowance	Zero
£11,001 to £43,000	Basic rate	20%
£43,001 to £161,000	Higher rate	40%
Over £161,000	Additional rate	45%

Table 5.4

UK tax bands and rates in 2016–17.

- Income £10,000 – This is under the personal allowance so no tax is due.
- Income £16,000 – The £5,000 over the personal allowance is taxed at 20%, so £1000 of tax is due.
- Income £43,000 – £32,000 is taxed at 20%, so £6,400 of tax is due.
- Income £48,000 – £32,000 is taxed at 20%, then the next £5,000 is taxed at 40% so tax due is £6,400 plus £2,000 which equals £8,400.

Tax on larger incomes is complicated by the additional rate and the reduction of the personal allowance limit above £100,000.

The UK budget for the financial year 2017–18 made two changes to the bands and rates in Table 5.4: the personal allowance was raised to £11,500 and the higher rate threshold was raised to £45,000. Aside from the effects of inflation, this means that anyone who earns more than £11,000 will pay less tax than in 2016–17.

The significant change introduced in the Scotland Act 2016 is that the Scottish government does not simply vary tax rates and bands set by Westminster budgets, but set their own above the personal allowance. In the first budget following the 2016 act, for the 2017–18 financial year, the Scottish government chose to copy tax rates for the rest of the UK but set the higher rate threshold at £43,000, the same as the UK's for 2016–17. This meant that although Scottish income tax payers still experienced a tax cut from the UK's increase in the personal allowance, there was no extra cut for those in the higher rate band. Someone with income £48,000 outside Scotland would pay £800 less income tax in 2017–18 than someone with the same income in Scotland.

In the draft budget for 2018–19 published in December 2017, the Scottish government created two new Scottish income tax bands and rates, as

Income	Name	Rate
Up to £11,850	Personal allowance	Zero
£11,851 to £13,850	Starter rate	19%
£13,851 to £24,000	Basic rate	20%
£24,001 to £44,273	Intermediate rate	21%
£44,274 to £161,000	Higher rate	41%
Over £161,000	Top rate	46%

Table 5.5
Scottish tax bands in the draft budget for 2018–19.

shown in Table 5.5, and increased the top two rates by 1 percentage point to 41% and 46%.

In contrast, the UK budget's income tax structure remained the same as before except that the personal allowance rose to £11,850 and the higher rate threshold rose to £46,350. Below an income of £26,000, a Scottish taxpayer will pay £20 or 0.1% less tax per year than someone on the same income elsewhere in the UK. Above £26,000, a Scottish taxpayer will pay more income tax, with the biggest gap in percentage terms being at £46,350 where 1.3% more income tax is paid. The additional tax revenue raised for the Scottish budget is estimated to be £164 million, or 0.4% of total managed expenditure.

The introduction of the new Scottish income tax regime may only have a small effect on incomes and the Scottish budget in percentage terms, but it does have important political significance. And, as always with such matters, it is not the actual details that are important, but how the changes are perceived. These changes can be presented as being progressive, albeit slightly, and also as making Scotland the highest taxed part of the UK, but again, only slightly.

There is also increased complexity in the tax system and it is not clear how some laws should be interpreted. For example, the legislation behind the Marriage Allowance effective from 2015 refers to the 'basic rate', but should that apply to just the 20% band in Scotland, or some or all of the 19%, 20% and 21% bands? Such issues will of course be resolved, and the calculations, though perhaps more annoying to perform, are easily done with a spreadsheet and provide extra business for accountants. But nevertheless, the extra complexity makes it harder for most people to understand and harder for academics, civil servants and journalists to explain to the public.

Another element of complexity is that the block grant needs to be adjusted to account for devolved and assigned revenues as well as respecting political commitments to retaining the Barnett formula. To this end, following the Scotland Act 2016, cross party discussions were held to agree on a **fiscal framework** based on a principle of 'no detriment', that is, that Scotland nor any other part of the UK would be disadvantaged as a result.[21] Unlike the Barnett formula, which is relatively simple, the resulting fiscal framework is a complex web of political compromise.

The operation of the fiscal framework can be summarised in greatly simplified form for a particular tax year as follows:

1 Apply the Barnett formula to calculate the block grant as described above.
2 Estimate the amount of revenue that is no longer collected and pooled at the UK level because it is devolved or assigned. This is done by looking at the last year before each tax was devolved, eg 2016–17 for income tax, and applying an adjustment for how its revenues would have grown or shrunk. This is sometimes called the Block Grant Adjustment or BGA. The BGA is provided by HM Treasury based on forecasts provided by the Office of Budgetary responsibility or OBR.
3 Estimate what is expected to be collected from devolved and assigned taxes. These estimates are provided by the Scottish Fiscal Commission or SFC.

The block grant is then calculated as (1) less (2) plus (3). Of course, there is much more to it than this, mostly arising from application of the no detriment principle. For example, as part of step 2 there is an adjustment to account for the fact that Scotland's population is growing more slowly than the rest of the UK's. Without this, there was likely to be a detriment to Scotland in the form of lower revenues per head, but as the rest of the UK currently raises more revenue per head than Scotland, it can be argued that the detriment is to the rest of the UK. In truth, it is impossible to ensure that no detriment occurs under all possible outcomes. The current fiscal framework applies until 2020–21 and, following a review that will take place 2021, it is likely to be revised.

After considering local government funding and spending, we'll bring together much of the above to construct a unified picture of how funding and spending are distributed across the three levels of government.

Devolution and spending

Table 5.6 shows how public spending per person has changed in real terms for Scotland and the whole UK. Changes are shown from the year before devolution began in 1998–99 to 2016–17, and also from 2006–07 after which the Scottish government (though it was called the executive then) changed from being run by a Labour and Liberal Democrat coalition to being run by the Scottish National Party.

Total public spending per head has increased in real terms over both these time ranges with Scotland seeing a larger increase since 1998–99 than the whole UK, though the opposite is true for the change since 2006–07.

Areas marked with an asterisk are reserved or relate to EU matters, and spending in all other areas is either completely or mostly under the devolved control of the Scottish government (see Table 5.2).

Social protection shows the largest change of all areas with Scotland's increase being slightly greater than that of the whole UK. The increase is mostly driven by a rise in state pension payments because the number of pensioners is growing.

Health is the next greatest area of spending increase, and again there are increases in Scotland and the UK as a whole. This is perhaps more surprising because, unlike social protection, health spending is devolved. But again, funding for health is not just a discretionary matter for governments, but is strongly driven by demand, and, as seen in Chapter 4, the demand is growing because of an ageing population. That said, from 2006–07, there is a noticeable difference with the increase in health spending per person being £119 lower in Scotland as compared to the whole UK.

Education and training also shows very little difference over the whole time range between Scotland and the whole UK, and although spending per head fell over the last decade for both, it fell by 50% more in

Change 1998–99 to 2016–17	Scotland	UK	Diff	Since 2006–07	Scotland	UK	Diff
Total	£4,117	£3,544	£573		£531	£569	-£38
Social protection*	£1,433	£1,247	£186		£634	£549	£85
Health	£1,024	£1,067	-£44		£220	£339	-£119
Accounting adjustments*	£397	£398	-£1		£22	£34	-£13
Education and training	£367	£363	£4		-£152	-£106	-£46
Transport	£352	£263	£89		-£49	£60	-£110
Public order and safety	£140	£25	£115		-£24	-£138	£115
Environment protection	£113	£68	£45		-£9	-£13	£4
EU Transactions*	£110	£135	-£25		£72	£107	-£35
Housing and community amenities	£103	£28	£75		-£78	-£65	-£13
International services*	£73	£72	£0		£26	£26	£0
Public and common services	£63	£26	£37		-£45	-£50	£4
Agriculture, forestry and fisheries	£57	-£25	£81		£37	-£19	£56
Science and technology	£23	£26	-£3		£4	£2	£2
Recreation, culture and religion	£15	£3	£12		-£50	-£47	-£3
Enterprise and economic development	-£7	£14	-£20		-£13	-£35	£23
Employment policies	-£14	-£32	£19		-£17	-£27	£10
Defence*	-£27	-£27	£1		-£68	-£69	£1
Public sector debt interest*	-£105	-£107	£2		£21	£20	£1

Table 5.6

Changes in real spending per person for Scotland and whole UK 1998–99 to 2016–17.

Scotland. *Transport* spending saw large rises in both Scotland and the UK since 1998–99 but this has slightly reversed in Scotland over the last ten years.

There are several areas where Scotland has seen greater rises in spending per person than the whole UK, notably *Public order and safety*, which includes policing, *Environment protection*, *Housing and community amenities* and *Agriculture, forestry and fishing*. All of these are devolved areas.

Local government funding

Local government in Scotland is made up of 32 councils, with each council's officers and various departments being accountable to an elected body of councillors. Following the council elections of May 2017 there were a total of 1227 representing 353 wards across Scotland.

Councils range in size from the smallest, Orkney with a population of 21,000, to the largest, Glasgow with 593,000. The smallest council on the mainland, Clackmannanshire, has a population of 51,000, less than a tenth of that of Glasgow (see Chapter 1).

Government at the local level is necessary because there are large variations in society within Scotland with obvious divides between urban and rural areas, as well as rich and poor. Consequently, health and education and welfare needs vary greatly too.

To give a few examples. Dundee is gaining a reputation for computer games and related digital businesses but is still dealing with a legacy of deprivation from its post-industrial decline. Leafy, suburban East Dunbartonshire is wealthy but has an ageing population and sits awkwardly next to the much larger but less prosperous city of Glasgow council area. Shetland is a group of islands remote from the mainland but like the city of Aberdeen, it has benefited greatly from the North Sea industry which faces an uncertain future.

One of the main functions of a council is to allocate spending on a number of essential services, such as schooling, social care, refuse collection, maintenance of roads, footpaths and other public spaces. Until 1 April 2013 (the start of financial year 2013–14) councils were also responsible for funding regional police, fire and rescue services which, at cost of over £1 billion per annum, made up around 10% of councils' total spending.

A difficulty in understanding a council's finances is that funding comes from a variety of sources: the Scottish government, the UK government, and taxes and charges from within the council area itself. Most of council funding comes from the Scottish government and as this is known in advance of each financial year, it is the main factor in determining each council's planned spending. Any excess in spending over funding from all sources is met by drawing on reserves or by borrowing.

The Scottish Local Government Financial Statistics[22] report is usually published by the Scottish government in February of the year after the financial year it covers. The information in this section is from the edition covering 2015–16.

Consider the simple-sounding question: how much was spent by councils in 2015–16? There are several answers to this depending on how you wish to define spending. You'll find a few different answers in the financial statistics report, and other ones in the Scottish budget and yet more in Audit Scotland's report [23]. Much of the confusion arises because of the distinctions between gross vs net spending and revenue vs capital spending, which is explained below.

One total for spending by all councils in 2015–16 is £14.7 billion. This is known as **gross revenue expenditure** which may sound a bit oxymoronic but in local government parlance 'revenue' refers to spending on day-to-day services. In Scottish and UK government finances the word 'resource' is used for this purpose.

In case this isn't confusing enough, the word 'gross' is used to distinguish this total from net totals which deduct certain incomes from expenditure totals. The motivation for this is that the net total is, with a few potential complications, the amount that councils need to fund from council tax and external sources.

Other necessary costs are the amounts that are spent paying back debt, which was about £0.7 billion in 2015–16, and paying interest on outstanding debt, which was about £0.8 billion. This brings the expenditure for all councils to £16.2 billion.

And to the revenue expenditure total we can add **capital expenditure** which amounted to £1.9 billion in 2015–16. This brings the total to £18.1 billion.

Councils are required by law to track spending and income from their housing stock separately in what is called the **Housing Revenue Account** or **HRA**. This isn't included in the totals just mentioned. We'll return to HRA again below.

Although I cannot pretend that understanding council finances can ever be simple, I can at least offer a route into thinking about it that makes most sense to me. To this end, let's start by looking at how the £16.2 billion of gross revenue expenditure plus costs of servicing debt is funded. This is shown in Table 5.7.

The **General revenue grant** from the Scottish government provides the single largest source of funding for councils, and funds almost half of their expenditure.

Non-domestic rates (NDR) are collected by each council from businesses with premises in their area, and given to the Scottish government which then redistributes them back to the councils. This helps ensure that councils receive funding in proportion to their needs, rather than being limited by their ability to raise revenue locally.

Council tax is money paid by residents with a home in the council area and is set according to the value of the property in the year 1991. Although council tax is perhaps the best known of local taxes, it only makes up 13% of funding for councils' gross revenue expenditure. In accord with Scottish government policy, often referred to as the **council tax freeze**, councils did not change council tax rates from 2007–08 until the freeze ended on 1 April 2017.

Revenue	£ billion	%	Notes
General revenue grant	7.1	44%	Block grant from Scottish government
Non-domestic rates	2.8	17%	From businesses
Council tax	2.1	13%	From residents
Other revenue	4.2	26%	From UK government, NHS, reserves, borrowing
Total	**16.2**	**100%**	

Table 5.7
Sources of funding for all councils 2015–16.

Other revenue makes up about a fifth of the total and is mostly (non-HRA) housing benefit payments from the UK government's Department of Work & Pensions. It also includes funds from the NHS for council-run social care, fees collected by the council (e.g. hiring council premises and for parking), borrowing and money moving to and from reserves. There was a surplus in the revenue budget of £0.45 billion in 2015–16 but most of this, some £0.34 billion, was used to fund capital expenditure with the remaining £0.11 billion being placed into reserves.

In real terms, total annual revenues to local government have fallen by £2.5 billion from 2009–10 to 2015–16. Around £1.7 billion of this was due to the police and fire services being removed to central control in 2013–14. After allowing for this, local government annual revenue has still decreased by £0.8 billion or 4% in real terms.

Figure 5.16 shows how the various sources of councils' revenue have changed in recent years.

This graph shows the main reason for the decrease in local government's total revenue is the drop in funding from the Scottish government. Allowing for the police and fire centralisation, the drop between 2009–10 and 2015–16 is about 10% in real terms.

Although council tax has been frozen, its revenues have decreased in real terms from £2.5 billion to £2.0 billion because of inflation. NDR is

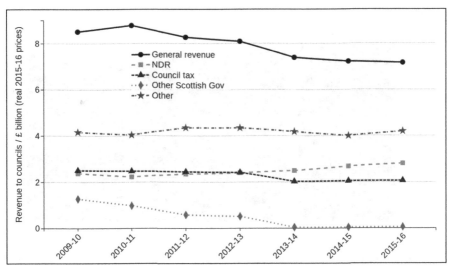

Figure 5.16
Sources of funding for all councils 2009–10 to 2015–16.

the only funding source to show a rise in real terms, increasing from £2.4 billion to £2.8 billion.

Local government spending

Figure 5.17 shows the total gross expenditure including debt servicing costs for all councils between 2009–10 and 2015–16.

Gross expenditure excluding police and fire has decreased in every year except the last, and has fallen by £0.75 billion in real terms over this time, or 4%. Police and fire expenditure decreased by £0.15 billion in real terms to 2012–13, or 9%.

Figure 5.18 shows the breakdown of councils' gross expenditure by area of spending for 2015–16. The 2012–13 figure for Police & fire in 2015–16 prices is shown for comparison.

The three largest areas of spending – education, social work and housing – make up 70% of total gross expenditure. The fourth largest area (following centralisation of police and fire) is paying interest on debt. This is separate to the public sector debt interest shown earlier in the GERS figures which relates only to UK-level debt.

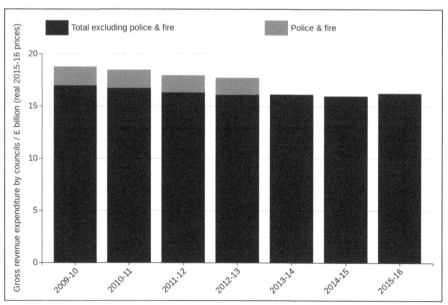

Figure 5.17
Gross revenue expenditure by all councils 2009–10 to 2015–16.

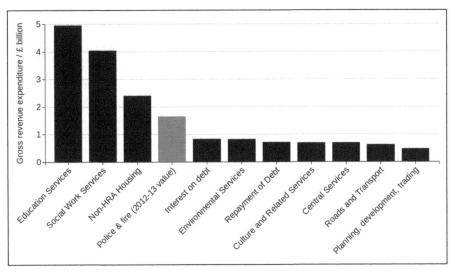

Figure 5.18
Gross expenditure for areas of council spending 2015–16.

HRA stands for **Housing Revenue Account** which covers income from renting council-owned homes and expenditure on maintaining them. By law, this must be accounted for separately in local government finances and accordingly they are excluded from all figures stated here. Although the flows of money into this account are large – it received £1.2 billion of rental and other income in 2015–16 – its balance does not change dramatically because its outgoings are similarly large with any surplus being reinvested in the HRA capital account. **Non-HRA Housing** is the third largest area of gross expenditure and is mostly made up of housing benefit payments from the UK government's Department of Work and Pensions.

Figure 5.19 shows how the major areas of council spending have changed since 2009–10.

Education, the largest single area of expenditure, experienced a real terms fall of £0.33 billion or 6%, though there was an increase in 2015–16. But most of the fall in total expenditure was concentrated in *Other* which fell by £0.8 billion or 19%. Within that, Planning & Economic Development and Central Services saw expenditure fall by £0.43 billion or 25%. Social Work saw a slight rise of £0.15 billion or 4% but the largest rise in expenditure was a £0.37 billion or 32% rise in Debt repayment and interest.

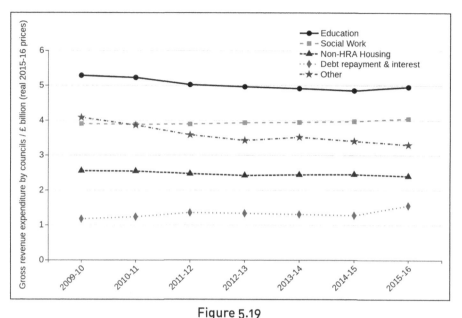

Figure 5.19

Gross expenditure for major areas of council spending 2009–10 to 2015–16.

Variation across councils

The figures above are totals for all councils in Scotland. There is of course significant variation from council to council both in expenditure and in how much revenue is received from different sources.

Figure 5.20 shows how the gross expenditure per person (including debt costs) for each council is funded by the four main revenue areas: the General revenue grant from the Scottish government, NDR, council tax and other revenue. The NDR figure here is the amount distributed back to each council and although it is mostly based on what the council collected, the redistribution typically alters it by 10%.

Most councils are within a few hundred pounds either way of the Scotland average figure of £3,000 per person.

Shetland is interesting: not only has it the largest expenditure per person at more than double the Scotland average, but an usually large proportion of its funding comes from Other revenue. This is likely due to the combination of its remote location, its role in the oil and gas industry, and its small permanent population. Also, its amount from Other revenue has dropped from £3,300 down to £2,100 between 2014–15

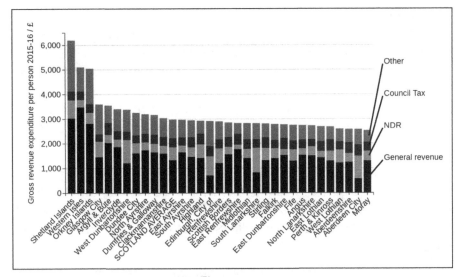

Figure 5.20

Breakdown of gross expenditure per person for each council
by funding source 2015–16.

and 2015–16. This is almost certainly due to the effect that the fall in oil price has had on the North Sea industry.

Orkney also has a very large expenditure per person and it too has a relatively large proportion of Other revenue but it has not dropped in the last year presumably because unlike Shetland its local economy is less dependent on the North Sea industry.

With the exception of the Western Isles, the other councils that have high expenditures per person are mostly urban and post-industrial areas. On average, most councils draw 44% of their funding from the General revenue grant, but Aberdeen City, which has the second lowest expenditure per person, draws only 22% of funding from it. Aberdeen has many oil and gas related businesses and these contribute to its high proportion of NDR and other revenue. Edinburgh's dependence on General revenue is similarly low at 24% and it too draws substantial NDR and other revenue from businesses based there. In contrast, the Western Isles has 68% of its gross expenditure funded by the General revenue grant with only a small contribution from NDR.

Who cut what?

From 2010–11 the UK government's stated intention was to reduce its budget deficit by cutting public spending. According to the GERS report, Scotland's public total expenditure across all levels of government has fallen by 2% between 2010–11 and 2016–17. The figure for all of the UK is almost exactly the same. To put this in longer term context, measured over the whole time range given in GERS from 1998–99 to 2016–17, expenditure has grown by over 50% for Scotland and the whole UK.

The fact that Scotland and the whole UK show similar public spending changes is not a surprise as much of Scotland's funding comes via the Barnett formula which is designed to reflect spending elsewhere in the UK, and most of the rest of spending in Scotland is reserved to the UK government.

The body that has most control over allocating public expenditure in Scotland is the Scottish government (that is, more than either the UK government or councils) and its expenditure in Scotland, as measured by outturn TME, has fallen by 1% between 2010–11 and 2016–17. The reason this cut is smaller in percentage terms than the 2% for total Scottish spending is due to the Scottish government using its borrowing powers that were introduced in the Scotland Act 2012.

Just as most of the Scottish government's funding comes from the level above it, most of council funding comes from the Scottish government. This is given in the 'Local Government' line of the budget, but, unlike the UK-Scottish government situation, there is no equivalent of the Barnett formula. Instead the Scottish government holds most of the power in deciding the size of the block grant to the councils, though some aspects are negotiated with the Convention of Scottish Local Authorities (COSLA).

In real terms, the outturn for local government in 2016–17 was 8% lower than the one for 2010–11, where, to ensure a fair comparison, the cost of police and fire is added to the 2016–17 local government figure. Alternatively, confining our attention to after the police and fire services were centralised, from 2013–14 to 2016–17, the local government figure has dropped by 4% (though remember, this is over three years rather than six). Either way, the drop appears to be significantly greater than the 1% in the total budget of the Scottish government.

Spending and revenue by level of government

In the preceding sections we looked at spending in three ways. The first, based on GERS, gave us totals irrespective of which level of government spent the money. Next, we looked at the Scottish government which budgets for most of Scotland's public spending. Finally, we looked at local government's finances.

We also saw how tax revenue was raised but, as mentioned at the start of this chapter, more money is spent than is received from revenues at any level of government. What we'll do now is summarise the fiscal flows of revenue and spending across all three levels of government.

Figure 5.21 shows taxes raised and totals spent in Scotland. Also shown are transfers between the levels of government, including the block grants. The estimates are based on outturn figures (actual amounts spent, not budgeted in advance) from the Scottish government and local government finance statistics. Complete data on this is only available

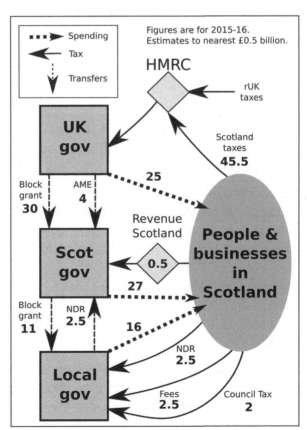

Figure 5.21
Fiscal flows in Scotland 2015–16.

5

up to the financial year 2015–16 but we'll discuss the effects of the significant post-2016 fiscal changes below. The UK block grant and AME amounts are cross-checked against the latest Scotland Office accounts[24] and also against GERS figures for 2015–16. I refer to the figures as 'estimates' as there are some grey areas where flows of public monies are not clear, but such uncertainties are likely to be below the rounding to the nearest £0.5 billion.

The main part of the diagram is the oval that represents all the people in Scotland, all its businesses and the public infrastructure and services that allow them to live their lives and do their work. As they work they will pay income tax, national insurance, VAT, corporation tax and so on. This is collected along with all UK taxes by HMRC.

Next, look to the UK government box. From it are two transfers going down to the Scottish government: the block grant of £30 billion and the AME component of £4 billion (most of AME is welfare in the UK government's spending but this amount covers, for example, public sector employee pensions administered by the Scottish government). The Scottish government also receives £0.5 billion via Revenue Scotland from the new taxes it started levying from April 2015, and also £2.5 billion of NDR (non-domestic rates) collected by local government from businesses.

Local government receives a block grant of £11 billion from the Scottish government which adds to £2 billion of council tax, and £2.5 of fees from various local income which includes fees and fines levied by councils.

The spending of each level of government is shown by the dotted arrows. The Scottish government spends the most at £27 billion. This is dominantly on health, with the rest divided between pensions, education (universities and colleges), infrastructure and justice. The UK government spends £25 billion, and this is almost entirely on pensions, benefit payments, defence and includes about £2 billion which is administered through the councils (see non-HRA housing above). Finally, local government spends £16 billion, with most of this going on school education and social work.

Table 5.8 summarises public revenue and spending together with transfers in and out of each level of government. The columns sum to give totals consistent with GERS, and the rows sum to give net balances

£ billion 2015–16	Revenue	Spend	Transfers out	Transfers in	Net balance
UK Government	45.5	-25	-34	-	-14
Scottish Government	0.5	-27	-11	36.5	-1
Local Government	7	-16	-2.5	11	0
Total	**53**	**-68**	-	-	**-15**

Table 5.8
Public revenue, spending and transfers 2015–16.

for each level of government (though rounding means they do not necessarily sum exactly to the nearest £0.5 billion).

It's clear that revenue does not equal spending at any level, and that £15 billion more is spent in Scotland than is raised in revenue. This accords with GERS figures for 2015–16 shown in Figure 5.5.

The first line of the table shows the UK government collecting much more revenue from Scotland than it spends, but it also transfers £34 billion to the Scottish government, which in turn transfers £11 billion to local government. In this way, the block grants and other transfers ensure that Scotland's funding matches its spending. Both Scottish and local governments can draw on reserves and are able to borrow though the amounts are limited and relatively small. In fact, the balances shown for Scottish and local government are at the level of rounding errors in these figures.

The negative £15 billion net fiscal balance, or deficit, was 9% of Scotland's GDP in 2015–16 (including North Sea revenues). The UK's deficit (which includes Scotland's) was 4% of UK GDP. The cause of Scotland's larger deficit is its higher per person public spending combined with the collapse in North Sea revenues. We'll look at deficits again Chapter 6.

It's important to realise that the arrows and boxes represent fiscal flows and do not imply control over how it is spent. For example, in no sense does HMRC control the £45.5 billion it collects, nor does the UK government control all the money flowing into it from HMRC; for one thing, its block grant to Scotland is determined by the Barnett formula, with little or no discretion from UK or Scottish government ministers. As such, the changes in devolution listed in Table 5.3 will not alter this diagram significantly. The main difference will be that Revenue Scotland will collect £1 billion more annually with a corresponding reduction in what HMRC collects.

Scottish public sector borrowing

There are a variety of approaches to borrowing across the three levels of government. We will look at borrowing and debt at the UK level more closely in Chapter 6 because it is quite different to the Scottish public sector borrowing which is considered here.

There are three main ways for the public sector to borrow: from another part of the public sector, by entering into public-private arrangement, or from the private sector. Only the last of these might involve conventional borrowing in which a bank lends a sum of money with a straightforward agreement to pay it back by a particular time with a specified amount of interest.

The Scotland Act 2012[25] gave the Scottish government powers to borrow to fund capital projects, such as building roads or hospitals. These were extended in the Scotland Act 2016[26] so that the Scottish government can incur its own debt to a total of £3 billion with up to 15% of this amount, or £450 million, being borrowed in any one year. There are three sources available to the Scottish government for borrowing.[27] There is the UK's National Loans Fund[28] which would likely offer the lowest rates of interest. There is conventional borrowing from private sector banks and the Scottish government can issue its own bonds which are essentially shares in its debt (see Chapter 6).

Public Private Partnership or PPP schemes have been used across the UK since the early 1990s and involve more than just borrowing. Not only were they intended to bring perceived efficiencies of private companies to public sector initiatives, but they were also intended to share the risks of unanticipated, but all too common cost overruns in such projects. Usually several companies would be involved in each project and obtain up-front business from the government in building public infrastructure, such as a school or hospital, and also an ongoing concern in maintaining it. Companies also invest their own money in the project with an expectation of getting it back in the future with interest or some other form of financial return. It is this element which constitutes lending to the public sector. Governments favoured this arrangement because it gave companies a vested interest in making sure their projects were well built in the first place. Also, these **Private Finance Initiatives** or PFIs, as they became known, allowed the government to borrow money without it adding to the official total of public debt measured by the Office for National Statistics.

In time it became apparent that PFI schemes had a number of problems. One is that they proved to be very complex with heavy administrative burdens. Also, there is little evidence that the premium paid for private over public financing of these projects was worth the risk-sharing and other benefits they were said to offer.[29] In 2016 it emerged that a number of Scottish schools built under a PFI scheme had serious structural flaws. Although these issues were caused by poor quality control rather than any intrinsic feature of PFI,[30] this example highlighted that the financial incentive for companies to build infrastructure well in the first place was no substitute for proper inspection regimes.

The Scottish government phased out use of PFI and set up an arms-length company called the Scottish Futures Trust (SFT) to manage its own form of PPP known as the Non-Profit Distributing or NPD model which is unique to Scotland, but this too has been found to incur relatively high costs and share some other drawbacks of PFI.[31] Some schemes, such as the bypass being built around Aberdeen were reclassified by the Office for National Statistics as being in the public sector[32] and so associated borrowing was counted as public debt. This would have caused problems for the Scottish government's budget but was resolved by restructuring the public-private make-up of the project.

Some thoughts

At present, governments can decide how various kinds of income and a small amount of wealth will be redistributed. What the government has far less control over is how much revenue is raised. That depends on the state of economy and the confidence of consumers and businesses which, as demonstrated by the financial crisis of 2008 and its aftermath, depends on factors beyond the control of any one country's government.

Governments are more restricted still. Their ability to vary tax rates and rules are limited by politics and by tax choices made in other countries. Tax rises are very difficult to sell to an electorate. Businesses and individuals on higher incomes who attract the highest tax rates, and pay the greatest share of tax, can find ways to avoid it without resorting to illegal tax evasion, most obviously by routing income through a lower-taxed country.

Similarly, governments have much less freedom on spending than it appears. A reduction in numbers of doctors or nurses will be noticed by an electorate fairly quickly. In fact, even though health spending has increased in real terms, it has not kept up with the demands of an ageing population and so it is perceived by the public as a cut in the service. Education however has seen its funding cut in real terms but its effects take years, perhaps as long as a generation to become apparent.

The point here is that in both taxation and spending, governments are constrained by the demands placed on public services and also by how quickly the public will begin to feel any change a policy creates. This does not mean how quickly opposition politicians point it out, nor on when or how it is exposed in the media, traditional or social, but when people experience it: when they realise their household budgets push them into debt, or when it takes too long to get an appointment with their GP, or when their local school has to turn to the community to fund essential equipment.

But within such limits, governments do have control over redistribution, both through taking of taxes and targeting of benefits. Currently our tax system is progressive on income in that, in percentage terms, we take more from those on higher incomes and provide public services for all, and means-tested welfare for those on the lowest incomes. Should income be taxed more or less progressively than at present? Can wealth be taxed more? There aren't objective answers to these questions and so they will continually be raised and debated.

Redistribution is not just amongst individual citizens. When looking at councils it is clear that wealthy council areas such as Edinburgh or Aberdeen raise more funds locally and receive less from central government than more deprived areas such as urban Glasgow or the Western Isles. And this takes place at the country level in the UK too. Scotland's large notional deficit is primarily explained by Scotland's high public spending per person. This was highlighted by the sudden fall of the oil price in 2014–15, a matter beyond any single government's control, but this problem was much diluted in the UK's much larger fiscal system.

But still there remains political tension. Some believe that our tax system should be more progressive, others believe that it should be less so. Some believe that Scotland's benefits from being inside the UK are over-stated, while others believe they are under-appreciated. And where an individual stands on such issues is not determined by them taking a cold, hard and rational look at the facts. The desire is more to collect and promote the facts, or fictions, that fit moral values and cultural identity. These are partially inherited from parents but also shaped by peer groups, and are fragmented and filamented through society. The reason governments are cautious about making significant changes to public spending and taxation is that the electorate shows no clear consensus on how they would respond at the ballot box.

Some questions to ponder:

- What evidence is there that Scotland's low population density (see Chapter 1) and health needs (see Chapter 4) necessitate higher spending per person?
- Currently, the Scottish government and councils effectively re-distribute money from councils with high tax revenue to fund those with lower tax revenue, but are there ways to boost the economy and tax revenue of low-income councils especially those in rural areas and islands where spending per person is higher?
- A similar situation exists in that Scotland's higher spending per person creates a large notional deficit which is funded by fiscal transfers from the UK government; should this deficit be closed or is the high public spending person necessary?
- Should the Scottish Government use the powers it gained in the Scotland Act 2012 to issue its own bonds, and should it seek to increase the limits on its borrowing and debt?
- Has Scotland's devolution settlement, and the fiscal framework in particular, become so complex that it impedes good governing and risks clouding key issues for politicians and the citizens who elect them?
- If Scotland leaves the UK, how do questions of deficit, borrowing and debt relate to issues of currency choice and trade?

Chapter 6

The political economy

6

The economy refers to all types of human activity that involve an exchange of goods, services or money. Businesses take investment and pay workers to make goods or offer services which are then bought by consumers. Those consumers buy those goods and services using money they earned by working for a business (possibly their own), or from dividends if they own shares in a profit-making business. In this sense, the economy is a system which recirculates money through itself.

Since the industrial revolution, economies have grown significantly because of technological improvements and efficiencies, but also due to increasing populations. This growth can be measured by looking at how money circulates through an economy. If we account for the inflation of prices correctly then this will be proportional to the growth in new goods and services being bought and sold. This is true economic growth.

Of course, such growth has not been uninterrupted. Recessions have occurred in which growth goes negative and the economy shrinks. The mechanisms that trigger recessions are varied and can seem complex, but they have one thing in common: a loss of business and consumer confidence. If consumers fear for the future and save money and reduce their spending on goods and services, businesses will make less money and cut back on their spending, including what they pay workers, possibly by dismissing them. Since workers are also consumers this can reverse the growth cycle and cause a recession.

The economy of a country is not a closed system but is linked to other economies through trade. Exports of goods and services allow the businesses of one country to access a wider pool of consumers in other countries. Imports allow consumers to obtain products that aren't made by domestic businesses, or perhaps buy them at a cheaper price. Such trade also permits businesses to spread their production over many countries which can bring efficiencies from choosing the most appropriate local resources and skills.

Public spending is an integral part of any modern economy. Without it we would lack educated and healthy workers and the infrastructure of roads, electricity and more needed for commerce to take place. Taxes together with state benefits serve to redistribute money and help ensure that almost all consumers have enough money to live, and in doing so they necessarily consume the goods and services of businesses.

Public spending is a flow from the public to the private sector, and taxation is a flow from the private to the public sector. Keep this in mind, as it can jolt your thinking out of common potential misconceptions. In particular, it allows for an alternative view on the thorny topics of fiscal deficit and how it is connected to private wealth, public debt and the trade deficit.

Economics deals with activities that can be measured, and the easiest, though not necessarily the best way to measure them is with money. But there are many types of activity that we value that do not involve money, such as sleeping, playing, singing a song or laughing with friends and family. As such there are many aspects of life that economics has difficulty in addressing, but the main one is human psychology: as mentioned above, a contagious lack of confidence in the future can, by itself, cause a recession.

Economics has come in for much criticism since the financial crisis of 2008, mainly because the mainstream of the discipline overlooked the important role of the banking system and its handling of the pricing of assets associated with risky loans. But there's a more fundamental issue that afflicts some economists, governments, politicians, civil servants, the media and the public too: economics is too often viewed as a technical discipline like a physical science when in fact it is a social science. And this is no criticism of economics, but of our expectations of it. It has technical aspects, and it is right that it draws on the skills of statisticians, scientists, engineers and mathematicians, but it lacks the predictive power of such disciplines. For example, we can land humans on the Moon with great precision by applying Newton's laws in physics, but such laws have no analogue in economics. We cannot 'land' the economy where we want it in any sense.

So to understand society, economics also needs expertise from psychologists, lawyers, artists and many other disciplines concerned with human behaviour in order to gain insight into the mass psychology of people, businesses and their politics. It is for this reason that I have reverted to the 19th century term for the subject in the chapter title – the political economy.

GDP is confusing and boring

Gross Domestic Product (GDP) is the most commonly discussed measurement of economic activity; it is the total of all value created in the economy.

Unless you already understand GDP, this definition is unlikely to be helpful. In fact, depending on what you understand by 'economic activity' and 'value created' it might well be misleading or even meaningless. I think it is fair to say that many people find GDP and related concepts both confusing and boring.

Take a breath, and imagine you are standing on the Isle of Skye. I see myself in Elgol with the Cuillins towering above me and the twisting road dropping towards the sea. But it can be anywhere you like.

In a shed at the back of a converted cottage, a new business is beginning. A recently retired teacher, who has settled on the island from Edinburgh having inherited a cottage and the attached village shop, has the idea of collecting driftwood from beaches, cleaning and shaping the pieces and then inserting clock mechanisms and selling the finished product. Making the clocks began as a hobby but they prove to be a hit with tourists, and the profit generated, although small, is important because the shop barely breaks even.

And, as small and humble as it is, it adds to Scotland's GDP. The wood costs nothing, but the clock components cost £6 per set and are bought from a local supplier. Each clock is sold for £10 so a value of £4 has been added for each clock sold. If the shop sells 100 such clocks in a year and the **value-added** for each one is £4, then this business's contribution to annual GDP is £400.

In time, other small shops on the island buy the product from her for £8 and sell them for £10. By selling through other businesses she gains income from many more sales, but it also shares the value that is added more widely (£2 for her, £2 for the shop owner), benefiting the local economy. The business grows and she calls it Drift Clocks and secures a deal with a large online retailer. Now customers from anywhere in the country can buy the clocks. As with local shops, she sells them to the retailer for £8, and they apply the same markup of £2. This totals to £10, as before. But, unlike local shops, because the online retailer is a much larger business it must apply VAT at 20% of £10, bringing the price the customer pays to £12. Despite the name, VAT is not a percentage of the value-added amount, but the sale price (excluding VAT). In summary, the customers pay £12: £2 goes to the government, £2 to the online retailer, and £8 to Drift Clocks, of which £2 is its value-added.

Drift Clocks grows, acquires larger premises with expenses such as rent and electricity bills, and its income from sales, that is, its turnover, has grown to the point where it must include VAT in its sale prices. For all these reasons its value-added drops to £1 per clock. The owner forms a company, receives investment with the investors getting shares of the company in return, and hires employees to grow the business and expand the product range beyond clocks. In its first year, its sales are £120,000, of which £20,000 is VAT (20% of £100,000) and another £40,000 goes on raw materials and other non-wage running costs. After VAT and these other expenses, what's left is the value-added, that is £60,000. The contribution to GDP, which includes VAT comes to £80,000.

We've worked out a GDP contribution by looking at production and sales, but it's also possible to view it in terms of income. If, say, Drift Clock's cost of paying employees, including all national insurance and income tax paid by employer is £50,000 then the breakdown of GDP in income is shown in Table 6.1.

The important point behind this is that one person's spending is another person's income. Here we are viewing the business in terms of incomes it generates for others. Note that the 'of government' line is not the total income to the government because other taxes are included in the lines above it, of which, more later.

At this point, so long as this example wasn't too boring or confusing, you can appreciate why value-added is used in constructing GDP. If we did not subtract the running costs, that is money Drift Clocks pays to other businesses, then we would end up double counting certain amounts when adding up GDP across all businesses. For example, we had to deduct the £6 per clock mechanism because some of that is the value-

Income	Amount	Description
of employees	£50,000	Wages, income tax, NI
of shareholders & others	£10,000	Profit & operating costs & corp tax
of government	£20,000	VAT on sales
Total income from business	**£80,000**	**Value-added plus VAT**

Table 6.1
GDP of Drift Clocks split by income.

added of the company that makes them, not Drift Clocks. Similarly, payments of electricity bills have to be subtracted because it includes the value-added of the electricity company. Wages are not treated this way because employees are individuals and individuals are, in a sense, end-points in an economy whereas businesses are intermediaries.

Real world examples are of course far more complicated than this Drift Clocks example, but if you understand it, then you've got the gist of what GDP means.

GDP is interesting

If you add up the value created by all businesses operating in a country, then that total is the country's **Gross Domestic Product** or GDP. This is called the **production approach** to estimating GDP. It also helps explain GDP's name:

- **product** because it concerns production.
- **domestic** because it only includes production inside one country.
- **gross** because an element of depreciation has not been deducted (e.g. wear and tear on the business's tools and machines).

The official GDP of Scotland in 2016 was £149 billion. This excludes North Sea industry, which we'll come to below. In other words, all economic activity in Scotland resulted in £149 billion of value being created in making physical products, like tables and chairs, or delivering services, such as legal advice or IT support.

Data on GDP and growth is available from the Scottish government in their quarterly national accounts.[1] All data in this chapter is taken from the spreadsheet provided with that report for 2017Q2 – second quarter, April, May and June 2017.

Economists sometimes use the term **output** to mean GDP but it is often used loosely and may mean **Gross Value Added or GVA**. GDP is equal to GVA plus taxes on products, such as Value Added Tax or VAT, less any subsidies. For Scotland, GDP is roughly 10% higher than GVA. GVA is useful in looking at regional variations where a breakdown on taxes on products and subsidies is not available.

Just as one person's spending is another's income, one country's output can be viewed as an input. So another way to interpret Scotland's £149 billion GDP, and to my mind the easiest for newcomers, is to think of it as a measure of income for the whole country. If we add up all wages, all profits paid out as dividends and all taxes – all types of income – then we will find this is also equal to GDP, as shown in Table 6.2.

Income	Amount / £ billion	Name in national accounts
of employees	£75.6	Compensation of employees
of shareholders & others	£53.1	Gross operating surplus
of government	£20.0	VAT + other production tax less subsidies
Total income of Scotland	**£149**	**GDP**

Table 6.2
GDP split by income 2016.

The national accounts show that compensation of employees has remained stable at just over half of GDP between 1998 and 2016, and gross operating surplus has been a little over a third of GDP.

Even with GDP broken down like this, amounts covering the whole country in billions of pounds still seem abstract and disconnected from our everyday lives. However, we can address that by dividing by the population to produce GDP per person, often called **GDP per capita** or per head. To go from the figures in Table 6.2 to the per person figures in Table 6.3, all we need to do is divide by Scotland's population. For mid-year 2016, it was 5,404,700.

Income per person	Amount / £	Name in national accounts
of employees	£14,000	Compensation of employees
of shareholders & others	£9,800	Gross operating surplus
of government	£3,700	VAT + other production tax less subsidies
Total income of Scotland	**£27,500**	**GDP per capita**

Table 6.3
GDP split by income, per person 2016.

Scotland's GDP per person, or total income per person, is £27,500. Around half of this – £14,000 – is income (before tax is deducted) received by employees. This figure may seem low to you, and it is in fact roughly half the median income of an employee, but this is because about half the population is not in paid employment. That half of the population include children, parents and others carers, the retired, those in prison as well as those seeking a job.

The next largest item is *Gross operating surplus* at £9,800 per person. It can loosely be thought of as operating costs and profits. Operating costs includes all business consumption, such as paying for postage or renting premises, which will mostly go to other businesses. Some of the profits will go on corporation tax and some may be retained and possibly invested in the future, say in building a new factory, buying new equipment or training a workforce. The remainder will be distributed to shareholders as dividends. These shareholders can be other businesses but ultimately, possibly through a chain of businesses, every profit-seeking business is owned by shareholders that are people. This means you can view an individual's income as coming from two distinct streams: income from work as an employee of a business, or income from owning shares in a business. Although richer folk tend to own more shares and so benefit directly from such dividends, less affluent employees who have a private pension may benefit indirectly because pension funds have significant shareholdings in companies.

The remaining £3,700 of GDP per person goes to the government as tax, mainly VAT, but also some other smaller taxes with deductions for subsidies and VAT amounts reclaimed by companies on purchases.

The government income is of course much higher than £3,700 per person: some of the employee's £14,000 will be paid as income tax and national insurance, and some of the £9,800 of gross operating surplus will be paid as corporation tax on company profits. Once these plus a few other smaller taxes are added together, Scotland's total tax revenue per person comes to £10,400 in the national accounts for the calendar year 2016. Unsurprisingly, this is similar to the GERS value for financial year 2016–17 of £10,700 (see Chapter 5).

Gross deceptive product

GDP and its change over the years can inform policy and yield clues about our society, but only if its uncertainties and limitations are appreciated.

The remarks at the opening of this chapter highlighted GDP's inability to capture many non-monetary aspects of our society, but GDP was never designed to measure these and, indeed, there are many human activities where such measurement is either inappropriate or impossible.

The modern concept of GDP was introduced in 1934 by Simon Kuznets as part of the United States government's struggle to escape the great depression. The data and methods behind measuring GDP took on a new significance in the following decade in assessing and planning war-time production. Towards the end of the war it gained acceptance as a primary economic measure at the Bretton Woods conference that laid foundations for global trade in the post-war years. The concept of GDP has its roots in an era which has nearly departed living memory and despite being carefully refined since then, there are fundamental problems with its application in our present economy, particularly with the 'D' for domestic and the 'P' for production.

One significant difference between then and now is that the economies of countries are more closely connected through both trade and move-ment of people and capital across borders. The word 'capital' used to refer specifically to assets associated with production, but these days capital means money used for almost any money-making purpose, inclu-ding speculation (betting) on currency. In 2016, trading in foreign exchange markets averaged at more than $5 trillion dollars *per day*, and was more than ten times larger than it was in 1988. For comparison, *annual* UK GDP, which was fifth largest in the world in 2016, was $2.6 trillion.

The huge flows of international capital mean that the D for domestic in GDP can be misleading. Production by a foreign owned business in a country will contribute to that country's GDP, but this will often include sizeable capital flows that leave the domestic economy. Ireland's setting of low corporation tax has attracted foreign businesses and this has led to distortions such as GDP apparently rising by 26% in 2015. This was not due to a miraculous surge in production that year but mostly due to Apple's movement of over €200 billion of intellectual property assets there to avoid tax.[2]

For Scotland, it has been estimated in experimental statistics for 2010 that net outflows would lower GDP by 5% (including a North Sea geographical share).[3] There is an adjusted version of GDP called Gross National Income or GNI that is obtained by subtracting capital flows to foreign owners from GDP and adding inflows for Scottish-owned assets abroad. The net outflow, often called the current account deficit, is routinely calculated for the UK as part of what is known as the balance of payments, and was 1.2% of GDP in 2010. In recent years, it increased to just over 2%, but the figure was negative before 2007, indicating an inflow of capital. Even for the UK as a whole there is much uncertainty associated with measuring such flows.

Although GDP can be estimated with more confidence than GNI, it is not free from uncertainty. Several estimates of GDP are released each year and the first ones to be released for a quarter should be treated with some caution. The initial Scottish GDP estimates are released three to four months after each quarter's end by the Scottish government, and the Office for National Statistics releases its preliminary estimate of UK GDP a month after each quarter's end. These estimates carry greater uncertainties because they are based on incomplete information from surveys, tax receipts and many other sources. Outright errors arising from mistakes are fairly rare, but subsequent revisions are quite common as more information becomes available. Through the early 2000s first estimates of UK GDP tended to be revised up slightly, whereas following the financial crisis first estimates tended to be revised down.[4]

There have been a few large revisions to Scottish GDP in recent years. Some of these reflect wider UK revisions, such as those that increased GDP for previous years by £4 billion or more (see the 2016Q1 edition of the Scottish national accounts).[5] Revisions of a few hundred million to a billion have occurred since then, but usually these alter subtotals rather than total GDP. Trade within the UK is subject to more uncertainty because there are no internal borders, and so revisions are common. In fact, the total of imports from the rest of the UK is treated as a balancing item which means that when two methods of estimating GDP cannot be reconciled, it is imports which is adjusted. As a consequence revisions to any part of GDP often end up with a roughly equal and opposite revision to imports from elsewhere in the UK. Such revisions are not large enough to alter the fact there is a large trade deficit with the rest of the UK.

Despite all these issues, GDP is still a useful quantity. But just as the weather cannot be described by one temperature reading alone, with data needed on precipitation, wind speed, cloud cover and humidity to build up a useful description, GDP must be understood in a wider context. When it is taken together with a history of statistics on employment, wage growth and interest rates, GDP can provide a useful summary of the economy. And we can push the weather analogy further in that no country can be understood outwith the context of the global climate. And this raises difficult questions. To what extent can governments independently control economies? Must they simply weather the short-lived economic storms? And if governments can exert some influence, do they know what the consequences of their actions will be for their countries in the short-term, let alone for the longer term economic climate?

Economic growth

When GDP is mentioned in the news, it's almost always in relation to its growth. GDP usually increases from one quarter to the next, and so from one year to the next. But, if it decreases for two quarters in a row then the economy is said to be in a **recession**. This almost certainly means that company profits and wages have fallen and some companies will decide to dismiss employees as a consequence, causing unemployment to rise. Growth, or lack of it, is therefore an important measure of the health of an economy.

The GDP of a country can grow for a number of reasons. First, if consumers wish to buy more goods and services than they did the year before, then companies will increase supply to meet that increased demand, and GDP will rise. This rise could occur simply due to an increase in population – more people will mean greater demand for food, TVs, cars, toys, homes, legal advice etc. This is called demographic growth.

Alternatively, even if the population remains unchanged, each person may decide to consume more, perhaps prompted by the availability of a new technology, such as the car or the smartphone, or because they are enjoying a rise in real incomes, or are being offered cheap finance deals or loans. This is economic growth driven by consumption.

In both cases, economic activity is increased, and although governing politicians may be quick to highlight the growth and link it to their policies, neither demographic nor consumption-driven growth are necessarily welcome news to an economist who will instead be more interested in a third type of growth, that is due to productivity.

Increased efficiency of production in an economy can drive GDP growth. Efficiencies can arise from an improvement in the skills of a workforce, or through better management of resources, and from new technology, such as the use of machinery and robots in factories. Such efficiencies will lead to a rise in what is called **labour productivity** or often just productivity, which is defined as the output per hour worked in an economy. This is the Office for National Statistic's main measure, but there are others, such as output per job or per worker. We'll return to productivity later when discussing employment.

Other consequences of technology are more subtle. For example, the affordability of home appliances such as washing machines has meant that it is easier now for both parents in a household to work than it was only a few generations ago. This boosted the available work force in Scotland, and with it household incomes, even when the population was not increasing.

An illusory way for GDP to grow is because prices rise. This is **inflation**. I say 'illusory' because this can happen without any corresponding increase in economic activity. In fact, if both prices and wages rise by the same proportion then GDP will go up but there will be no change in the economy's production. That said, if people are unaware that it is only inflation which is raising their incomes, then they may feel better off and increase their consumption. In other words, people are not rational and may well respond to an illusion and that could in turn affect the overall economy.

Scotland's GDP has grown from £78 billion in 1998 to £149 billion in 2016 (excluding North Sea activity). But the £71 billion growth implied by these figures is a mixture of actual growth and inflation. These figures are for Scotland's **nominal GDP**.

GDP can be calculated to account for rising prices to give what is called **real GDP**. It is real in the sense that a change in GDP is due to an actual change in economic activity, not due to inflation.

Figure 6.1 shows Scotland's nominal and real onshore GDP. It's called **onshore** because it excludes the North Sea, which we'll come to later. Remember that real amounts always relate to prices in a specific year, and here they are in 2016 prices.

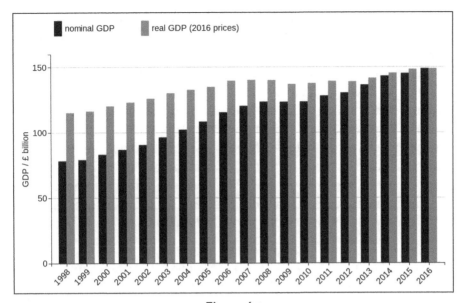

Figure 6.1
Nominal and real onshore GDP for Scotland 1998–2016.

Because we're working in 2016 prices, real and nominal GDP in 2016 are both £149 billion. The further back we go, the larger the difference, so that, for example, nominal GDP was £78 billion in 1998, but real GDP was £115 billion in 2016 prices. This highlights the importance of using real GDP when making long-term comparisons. For the rest of this chapter, assume all values are in real terms unless otherwise stated.

Real GDP grew from 1998 to 2007, then fell in the recession following the 2008 financial crisis but has since grown albeit more slowly. In 2016, GDP was £9 billion larger than its pre-recession 2007 peak.

Unfortunately, things can get a bit confusing when reading about GDP because there are a number of terms which mean the same thing, such as nominal GDP, GDP in current prices, and GDP in cash terms. Like-wise, the following all refer to real GDP: GDP in constant prices, GDP in volume terms or chain-volume measure GDP.

Real GDP is not computed by taking nominal GDP and just multiplying by an inflation factor. Instead, real GDP is calculated separately by a different method in which price changes specific to each type of product in the economy are treated separately. This throws up all kinds of difficult problems. One of the biggest challenges comes from dealing with dramatic changes in technologies and costs associated with them. For example, in the space of a few years, a computer went from being a costly item that sat on a desk to being an everyday object that most people carried about in their pockets in the form of a smart phone. And a couple of decades further back in time, the equivalent computing power of the humblest modern phone would cost millions and fill the space of a typical house. To deal with such problems, price changes concerning some technologies have to be smoothed out over time. This process is used in the most common method of estimating real GDP, the chained volume measure or CVM. If you want to learn more about this and other aspects of how GDP is estimated then an accessible but thorough account is given in the book *Understanding National Accounts* published by the OECD.[6]

To convert a nominal amount from a previous year to real terms, you can use something called a **deflator**. For example, consider £10.0 billion in 2007. The deflator for 2007 in 2016 prices is 70.9. Here 'in 2016 prices' means the deflator for 2016 is, by definition, equal to 100. So the recipe for conversion is to multiply by 100 and divide by the deflator, like this:

£10 billion in 2007 at 2016 prices = £10.0 billion × 100 ÷ 70.9 = £14.1 billion

You can also understand a deflator by thinking of it as a percentage. In this example, £10.0 billion is 70.9% of £14.1 billion. Hence the name: you can use it to deflate a current amount back to an amount in a previous year. Actually, the name is a bit annoying because a deflator is most usually used, as in this book, to inflate an amount from a past year into this year's prices.

Deflators are actually quite simple to calculate: they are just 100 times the nominal GDP for a year divided by the real GDP. But you don't need to calculate them as HM Treasury (the department of the UK government responsible for fiscal matters) publish the most widely used set of UK deflators. But, like GDP, they can be subject to revision. This book uses September 2017 edition deflators.[7] Scottish national accounts publish their own deflators but the differences between Scottish and UK deflators are quite small, and would not alter any of the trends discussed in this book.

The annual growth in GDP for a year is measured as the percentage change between that year and the one before. For example, for 2016, it

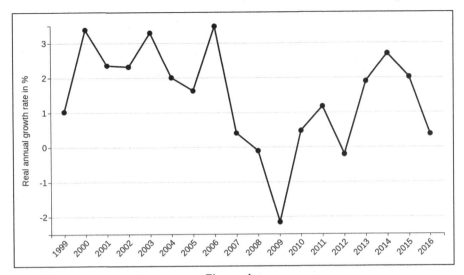

Figure 6.2
Real growth rates for onshore GDP 1999–2016.

is 2016's GDP less 2015's GDP divided by 2015's GDP times 100. Figure 6.2 shows the annual growth rate for real onshore GDP.

The most prominent feature on this graph is the 2008 financial crisis which triggered a recession in which the real growth rate dropped to -2.2% in 2009. A negative growth rate means that the economy shrunk or contracted. Growth before the financial crisis was stronger than growth after it: growth rates from 1999 to 2006 average 2.4% and those for 2010 to 2016 average 1.2%.

North Sea and GDP

The European Union specifies the system of national accounting called ESA10 that is used to produce Scotland and the UK's GDP figures. This involves classifying offshore oil and gas activity in the North Sea as *ex-regio*, that is, it's placed in its own special region of the UK that lies outside all the UK's countries. In this sense, onshore GDP is the official figure for Scotland, and so is most often quoted in the media.

Figure 6.3 shows North Sea GDP assigned to Scotland on a geographical basis (see Chapter 5) as a percentage of Scotland's onshore GDP.

The share of North Sea GDP as a percentage of onshore GDP was 10% in 1998, and then grew to peak at 21% in 2008. From that peak, North Sea

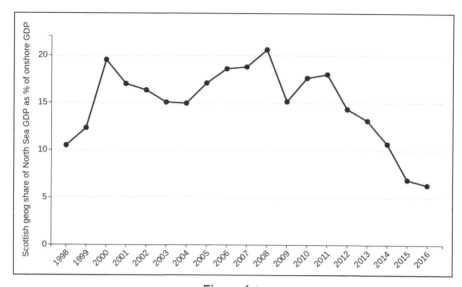

Figure 6.3
North Sea GDP assigned to Scotland on a geographical basis 1998–2016.

GDP declined to just 6% of onshore GDP in 2016. This fall was due to falling production until 2013 and then in 2014 and 2015 was mainly due to the dramatic fall in the oil price (see Chapter 5 for more detail).

Figure 6.4 shows growth rates with and without the North Sea along with the UK growth rate for GDP (which includes all North Sea GDP).

The most striking feature is that the line for Scotland including the North Sea has larger spikes, with growth at 10% in 2000 and falling to below -6% in 2009. This volatility of North Sea GDP is mainly caused by the oil price. Its effect on UK GDP is barely noticeable because North Sea GDP is a much smaller fraction of its total (typically 1.5% for the UK compared to about 15% for Scotland).

Scotland's onshore growth appears to be more variable than that of the UK. Some peaks and troughs in onshore GDP are coincident with, but smaller than corresponding ones in the North Sea GDP, notably in 2000, 2006 and 2012. It's likely this is because the North Sea industry feeds into many service industries onshore, including some that provide services to the industry directly, such as maintaining pipelines and oil rigs, and less directly in the form of software, finance, consultancy, and also for accommodation, travel and food for people involved in the industry.

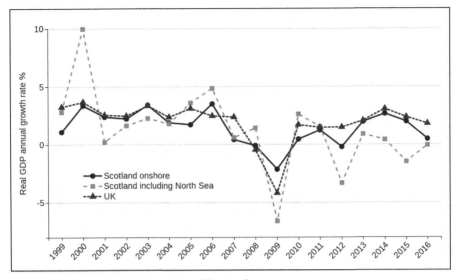

Figure 6.4
Growth rates for Scotland's GDP with and without North Sea
and UK GDP 1999–2016.

The connection between offshore and onshore economies became clear after 2014 following the oil price drop. A decrease in North Sea industry expenditure depleted the onshore economy of business, most obviously in Aberdeen where employment, house prices, restaurants and hotels all showed clear signs of an economic slowdown. It is likely that much of Scotland's weaker onshore growth compared to the whole UK from 2014 onwards is due to the North Sea slowdown.

The national accounts also contains onshore GDP on a quarterly basis, and at time of writing this extends to the 2017Q2 (April to June) and sheds a little more light on the recent trends in the last graph. Unfortunately, reliable data for real North Sea GDP growth per quarter isn't available.

Figure 6.5 shows Scotland's quarterly GDP. (Bars are used here only because quarterly variability makes lines and points harder to read.)

A quick glance at this graph shows you that the left and right halves of it are different. There are 18 quarters on this graph. Of the first nine quarters, four have whole UK growth higher, and five have Scotland's growth higher. There is no discernible pattern. But in the next nine

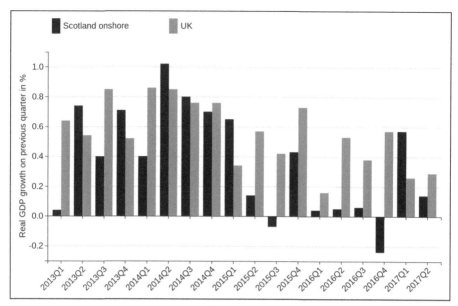

Figure 6.5
Onshore Scottish GDP and UK GDP 2013Q1 to 2017Q2.

quarters only one quarter, 2017Q1, sees Scotland with higher growth. Not only that but Scotland's onshore economy contracts in 2015Q3 and 2016Q4, and shows almost no growth through 2016. The timing matches the fall in the oil price that began in late 2014, and continued through all of 2015 and into 2016.

That said, Scotland has not technically been in recession because there were no two consecutive quarters with negative growth. Although Figure 6.5 doesn't show quarterly growth rates for it, Figure 6.4 shows that Scotland's real GDP including a geographical share of the North Sea shrank by 1.5% in 2015 with negligible growth in both 2014 and 2016.

As mentioned above, one source of economic growth is demographic. If the economy grows at the same rate as the population then, on average, no one is actually better off. The easiest way to account for this is to look at GDP per person. This is shown in Figure 6.6 for Scotland, with and without North Sea GDP, and the whole UK including North Sea GDP.

Scotland's onshore GDP per person sits a little bit below the UK's, but this is not surprising as the UK value includes the North Sea GDP. When a geographical share is included, Scotland's GDP per person sits well

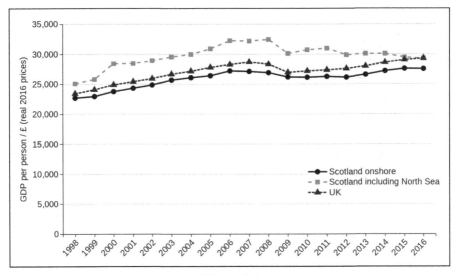

Figure 6.6
GDP per person for Scotland and the UK 1998 to 2016.

above that of the UK, with the gap being as large as £4,100 in 2008. However, as a consequence of the oil price fall in 2014 and 2015, Scotland's GDP per person including the North Sea fell slightly below the UK's in 2016, which is the only year in this record where this has happened.

GDP by industry

Figure 6.7 shows the contribution from all major industries to GDP. The *Total taxes less subsidies on products* amount is the difference between GVA and GDP.

The lion's share of GDP in 2016 – two-thirds of it – comes from *Services*. This includes all types of business in which there isn't a physical product, such as advice given by lawyers, or telephone call centre services for banks.

Figure 6.8 shows how contributions to GDP from broad sectors of industry have varied over time.

In 2016, all sectors other than *Services* each account for less than 10% of GDP, with the next largest being manufacturing at 9% followed by construction at 6%. *Everything else* is comprised of agriculture, forestry and fishing; mining and quarrying; electricity and gas supply; water supply and waste; and taxes less subsidies on products (see above).

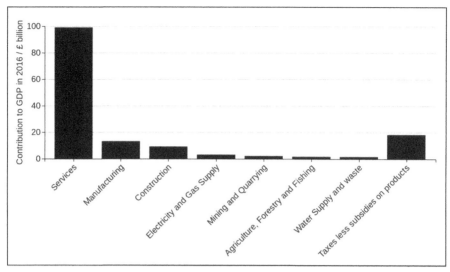

Figure 6.7
GDP by industry 2016.

Services expanded from 61% in 1998 to stabilise at 67% from 2004 onwards. *Manufacturing* declined from 16% in 1998 but levelled out around 10% from 2004 to 2014, followed by a slight drop in 2015 and 2016. *Construction* has varied around 6% of GDP though it rose to touch 7% in 2007 but then fell back to around 6% during the recession. The slight growth of *Everything else* is almost entirely due to taxes on products which makes up more than half of it, and that in turn is in good part due to the VAT rate rising to 20% in 2011.

The decline of manufacturing between 1998 and 2004 is in fact the tail end of a trend spanning much of the 20th century. It is also exhibited by the whole UK and many other wealthy countries. From 1973 to 2009 manufacturing declined from making up a quarter of Scotland's GDP to only a tenth.[8]

Employment

For many people, the most tangible effect of a struggling economy is the fear of becoming unemployed. Ironically, as explained at the start of the chapter, such fear can trigger or exacerbate an economic slowdown. Usually, employment is high when the economy is doing well, and lower when it isn't, but recent years have been unusual in this respect, as we'll see.

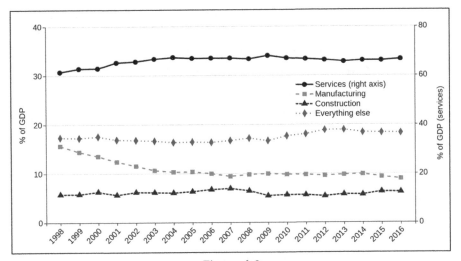

Figure 6.8
GDP by sector of industry 1998 to 2016.

Information on employment is available from the Office for National Statistics or ONS which publishes several UK Labour Market bulletins[9] a year, and figures for Scotland and other UK countries and regions can be found in the regional version of the bulletin.

Figure 6.9 shows the employment rate of Scotland and the UK.

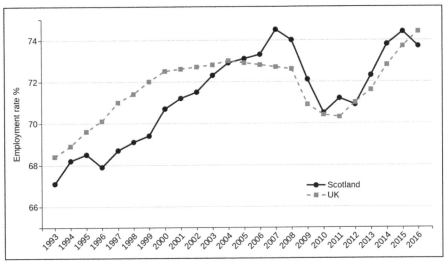

Figure 6.9
Employment rate for Scotland and the UK 1993 to 2016.

The **employment rate** is the percentage of people aged from 16 to 64 who are in work. The vast majority of these people are in paid employment, but also included are a small minority who are not paid explicitly, such as those who work for family businesses.

Scotland's employment rate rose from 67.1% in 1993 to peak at 74.5% in 2007. It fell after the 2008 financial crisis to a low of 70.9% in 2012 and recovered to 74.4% in 2015, just below the pre-crisis peak, but then fell again, possibly as the result of the North Sea slowdown.

The UK shows a similar pattern, but until 2004 its employment rate was as much as 2 percentage points higher than Scotland's. Since then, Scotland's employment rate has mostly remained slightly higher than the UK's with the notable exception of 2016.

The **unemployment rate** is the percentage of people who are unemployed out of all employed and unemployed people. The ONS follows the International Labour Organisation (ILO)[10] definition which classes someone as unemployed if they are available for work and seeking employment. People who are either employed or classed as unemployed are called **economically active**, and those who are not are said to be economically inactive. If everyone who was willing and able to work had a job then the unemployment rate would be 0%.

Figure 6.10 shows the unemployment rate of Scotland and the UK.

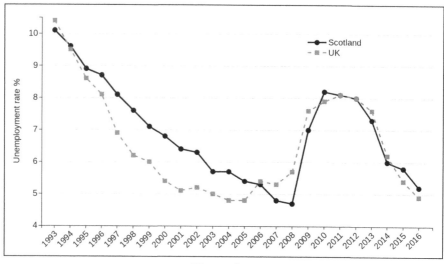

Figure 6.10
Unemployment rate for Scotland and the UK 1993 to 2016.

The profile for both the UK and Scotland in Figure 6.10 is similar to that of Figure 6.9 turned upside down. Unemployment falls from around 10% in 1993, reaches a low of under 5% before increasing sharply after the 2008 financial crisis. Unemployment then peaks at 8% and falls to around 5% by 2016.

One surprising feature of these graphs is that in 2015 Scotland's employment rate *and* its unemployment rate were greater than that of the UK. Also, between 2015 and 2016, both the unemployment rate and employment rate fell in Scotland. These apparent contradictions can occur because the two rates are not percentages of the same total: one is of the working age population, and the other is of those who are economically active.

Figure 6.11 shows the economic activity rate.

The percentage of the population aged 16-64 who are economically active – either employed or classed as unemployed – is called the **economic activity rate**.

Both Scotland and the UK show an overall increasing trend but Scotland's rate has increased by over 4 percentage points in the last two decades, peaking at just over 79%. Scotland's fall by over a percentage point in 2016 seems mostly to be reversed according to the first data available for 2017.

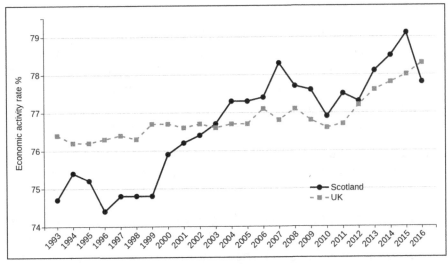

Figure 6.11
Economic activity rate for Scotland and the UK 1993 to 2016.

The UK's change is less dramatic, increasing by less than 2 percentage points but from a higher starting point. The result is that both Scotland and the whole UK have an activity rate of about 78% in 2016. The effect of the 2008 financial crisis is less noticeable on this graph; it only interrupts the increasing trend for a few years.

The rise in employment and economic activity is mostly due to the rise in the number of women seeking work. Also, there has been a pronounced rise in self-employment and again this seems to involve women more than men, especially since the 2008 crisis.

The employment rate is near record highs and the unemployment rate is similarly very low, but unlike similar periods in history, economic growth is poor, and more so in recent years in Scotland than for the whole UK. Part of this is because of the Scottish economy's stronger links to the troubled North Sea industry, but the part in common with the rest of the UK is to do with productivity. Productivity, the amount of economic output per hour of work, has failed to increase, meaning that the slight growth in GDP in recent years is due almost entirely to the fact that more people are working. We'll return to productivity again later.

For more detailed analysis on employment, see the Scottish Labour Market Trends report which is published by the The Fraser of Allander Institute (FAI) and The Scottish Centre for Employment Research (SCER).[11]

Inflation

We've encountered inflation many times so far and have tried to remove its effects using the Consumer Prices Index (CPI) and HM Treasury deflators. It's worth pausing for a moment to consider what inflation actually is, what might cause it and when we shouldn't ignore it. As with many things (notably the idea of time itself) inflation seems easy enough to comprehend until, that is, you start thinking about it more carefully.

The rate at which an index like CPI grows is known as the inflation rate. Amounts of money uncorrected for inflation are said to be 'nominal' or in 'current prices', or 'real' or in 'constant prices' if adjusted for inflation.

Inflation is the rise of prices over time. If you could buy a bread loaf for £1 last year but find the exact same type of loaf costs £1.10 this year, then you are experiencing inflation. There are many possible causes. It might be that the bread now costs more to make. Perhaps wheat has increased in price, or maybe bakery staff need to be paid more, or it could be that the costs of powering the ovens have gone up. Alternatively, there may be no change in the cost of making bread but demand for bread has increased allowing shops to hike prices because customers are willing to pay more.

Notice that none of these examples explains why inflation is occurring in the first place. Rather they move the cause of inflation elsewhere. That's not a minor point but highlights the fact that inflation often has no easily identifiable cause. Instead it emerges from a complex web of interactions. To look for a single reason for inflation can be as futile as trying to find a simple reason for why consumers prefer to buy red cars one year and black cars the next.

If inflation is uniform across the economy including people's incomes then *in theory* there is no change other than larger numbers appearing on receipts and payslips; activity in the economy is the same. But, in practice, inflation may have psychological consequences. For example, if an employer cut wages by 10% in a year there would be an outcry, yet protest might be muted if an employer left nominal wages unchanged and let inflation of 1% to 2% result in a 10% cut to real wages over several years.

Higher inflation can cause people to spend the money more quickly if they become aware it buys them less over times. The opposite is true of deflation in which prices fall. This is a rarer beast in modern times but it is feared because if people think their money will buy more tomorrow than it will today they might delay purchases and that could trigger a recession.

It's often said that inflation is caused by printing too much money, with historical examples offered of the Weimar republic in inter-war Germany, or Scotsman John Law championing the introduction of paper money in 18th century France. These lessons from history are worth heeding but their circumstances are very different from our current, more complex economic and monetary systems. More recent examples in Zimbabwe and Venezuela are perhaps more relevant, but aside from a few such exceptional cases, it's not obvious what 'too much money' might mean. One approach is to say that inflation will occur if more money is in circulation than current economic production requires, sometimes referred to as the economy overheating. The problem is the definition risks being circular because inflation is also used as a signal that there is overheating.

In practice, even if inflation cannot be adequately explained, it can be measured and perhaps managed. The routine inflation we usually experience is not only expected but desired as long as it stays within a percentage point of 2%. This is the target that the UK's central bank (misleadingly called the Bank of England for historical reasons) tries to meet by setting interest rates and in buying and selling government bonds.

Another source of inflation is caused by shifts in global trade and particularly the behaviour of the oil price. Even expectations of change can have a noticeable effect. When the result of the UK's 2016 EU referendum became known, the pound fell in value against the dollar and Euro almost immediately. This can be interpreted as international investors and businesses seeing that they would have less use for pounds in the future. The pound's lower value meant that imports into the UK became more expensive leading to a subsequent rise in inflation. Once the prices in the UK have adjusted to reflect the jump in import prices, inflation is likely to drop again. Also the pound's value against the dollar and euro varied in quite different ways due to events elsewhere in the world. Inflation is now bound up with the changeable winds of global trade.

If you have money then inflation will erode its value, but if you are in debt then inflation will erode that too. Whether that will help or hinder inequality in wealth or income depends on interest rates and the level of growth in the economy. This is given much attention by Piketty who also noted that before the First World War there was no tendency for inflation overall, instead there were periods of inflation and deflation that averaged out to about zero. It seems inflation is an economic phenomenon that took hold in the early 20th century and there is no reason to believe that it will continue indefinitely.

Earnings, income and inflation

Working for an employer is akin to renting out your time, and for most people it will be a significant amount of each waking day for most days in each year. Depending on your circumstances and qualifications and how much you enjoy the work, you may deem certain rates of pay as being inadequate for you to yield your time to an employer. And just as there is a market for property, there is a market for labour in which supply and demand can wax and wane. If there are many workers applying for a certain kind of job, employers may, in time, decide to reduce the wages on offer. The employees may accept these lower wages for fear of becoming unemployed. Conversely, if there are few suitable candidates for a certain kind of a job, then employers may compete with each other causing wages to rise. This is how employment is viewed in the discipline of economics and it bears a few similarities with reality.

A subtle but important point is to distinguish between earnings and income. Earnings suggests that the money received is in return for some kind of work – that you have done something to 'earn' it. Income, however, has a broader meaning. If you are born into a wealthy family and live off the returns from inherited assets, then you have an income but in a literal sense they are not earnings. And, as described in Chapter 3, those on lowest incomes in society draw an important part of their income from welfare payments.

In practice this distinction is not always made between income and earnings, but usually earnings does refer to income from employment or some kind of productive activity. In either case, it's important to be clear whether tax has been deducted and benefits are added because they have a profoundly progressive effect (see Chapter 3).

Information related to earnings in this section is drawn from the ONS report on its Annual Survey of Hours and Earnings (ASHE).[12] Figure 6.12 shows earnings for all countries and regions in the UK for 1999 and 2016. The earnings are 'gross' in that they are before tax is deducted and benefits added.

Real earnings have risen considerably in all areas of the UK. For a full-time employee in Scotland, the median income has risen by 18%, from £23,600 in 1999 to £27,900 in 2016 in real terms at 2016 prices. The UK median started higher at £24,900 in 1999 but only rose by 13% to be slightly higher than Scotland's at £28,200 in 2016. In fact, Scotland's median had risen slightly above the UK's for the first time in 2015 but this was undone because of slower Scottish growth in 2016. Although earnings did fall following the 2008 financial crisis, the fall was smaller than the rise in real earnings since 1999.

London has significantly higher median earnings than any other part of the UK. All other English regions, except the South East, have earnings below that of Scotland.

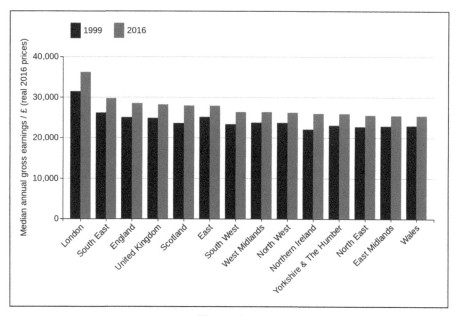

Figure 6.12
Median annual pre-tax earnings by UK country and region 1999 and 2016.

We see here what we saw in Chapter 3: since 1998 earnings have grown in real terms. In fact, this is true for much of the post-war period in the 20th century. This is a consequence of economic growth and the fact that GDP per person has been growing in real terms, as seen in Figure 6.6.

Figure 6.13 shows the labour productivity in £ of output per hour worked. It is calculated by dividing GVA by the number of hours worked in each year.

This shows that labour productivity grew from 1998, with growth slowing from 2004. Since the financial crisis there has been almost no growth in productivity. Both the UK and Scotland show much the same trend but Scotland's productivity is a little lower than that of the whole UK, though the gap reduced noticeably after 2008.

The lack of post-2008 growth in productivity is often referred to as the productivity puzzle. Other countries have experienced it too, but to a lesser extent. The solution to the puzzle is likely a combination of factors. One is that a lack of investment has meant that work practices have not increased in efficiency. Also, productivity is harder to quantify in the services sector than say for manufacturing, and services dominate in Scotland as throughout the UK. For example, the number of employee

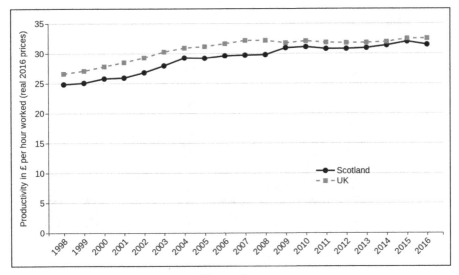

Figure 6.13
Labour productivity for Scotland and the UK in £ per hour 1998 to 2016.

hours needed to manufacture a mobile phone (usually somewhere in Asia) is easier to estimate than those for the services of a software engineer to write apps for it, because some software can be reused at the click of mouse. And, unlike the phone it runs on, once an app is written, each sale can be made with zero manufacturing cost. A similar situation exists with music that is streamed or downloaded.

Whatever the reasons, the lack of productivity since the 2008 financial crisis is is behind the weak growth of GDP. What growth there has been has come from increasing the number of hours worked, which also explains why the employment rate is unexpectedly high despite the weak recovery from 2008. A problem arising from this situation is that if workers are not producing more for each hour worked, there is little incentive for business to raise pay. As inflation has been low in recent years, this has not caused a significant problem, but as inflation rose in 2017 there was more concern that real wages would stagnate or fall.

Figure 6.14 shows the **gender gap** in earnings between men and women.

For full-time employees, males earn more than females with a gender gap of £4,750 in Scotland and a larger one of £5,800 in the UK. For part-time employees, the gender gap reverses and women earn slightly

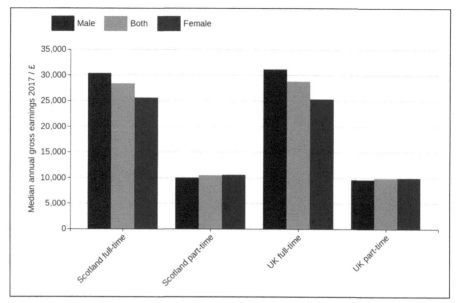

Figure 6.14
Median pay by gender for Scotland and the UK 2017.

more than men. A likely explanation is that mothers with higher earning jobs are more likely to return to work part-time than fathers after becoming parents. The number of women in part time jobs is almost four times that for men.

To round off this discussion of income, let's look at how trends in household income and spending compare in real terms over time. Figure 6.15 shows data from Chapter 3 on median real income after tax is deducted and benefits are added and compares it to a measure of total household consumer expenditure in the economy from the national accounts called Household Final Consumption Expenditure or HHFCE. Financial year data is used and the data indexed to be 100 in 1998–99.

Both show strong growth from 1998–99 but expenditure stops growing after its pre-crisis peak in 2006–07 and drops. Such behaviour by consumers is a normal prelude to recession in that once it becomes clear there is an economic problem they will begin to fear for the future and rein in spending. Employers, although also nervous of the future, cannot respond so quickly as contracts must run their course, and employment law restricts how quickly, and cheaply, they can lay off workers. For this reason, and perhaps also because rising government

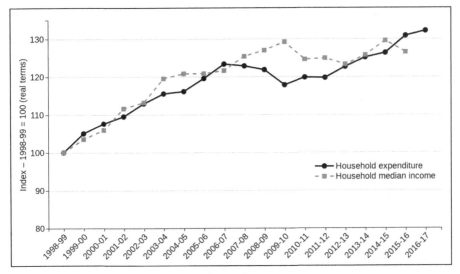

Figure 6.15
Household expenditure and income 1998–99 to 2016–17.

spending helped the economy prior to 2010–11 (see Chapter 5), household income continued to grow until 2009–10.

Household expenditure has grown consistently in recent years, exceeding its pre-recession peak. Income, however, has not. To some extent this disparity has occurred because the recession resulted in a greater fall in expenditure than income.

Household Final Consumption Expenditure comprises 64% of GDP, and dwarfs both government spending and spending by business. With this in mind you can also understand that the fall in expenditure after 2006–07 removed a small but important amount of activity from the economy. The effects of this are visible in the graphs of economic growth rates and employment given earlier in this chapter, and the fall of real incomes in the above graph.

It is important to appreciate that not all types of household spending are at the discretion of the householder. For example, if rent or mortgage payments go up, the extra expense often has to be accepted, albeit grudgingly, because moving house is disruptive and brings large expenses of its own. Similar reasoning applies if the cost of travelling to school or work increases. If the household budget is to be trimmed, then savings will be found from trips to the cinema, eating at a restaurant, going on holiday, or perhaps by postponing big ticket purchases, such as a car or a new kitchen.

Figure 6.16 shows the four largest areas of household expenditure in real terms. Together *Housing* and *Transport* make up just over a third of total house expenditure, and all four areas made up half of expenditure in 1998, rising to nearly 60% by 2016.

All areas show strong growth until 2006 but different behaviours afterwards. *Housing* expenditure growth continues through the crisis and the recession with a peak in 2011 and a subsequent fall. This may seem surprising because the Bank of England interest rate, which is used as the basis for setting most mortgage rates, fell to its historic low (at least at the time) of 0.5% in 2009. The delay in affecting housing costs has a few possible explanations. It could be that many mortgages remained on fixed rates or it could be that the private rental market only responded once household incomes decreased in 2010–11.

The fall in *Recreation and culture* is entirely consistent with the discussion above, in that it begins to fall upon the first signs of economic woes in 2007 and suffers the longest and deepest fall of the four categories. The smaller and shorter fall in *Transport* is likely due to the rise in unemployment following the recession which resulted in fewer passengers commuting to work.

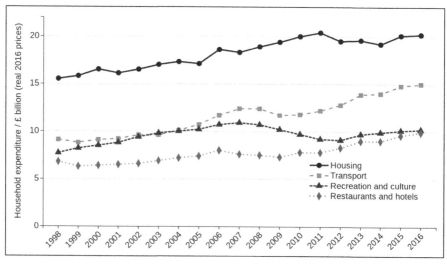

Figure 6.16
Major areas of household spending 1998 to 2016.

Recent economic growth, which has been weak by historical standards, has relied mainly on household expenditure. A glance at the last few years of household income and expenditure in Figure 6.15 does not bode well for the years ahead.

Trade unions

Members of a trade union are employees from many companies across an industry who come together to further common interests in their working conditions. In 2017, 28.1% of employees in Scotland belonged to a trade union though this has declined from 39.0% in 1995. Figures for England are a few percentage points lower and those of Wales and Northern Ireland are a few percentage points higher. The declining trend is seen across the UK and began in the early 1980s. These figures and much more data can be found in the Trade union statistics report[13] published by the ONS and UK government.

Examples of unions include the Educational Institute of Scotland (EIS) for teachers and lecturers, the Fire Bridges Union (FBU), Musicians' Union, National Union of Journalists (NUJ) and UNISON for employees in the public sector. A total of 39 unions are affiliated with Scottish Trade Union Congress (STUC) which coordinates activity across unions. It is a separate body from the Trade Union Congress of England and Wales having split from it in 1897 due to political tensions related to the formation of the Labour party.

Trade unions play an economic role because they collectively bargain on behalf of their members for fair wages. If prices are rising due to inflation but employers do not raise wages in response then unions will raise this with employers and if negotiations are not fruitful then strikes can result. Because complex economic issues such as inflation and productivity are needed to make the case for a wage rise, trade unions often seek advice on economic matters and some even employ economists.

Trade unions could equally well have featured in this book in Chapter 4 as they play an important role in society. Events such as the Upper Clyde Shipbuilding dispute in 1971 and the miners' strike in the 1980s are important landmarks in our social history. The former attracted attention from beyond Scotland with cab drivers in London sending their tips and John Lennon sending £5,000 to sustain the workers who had occupied and were running the shipbuilding yards. This example showed that although unions could not arrest the prevailing long-term shift from a manufacturing economy to a services-based one, they had the power to challenge not only employers, but also the government. The decline of union membership through the 1980s is partly explicable by this shift away from manufacturing but it was also caused by the political response of Margaret Thatcher's Conservative government to unions' show of power in the 1970s.

Despite the decline, trade unions are still an important force in society with some 629,000 employees in Scotland being members of a union in 2017. But the stereotype of trade unionists as gruff, shop-floor factory workers from the west of Scotland is receding into the past. The rise of the 'gig economy' with its temporary and insecure work practices has led to the emergence of organisations such as Better Than Zero which can be viewed as a new form of union. Although the mostly youthful members of these movements were not born when Jimmy Reid, the trade unionist prominent in the Upper Clyde Shipbuilding work-in, gave his famous speech entitled Alienation as Glasgow University's Rector in 1972,[14] they share his belief that work is about more than just fair pay:

> Let me right at the outset define what I mean by alienation. It is the cry of men who feel themselves the victims of blind economic forces beyond their control. It's the frustration of ordinary people excluded from the processes of decision making. The feeling of despair and hopelessness that pervades people who feel with justification that they have no real say in shaping or determining their own destinies.

Exports and imports

Economies of different countries are connected by trade. A country aiming for complete economic independence, such as North Korea, is called an autarky and is moving very much against the tide of globalisation.

Importing gives a country access to goods and services it cannot produce itself, or perhaps at lower prices than domestic costs allow. Too much importing may harm a country's businesses however, especially if they struggle to compete on price.

Exporting gives a country access to a larger pool of customers. A rise in exports is generally viewed as good thing for an economy as it can encourage growth of the country's GDP. But too much exporting can have a downside in that it may disrupt the economies of the importing countries, and the exporting country will be vulnerable to any disruptions in those economies.

Figure 6.17 show figures from Scotland's national accounts on imports and exports as a fraction of onshore GDP. Exports are shown as positive numbers and imports as negatives. This reflects the fact that exports involve a flow of money into Scotland, and imports are a flow out. These figures relate to Scotland's onshore economy.

Scotland is a net importer with the rest of the UK in that more is imported than is exported. The situation is more balanced for the rest of the world where imports and exports are roughly equal. Taking all exports and imports together gives us *Net trade* and the fact this is negative in every year tells us that Scotland's onshore economy imports more than it exports.

More detail on exports are given in the Export Statistics Scotland report 2015[15] that was published in January 2017 by the Scottish government. Its figures are calculated on a slightly different basis from those in the national accounts and as such are generally larger, though they show similar trends over time.

Table 6.4 shows the breakdown of Scottish exports by destination in 2015.

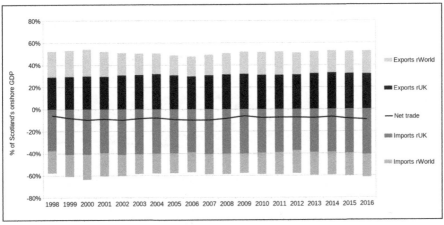

Figure 6.17
Imports and exports to the rest of the UK and the world 1998–2016.

Destination	Exports £ billion	% of total	% of GDP
Rest of UK	49.8	63%	34%
Rest of EU	12.3	16%	8.5%
Rest of Europe	2.8	3.6%	1.9%
Rest of world	13.6	17%	9.4%
Total	**78.6**	**100%**	**54.2%**

Table 6.4
Scottish exports by destination 2014.

Most exports – almost two-thirds – are to the rest of the UK. This equates to 34% or just over a third of Scotland's GDP. Most of the remainder is split roughly equally between the rest of Europe and the world.

Figure 6.18 shows the history of exports to the rest of the UK, the rest of the EU, and everywhere outside the EU.

Exports to the rest of the UK have trended upwards slightly rising from 32% to 34% of GDP. Exports to the rest of the EU have trended downwards from 12.6% to 8.5% of GDP. Exports to the rest of the world

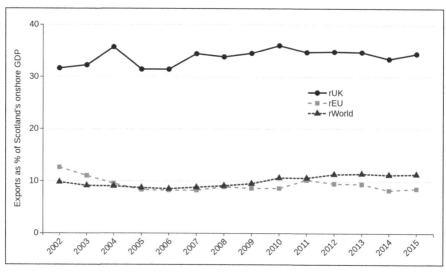

Figure 6.18
Exports to the rest of the UK, EU and world 2002 to 2015.

(including non-EU Europe) having risen from 10% to 11% and overtook EU exports in 2005.

Figure 6.19 shows exports by major sectors of industry as a percentage of GDP.

Manufacturing exports declined significantly between 2002 and 2006 falling from 26% to 18% of GDP and despite a rise in following years they have fallen back to 18% again in 2014 and 2015. This trend is the same as that for manufacturing production in Figure 6.8.

You might wonder why manufacturing was only 9% in the GDP break-down of Figure 6.8 but 18% of GDP in this one. This is because exports are measured on the sale price whereas the contribution to GDP in production shown in Figure 6.8 only includes the value added (see the Drift Clocks example at the start of the chapter). This is still useful though because not only does it side-step the issue of inflation, it also tells us how exports are growing relative to GDP. For example, Figure 6.18 shows that exports to the rest of UK are growing in line Scotland's onshore economy, but exports to the rest of the world are growing faster, and exports to the rest of the EU are growing more slowly than Scotland's economy.

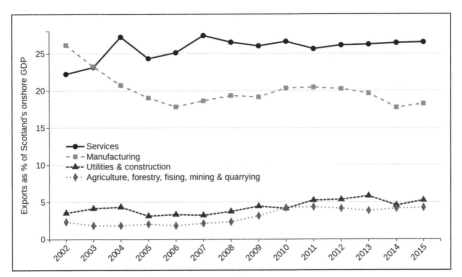

Figure 6.19
Exports as a percentage of GDP for broad sectors of industry 2002 to 2015.

Exports of services rose as a share of GDP from 22% and 27%, overtaking declining manufacturing exports in 2004. Services are exported in the sense that a foreign buyer pays for a service from a company or individual located in Scotland, such as banking support, advice from a Scottish lawyer, or handling of phone calls at a call centre based in Scotland.

Exports in other sectors also show slight rises in recent years and this slightly lessened the combined dominance of services and manufacturing which was 89% in 2002 but down to 83% in 2015.

Comparing Figures 6.18 and 6.19 shows that the profile of the *rUK* and *Services* lines are very similar. This is because services dominates exports to the rest of the UK making up 55% of all exports to rUK. The reverse is true for exports to the rest of the EU in which 61% of exports are manufacturing. Currently exports outside the EU are similar for manufacturing and services at 46% and 43% respectively.

Figure 6.20 shows specific sectors of exports that have changed notably between 2002 and 2015. Two are manufactured products and the other two are services. Together these exports made up 41% of all exports in 2002, but this dropped steadily to reach 35% in 2015.

Much of the decline in manufacturing evident in Figure 6.19 can be traced to just one sector: *Computer, electronic and optical*. It was the single

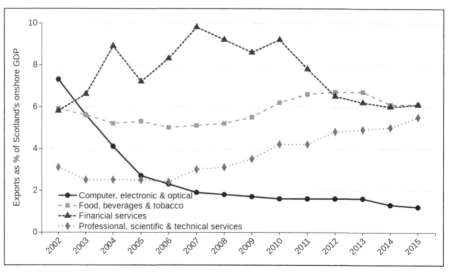

Figure 6.20
Notable sectors of Scottish exports 2002 to 2016.

biggest sector of exports in 2002 but dropped from 7.3% of GDP that year to just 1.2% in 2015.

One of the manufacturing sectors that has fared best is *Food, beverage and tobacco*, which includes two of Scotland's most famous exports: whisky, which makes up half of the whole sector, and salmon. *Food, beverage and tobacco* exports grew from 2008 but have since declined back to 6.1% of GDP which is roughly where it was in 2002.

Although services have seen substantial growth, its largest sub-sector, *Financial services*, shows a more complex history. It reached its peak in 2007 at 9.8% of exports and was by far the largest single export sector that year. Since the financial crisis of 2008, its share has dropped markedly, stabilising at about 6% of GDP in 2014 and 2015. The *Professional, scientific & technical services* sub-sector is very broad and includes legal, accounting, management, architecture, engineering, technical testing and analysis activities. It has doubled its GDP share of exports between 2002 and 2015, and its growth has helped offset the fall caused by financial services in the overall services total.

Sectors of the economy

To understand the economy of a country, you need to understand how public spending and taxation affects its consumers and businesses, and as no country is isolated, that necessarily involves trade with other countries. The **sectoral balance** approach brings these aspects together and, if applied correctly, is a great help in seeing the economic forest for the trees. We'll consider the whole UK first as this will help highlight Scotland's current context and potential differences if it became a separate state.

The **public sector** includes all levels of government and public owned institutions such as the Bank of England, Scottish Water and Network Rail. The **private sector** includes everything else in the domestic economy, which means businesses and individual consumers. To this we need to add the **foreign sector** which is connected to the domestic public and private sectors through imports and exports.

If you pause to think on it, a country's public sector plus its private sector plus the foreign sector represents the entire global economy (assuming there is no secret trade with an alien race). This means that the flows between the public, private and foreign sectors must balance.

For example, the net flow of money out of the public sector must go to the private and foreign sectors; it literally has nowhere else to go.

Figure 6.21 shows the three sectors and the flows between them.

To start with, for simplicity, let's restrict our attention to just the private and public sectors and assume that flows to the foreign sector are balanced, ie imports equals exports. The money flowing from the public sector to the private sector is public spending. Let's call this G. The money flowing from the private sector to public sector is tax (strictly it is all public revenues). Let's call that T. If public spending exceeds taxation – G exceeds T – then the net flow of money into the private sector is G minus T. This means that this flow must increase the wealth of the private sector by G minus T. The wealth of the private sector may change in other ways of course, most obviously from the wealth created in economic growth.

And, if it hasn't already occurred to you, G minus T – that is, public spending less taxation – is also the fiscal or budget deficit. For many people this seems like a jarring contradiction because politically a fiscal deficit is usually portrayed as a bad thing because it is only viewed as a net drain on public finances. What we see here is that the drain pipe leads to the individuals and businesses that make up the private sector. In other words, a fiscal deficit is equal to the net income of the private sector (if trade and other flows are balanced).

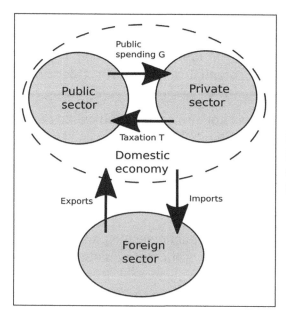

Figure 6.21
Private, public and foreign sectors and flows between them.

Does this mean a fiscal deficit is a good thing? That depends. For example, imagine you notice that the fiscal deficit rises in a year because government spending on health shoots up. If this is due to the building of a hospital or hiring more nurses to cope with an increased demand on the NHS then politicians would find this relatively easy to justify to the public. If, however, the extra government spending went to pay private firms for health care services, then there would be public concern about privatisation of the NHS. Sectoral balances give us a fresh insight, but, as we've seen throughout this book, we need to look at the details and consider moral arguments to judge whether they are good or bad.

So, with the foreign sector playing no role, the effect of public spending and taxation can be summarised as:

Net flow into private sector = Fiscal deficit

Let's now add in the foreign sector. There will be an outflow from the domestic economy to the foreign sector due to the money paid to foreign suppliers for imports. And there will be an inflow of money from selling exports to foreign customers. The trade deficit is the amount spent on imports less what is received from exports and can be thought of as a net flow out of the domestic economy. For simplicity, but without deviating far from reality, let's also suppose that the public sector deals exclusively with its domestic private sector which has suppliers that handle necessary public sector imports such as medical equipment for hospitals. This means we can revise the equation above to include the foreign sector by subtracting the trade deficit like this:

Net flow into private sector = Fiscal deficit – trade deficit

This is an identity – the mathematical equivalent of saying 'what goes in, must come out, or stay inside'. It's not roughly true, and does not depend on some theory, but is true by definition. What this identity tells us is that the private sector of a domestic economy has an inflow which is the fiscal deficit and an outflow which is the trade deficit.

We could instead talk about the fiscal surplus which is taxation less spending or the negative of the fiscal deficit. This is rarely done because fiscal surpluses are rare: the UK has run a deficit in 54 of the last 62 years.[16] Also, the UK has run an annual trade deficit in each of the last 30 years.

Sectoral balances and the above identity are useful in helping us understand potential consequences of running deficits or surpluses. A country that runs a trade deficit but has a balanced budget, that is a zero fiscal deficit, will have wealth drained out of its private sector, all else being equal. However, if that country were to run a fiscal deficit equal to its trade deficit then the drain on its private sector would cease.

Caution is required with cause and effect. For example, if, as can often be the case, you notice that a country is running a trade deficit and fiscal deficit of comparable sizes, it is tempting to think that one caused the other. Perhaps the government chose to run the fiscal deficit to match the trade deficit? But sectoral balances by themselves cannot answer such questions. In fact, governments cannot easily control the size of their deficits. If a government tries to reduce a deficit by cutting spending that in turn is likely to have an effect on the economy which will affect its tax take, and, all else being equal, it is likely to reduce it. In truth, it is very hard to be certain what changes in fiscal policy will do. This is because the government cannot control or even predict how consumers and businesses will respond. Similarly, it is very difficult for a government to deploy policies that will control its trade deficit, because not only does that depend on its domestic citizens spending preferences on imports, it also depends on actions of foreign governments and their citizens and businesses in buying exports, and also exchange rates of currency.

It is over-simplistic to assert that a fiscal deficit is always bad thing, or indeed that fiscal deficits are never a problem. The sectoral balance approach offers a way to put the fiscal deficit in a wider context which helps structure thinking about the economy. It is also useful in telling you what cannot happen. For example, if the government says it is going to move from a fiscal deficit to a surplus, the private sector cannot expect its net income to increase as a direct result.

The UK government, in common with most states, chooses to match the fiscal deficit with borrowing which then adds to the public debt. Notice my choice of words 'chooses to match'. The government could decide to create some or all of the money required for public spending at its central bank, which for the UK is The Bank of England. One often stated reason why it doesn't is because the central bank's primary task is to control the currency, interest rates and inflation, and too much money creation can cause inflation (and beware of glib interpretations of 'too' in that sentence). Also, although it is sometimes pointed out that article 123 of the Lisbon Treaty[17] – the treaty that forms the legal basis for the European Union – forbids an EU member state from using its central bank to create money to fund public spending, the UK has been exempted from this restriction.

When the UK decides to borrow, it carves its newly created debt up into £100 chunks called government bonds (often called gilts for the UK) and sells them. Unlike other forms of lending, the holder of the bond is not paid interest as a percentage but gets a fixed payment every six months. For example, if you hold a £100, you might get what's called a coupon payment of £1 every six months. Who buys the bonds? It has to be someone in the private or foreign sectors because there is literally no one else to buy them (actually, the government can purchase its own debt by creating money, and did exactly this in quantitative easing, but that's another story). As it happens, government debt is usually preferentially bought by investment companies in its domestic private sector and many of those are concerned with managing private pension funds.

There are a few reasons why the government can expect the private sector to buy its bonds. The first is that the private sector is likely to have the means to do so as it receives an inflow exactly equal to the deficit, by definition. But the reason the private sector is keen to lend to the government is because its bonds are trusted as being the safest of investments. Whereas shares of a company can suddenly fall and become worthless when it goes bust, this is almost impossible with government bonds because they are backed by a state with a central bank that can create money. (That's not to say a government with its own currency and central bank are immune from crises, see Venezuela for example, which incurred debts priced in foreign currencies.)

Private investors see government bonds as a safe bedrock of investment for their portfolios and so they tend to buy more of them in times of economic uncertainty. The greater demand pushes the resale price of each bond up above its starting price of £100, and because the amount paid on each bond is fixed, the effective interest rate, known as the yield, goes down. For example, if you buy a bond directly from the government for £100 and it pays £2 each year, its yield is 2% (£2 out of £100). If you are lucky enough to sell it on for £200 when bonds are in demand, the less lucky recipient will still get £2 a year on it, so their yield will be 1% (£2 out of £200). From the government's perspective this means the effective interest rate on government debt also goes down from 2% to 1%. This effect is behind the remarkable fact noted in Chapter 5 which is worth repeating here: between 1998–99 and 2016–17, payments of UK public sector debt interest decreased in real terms by 5% whereas the ONS tells us the UK's public debt (specifically, PSNDex) more than tripled.[18] Despite the dramatic increase in this debt, the effective annual interest rate on it dropped dramatically from about 8% to 2% with the overall effect that interest payments decreased.

Taking a step back, it should be clear that government debt is not really debt in the sense that an individual or household would understand;[19] government debt is treated much more like an investment. Even the language used in the bond market highlights this: you do not talk of interest on the debt, but the yield on gilt-edged securities. If you are doubtful of any of the above statements concerning money creation, borrowing and debt, then go to the horse's mouth and see the clear explanations given by the Bank of England itself.[20]

What we have not discussed here is how currency is involved and its interplay with international trade and foreign sector ownership of UK government bonds. Nor have we considered interest rates or the central bank and, as is crucial for understanding the 2008 financial crisis and the operation of the economy, the role of private banks in money creation. Also absent from the discussion above are the huge flows of money that flow around the world[21] as returns on assets and from speculations on currencies. Keeping these limitations in mind we can make a few statements specific to Scotland.

Sectors for Scotland

We can consider the domestic economy of Scotland and its foreign sector, which includes the rest of the UK, and apply the sectoral balances approach. The crucial difference is that Scotland does not have a separate currency and central bank and the bulk of public borrowing is managed at the UK level. If Scotland were to become a separate state then it could, if it chose, have its own currency, central bank and operate its own fiscal and monetary policies and issue its own government bonds. What choices might be made here are not clear, nor is it clear how they would interact with the rest of the UK or the rest of the EU. We can however consider what Scotland's sectoral balances looked like in recent years.

Scotland's fiscal deficit, that is the negative of the net fiscal balance in GERS (see chapter 5), for 2016–17 was £13.5 billion. According to Scottish government National Accounts the trade deficit that year was £13.9 billion. In other words, £13.9 billion flowed into the private sector from the public sector, and £13.3 billion left Scotland's onshore economy, mostly from the private sector, for the foreign sector.

The above figures all relate to the onshore economy. Including the North Sea industry (on a geographical basis) slightly alters the 2016–17 fiscal deficit, reducing it to £13.3 billion. In previous years the change would have been billions of pounds and in 2000-01 it was enough to turn a £3.6 billion budget deficit (in that year's prices) into a small surplus.

The effect of including the North Sea industry on the trade deficit is more uncertain, but tentative estimates suggest that in the North Sea industry's best years, such as 2010–11, its net exports would have roughly matched Scotland's onshore trade deficit.[22] Since then North Sea exports have fallen so that even with them, Scotland would be a net importer, albeit with a much smaller trade deficit. Much of the North Sea industry is foreign owned so there are also large capital outflows associated with it but their sizes are very uncertain, as are those of the onshore economy mentioned above (see the Gross Deceptive Product section).

Whatever the difficulties in establishing the exact level, it seems likely that Scotland has a large net outflow amounting to billions of pounds, just as there is for the whole UK. And this means that foreign businesses and individuals have a growing stock of pounds, and that they will likely be used to invest in our domestic assets. This can take many forms: buying shares, investing directly in an existing foreign-owned business or even buying UK government bonds, and, if Scotland were independent, buying Scottish government bonds. In these ways, a persistent trade deficit can lead to a country's assets increasingly ending up in foreign ownership. Whether this is problematic or not depends both on international and domestic politics and the public's perception of it, though it has the potential to limit a country's fiscal flexibility and control over its currency.

Some thoughts

Scotland's economy and its wider society do not exist in isolation. They are, for the time being at least, nested within the economy and society of the UK, which is in turn part of the European Union. Even without such explicit unions of countries, links extend globally through travel, trade and modern communications. For that reason alone, it's worth zooming out and giving thought to the wider context.

The words 'economy', 'market' and 'society' are usually used in the singular (I'll leave it to linguists to explain why society is rarely prefixed with an article such as 'a' or 'the'). When someone says 'it will benefit the economy', you have to decide from the context what part of the economy they might be referring to, or indeed which country is being discussed; and when you hear 'leave it to the market to decide' it's rarely clear what market is meant.

This is important because how we talk about such matters reflects and influences our thinking. An 'individual' is singular, as is an 'economy', but an economy is composed of many individual people and their interactions generate emergent behaviours that cannot be understood at the individual level. Indeed, behaviours of an economy can seem alien and surprising to the people from which it is composed. The most famous example of this is the paradox of thrift: people perceive the economy to be weakening and reduce their spending to save money for an uncertain future, but this reduces total consumer spending, starves business of revenue and so produces a real slowdown in the economy. What a rational individual may correctly decide is best in their own interests may lead the economy as a whole in a direction that is in no one's interest.

Real instances of paradoxical economic thinking are not hard to find. One example came from UK Prime Minister David Cameron in a speech released to journalists to drum up publicity prior to his 2011 Conservative party conference speech:

> The only way out of a debt crisis is to deal with your debts. That means households – all of us – paying off the credit card and store card bills.

Advisers rushed to rewrite this because if people had taken the Prime Minister's advice, consumer spending would have dropped and likely put the UK back into the recession from which it had just escaped. The revised version removed both the urgency and the instruction from the statement:

> That is why households are paying down the credit card and store card bills.

By 2011, with a few years of hindsight, it was clear that the crisis had its roots in loans being extended to people who could not afford to pay them back. These loans took many forms, though it was clouding of the risk around sub-prime mortgages in the United States that was more to blame than credit or store cards. So although expressing concern about repeating mistakes involving loans and credit prior to 2008 would certainly be appropriate in 2011, a blunt message that would divert money away from consumer spending was in no-one's interests.

What this example highlights however, is that politicians, especially governing ones, have some power to influence business and consumer confidence. Not only that, but when both consumers and businesses lack confidence to spend and invest because they enter a paradoxical thrift spiral, the government can, if it chooses, act in a concerted way to counteract that through its public spending and tax policies. This is often referred to as Keynesian fiscal stimulus, though it is a highly simplified version of the nuanced theories advanced by English economist John Maynard Keynes in the years following the Great Depression in the 1930s.

When public spending cuts began in 2011 and 2012, economic growth remained fairly weak (see Figure 6.4), and was much lower than would be expected when judged against recoveries from past recessions. But caution is required in blaming this solely on UK austerity policies because the UK economy was almost certainly affected by the Eurozone crisis that unfolded at about the same time. That crisis also had its roots in 2008 but Eurozone countries, particularly smaller ones, were restricted in dealing with mounting public debt because they did not have their own currencies and were compelled to follow EU fiscal rules. Although not involved in this crisis directly, the UK was affected through its trade connections. Restrictions on public spending were eased in 2013 and 2014 and this may be why growth improved in those years.

Objections to using government spending to counteract slowdowns are made for a few reasons. One is simply that it will lead to high public debt, but austerity policies have failed to reduce the deficit as expected, nor have warnings of high interest payments yet materialised, in fact total interest paid has fallen, as we saw earlier in this chapter. The public debt of countries with their own currency is usually not at all like debt in other contexts, such as that of a household or a business.

Another more interesting objection to state intervention comes from the idea of creative destructive in which some of society's practices, particularly those of businesses, are destroyed and reformed by an economic crisis. Old and ingrained inefficiencies are removed and new, possibly improved ones emerge in their place. This can be viewed as a natural process, in that it is an emergent behaviour of society, not the result of a deliberate policy, and for this reason it is sometimes referred to as Schumpeter's Gale. Joseph Schumpeter was an American-Austrian economist who explored and popularised the idea but he had adapted it from the work of the German (but later stateless) economist and philosopher Karl Marx.

To understand the economy of a country, you need to look at how it is governed, the culture and values of its public and its international activities. So it should not be surprising that the discipline of economics is an inherently international one. To the gallery of political economists from the various countries that I have mentioned in this chapter, I'd like to add a Scot, Adam Smith, and note the plural that appears in the title of his famous book *The Wealth of Nations*.

Some questions to ponder:

- Should less emphasis be given to GDP, and how do we capture non-economic but socially valuable activities in national statistics?
- Why does inflation occur and does working with figures in real terms risk throwing some baby out with the bath water?
- Scotland and the whole UK have transformed from a manufacturing based economy to one based on services; is this a concern?
- Is Scotland's large trade deficit connected to its large fiscal deficit and what implications does this have for the currency choice if Scotland becomes independent?
- Can government policies produce significant change in sectors of the economy, for example, to promote growth and boost exports for whisky or salmon?

- Exports are often viewed as a flow into the economy and imports a drain, but this is over-simplistic in a world inter-connected with trade; should Scotland and other countries take a wider view?
- Is it necessary for the economy to grow in order for society to improve?
- How do we reconcile the desire for continued GDP growth against environmental concerns such as climate change?

Chapter 7

An electoral long view

Democracy is often discussed as if it was synonymous with voting, but democracy involves a good deal more. Elections need to be free and fair with results that are trusted and respected. Beyond elections, a democracy needs institutions of parliament and government that function in a manner that is transparent and accountable enough so that the electorate can form an opinion on how the country has been governed. It is the perception of that which gives rise to the most important single consequence of an election: will the sitting government continue or be replaced?

Results of most elections presented in this chapter are drawn from the House of Commons Library's paper entitled UK Election Statistics: 1918–2017.[1]

Before delving into the detail of election results it is worth pausing to reflect on how different society and politics were a century ago at a time when many countries were still reeling from the shock of the First World War. Most women first got the right to vote in the 1918 general election though full parity with men's voting rights did not come until 1928. There was no NHS, only an embryonic welfare state, and levels of education and literacy were much lower than today's. Poverty of a kind that is all but banished from our modern society still existed in the sense of being deprived of food, warmth and shelter. There was no broadcast media but newspapers, pamphlets, public gatherings and word of mouth circulated new information to the populous. And just as today, interested parties with money and ties to power tried to control such news, with varying degrees of success.

Today you can produce a small, electronic slab from your pocket and share in the opinions of millions of others, or download a set of national accounts to muse upon. More usually though, the slab offers you a spectrum of ways to distract yourself from thinking about anything at all.

Although our technology has progressed dramatically there are some important aspects that we have in common with our electoral ancestors. We enter a polling booth and mark paper with pencil to choose a single human to represent thousands of other humans who live in the same area. Soon technology will change that physical process, but arguably, it will have less impact on how we decide to vote. We do so under the influence of information and values from our family, friends, peers and tribal groups. Humans are undeniably a social species.

Members of Parliament

Scotland currently sends 59 Members of Parliament or MPs to the House of Commons at Westminster in London. This is 9.1% of the UK total whereas Scotland has 8.2% of the UK's population, meaning that Scotland is slightly over-represented in numerical terms. If seats were allocated strictly on a population share basis of the UK's 650 MPs, Scotland would have 53 MPs. The situation was more extreme with Scotland having 72 MPs between 1983 and 2005, and 71 MPs before that. Part of the reason for the over-representation is the low population density. For example, Scotland has three island constituencies with much smaller populations than most on the mainland – Orkney, Shetland and the Western Isles – and it makes sense for them to have an MP each to address their differing needs.

Figure 7.1 shows the vote share by party in Scotland for all general elections from 1918 to 2017.

It's important to realise that only two of the parties of the mid-20th century directly correspond to the ones we know today: *The Labour Party* and *The Scottish National Party* or SNP. The modern Conservative party in Scotland is part of the UK party but its full title of *The Scottish Conservative and Unionist Party* retains clues to its roots. Before 1965, the vote share represented by 'Con' on this graph would mostly have

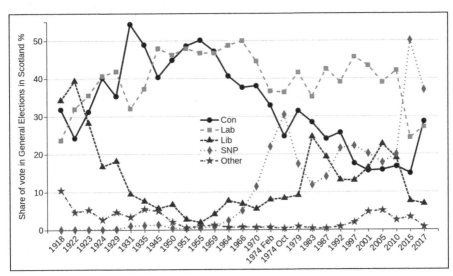

Figure 7.1
Vote share in Scotland by party in general elections 1918 to 2017.

comprised of votes for candidates from *The Unionist Party*, a Scottish party distinct and run separately from *The Conservative Party* in England and Wales. When at work in Westminster, Unionist MPs would have been under the Conservative whip and when Scottish Unionist Prime Ministers Andrew Bonar Law and Sir Alec Douglas-Home were in office, they were viewed as Conservative Prime Ministers by most of the UK's population. The Union in the party name was not that of the United Kingdom of Great Britain and Northern Ireland formed in 1707, though that association sits well with current Scottish Conservatives, but the Union of Great Britain and Ireland of 1800.

The present *Liberal Democrat Party* formed from the 1988 merger of *The Liberal Party* and *The Social Democratic Party* or SDP, which split from the Labour Party in 1981. *The Liberal Party* was founded in 1859 and was until the early 20th century one of two dominant parties in the UK. All of these parties are counted towards the 'Lib' vote on the graph. Votes for the smaller *National Liberal Party* that split from the Liberal party in 1931 are counted under 'Con' as they formed some alliances with the Unionist Party in Scotland and ultimately merged with the Conservatives in 1968.

The start of the graph in 1918 shows the tail end of the old two-party dominance of the Conservatives and the Liberals. As the Liberals declined in vote share from almost 40% in 1922 to under 10% in 1931, Labour rose to exceed 40% in both 1924 and 1929. Although Labour had the highest vote share in Scotland in 1929, the Conservatives had a slender 1 percentage point lead in the UK overall. Despite that, Labour won the most seats resulting in a hung parliament from which a Labour minority government was formed with the Scot and Labour party co-founder, Ramsay MacDonald as Prime Minister.

The aftermath of the 1929 Wall Street crash created fiscal problems that eventually led to the Labour government being replaced by the so-called National Government in 1931 which contained ministers from all main parties. MacDonald continued as Prime Minister but tensions within the Labour party ultimately resulted in his expulsion. The 1931 election took place shortly after formation of the National Government and bolstered its position with Conservatives achieving a UK-wide vote share of 55%. No party has since achieved an absolute majority of the votes in a UK general election. Surprisingly, MacDonald continued as Prime Minister until 1935 when he was succeeded by Stanley Baldwin.

The 1929 election is notable for a few other reasons. Firstly, because it was the first where all women over the age of 21 could vote, the limit having been at 30 since 1918. Secondly, it took place a few months prior to the onset of the Great Depression which continued well into the 1930s and helped revive Conservative electoral fortunes in 1931. Thirdly, in 1929 the graph has its first data-point for the SNP. Although the SNP did not come into existence until 1934, one of its forerunners, the National Party of Scotland or NPS stood two candidates in the 1929 election in Glasgow Camlachie and West Renfrewshire.

From 1924, Scotland, like the rest of the UK, entered a new phase of two party politics with the Conservatives and Labour Party vying for over 80% of the vote. The Liberals were relegated to a distant third place, and the nascent SNP made little headway for its first three decades. As a result, the patterns of vote share in Scotland were similar to that of the UK until 1959.

The 1950s saw the height of Con-Lab two party dominance with all four general elections in that decade seeing them take well over 90% of the vote in Scotland. In 1955 the Conservative vote in Scotland, with much of it being for Unionist Party candidates, achieved an absolute majority with a vote share of 50.1%. This, however, turned out to be a peak from which there would be a descent lasting 50 years.

As British society and culture went through a renewal in the 1960s, so too did politics and two party dominance waned with smaller parties, notably the Liberals, enjoying modest gains. But party politics began to diverge across the England-Scotland border as the SNP saw its vote share rise from being less than 1% of the Scottish total to 5% in 1966. During this time the Conservative vote share plummeted from the 50.1% high of 1955 to 37.8% in 1966. Labour's vote share rose slightly to peak at 49.9% that year.

In 1967, Winnie Ewing won the SNP's first seat in the Hamilton by-election. Although she lost it at the 1970 general election, the SNP more than doubled their 1966 vote share obtaining 11.4% of Scottish votes. This success continued into the 1970s with the SNP vote share peaking at 30.4% in the second general election of 1974. Figure 7.1 shows that the rise of the SNP vote share of 30 percentage points from 1955 to October 1974 is coincident with a 25 percentage point decline for the Conservative vote and a 10 percentage point drop for Labour. The liberals also gained several percentage points over this time in Scotland.

In 1979, following the first referendum on Scottish devolution, SNP MPs tabled a motion of no confidence in James Callaghan's Labour government. This was then superseded by another no confidence motion from the leader of the Conservatives, Margaret Thatcher. This motion, supported by SNP and Liberal MPs, carried by one vote and brought down the government, triggering the 1979 general election.

The result of the 1979 general election set the scene for the next three decades in Scotland with Labour remaining dominant with a fairly stable 40% of the vote from 1979 to 2010, and the other three parties competing for a distant second place. At the UK level, the Conservatives held their vote share for over a decade with it only dropping from 43.9% in 1979 to 41.9% in 1992. Labour struggled during this time, and their UK fortunes fell to a low point in 1983 with a vote share of 27.6%. Not only was this their lowest vote share since 1918, but they were closely challenged for second place by the SDP-Liberal alliance who gained 25.4% of the UK vote.

Through the 1980s and 1990s, the Scottish Conservative vote share decreased further and the SNP vote share rose. When Labour won its UK landslide victory in 1997 under Tony Blair, the SNP, now led by Alex Salmond, had gained 22.1% of the vote to achieve second place with the Conservatives trailing in third on 17.5%. While so-called New Labour was in government from 1997 to 2010, they continued to enjoy electoral dominance in Scotland with around 40% of the vote while the SNP, the Liberal Democrats and the Conservatives had vote shares varying from the teens to the low twenties.

Taking a step back from the detail, Figure 7.1 shows several transitions between political eras in Scotland's politics. There's the transition from Con-Lib to Con-Lab two party dominance in the 1920s, and then to Labour party dominance in the 1970s. In the wake of the 2014 independence referendum, a much more sudden transition occurred with the SNP vote jumping to 50.0% in the 2015 general election. Many Labour voters who had voted for independence in 2014 now turned to the SNP. This was also true to an extent for the Liberal Democrats but they also lost votes because they had entered into the 2010 coalition government with the Conservatives. The Conservative vote only dropped slightly in that election, remaining in the mid-teens where it had been since 1997.

The general election of 2017 brought another dramatic change with the SNP dropping 13.1 percentage points and the Conservatives gaining 13.7. In contrast, the shares for Labour and Liberal Democrats hardly changed.

Figure 7.2 shows how the number of MPs has varied in Scotland.

Elections for members of parliament operate on the first past the post system in which the candidate in a constituency with the most votes becomes the MP. Although this system has the virtue of simplicity, it means that parties with large shares of the vote will gain disproportionate numbers of MPs and smaller parties will have disproportionately fewer MPs. The most extreme example is of the SNP in 2015 which won 56 of 59 seats or 94.9% of them with 50.0% of the vote. The other parties together won 50% of the vote but gained just three MPs between them.

Another argument made by proponents of first past the post is that its disproportionate benefit to the winning party is likely to produce stronger governments because they will have substantial majorities of MPs. Although the historical record mostly bears this out, two recent general elections – 2010 and 2017 – produced a hung parliament in which no party had a majority of MPs. In fact, the first past the post

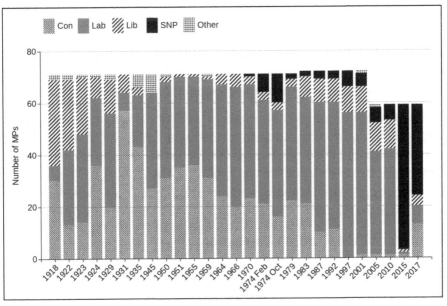

Figure 7.2
MPs by party in general elections 1918 to 2017.

system produces more balanced results when there are only two dominant parties. Such was the case in 1955 when the Conservatives achieved the record 50.1% vote share in Scotland. This resulted in 36 seats for them, 34 for Labour on 46.7% of the vote, and 1 for the liberals on 1.9%. Contrast this with the situation in 2015 mentioned above, or with 2017, when the SNP won 35 seats with 36.9% of the vote, and the other parties gained 24 with 63.1%.

The first past the post system makes it very difficult to predict the number of MPs won by each party from the overall vote share because the details of what happens in each constituency are important. Consider a simple example with ten constituencies each with 100 voters and two parties called Nice and Naughty. Imagine that Nice win in each constituency by two votes, that is 51 to 49. Despite the vote share being 51% to 49%, Nice win all ten seats. If just two voters in each constituency switch from Nice to Naughty then the vote share moves to 51% in Naughty's favour and they win all ten seats.

Another instructive example is to consider Naughty gaining an overall 50% vote share, perhaps by promising inexhaustible supplies of cake for the populous to eat, and Nice having a 40% share by promising a fiscally prudent amount of cake, and a third party, let's call it Honest, on 10%, promising to tax cakes because they are unhealthy. If votes to Naughty, Nice and Honest go exactly according to this vote share in each constituency – 50, 40 and 10 votes – then Naughty wins all ten seats despite Nice being only 10 percentage points behind them.

But a quite different outcome can arise from the same overall vote share of 50%/40%/10%. Suppose that Naughty still wins 50 votes in each constituency, but the other two parties focus their efforts only on certain seats. It's possible for Nice to win seven constituencies and Honest one constituency, leaving Naughty with only two despite having 50% of vote. I'll leave how this can be worked out as an exercise to you, dear reader.

Members of the Scottish Parliament

The Scottish Parliament sits in Holyrood in Edinburgh and came into being following the 1997 referendum on devolution. The first election of the 129 Members of the Scottish Parliament or MSPs took place in 1999.

Scottish parliament elections use a proportional representation system with each voter making two votes on the ballot paper. The first vote is for a local constituency MSP. This is operated on a first past the post system, but as there are 73 constituencies for the Scottish Parliament but only 59 for Westminster, the constituency areas differ.

Figure 7.3 shows the shares for the constituency vote.

In the first two Scottish Parliament elections in 1999 and 2003, the voting pattern for its constituencies was similar to that for Westminster constituencies, though the Labour vote was somewhat lower and the SNP a little higher. The SNP's vote share declined in 2003 but increased markedly in 2007 by 9 percentage points and then by another 12 in 2011 to reach a vote share of 45.4% which was slightly increased in 2016 to 46.5%.

The waning of Labour's vote share in Scotland is clear in the constituency vote from 1999 and the same is true for general elections in Figure 7.1, except 2010 which saw a slight increase. This might be because the then Labour leader and Prime Minister, Gordon Brown, was Scottish, but it is also likely that after decade of its existence, perceptions of the Scottish Parliament had shifted and were now distinct from the one in Westminster. The most striking evidence of this is that the sudden increase in the SNP vote share between the 2010 and 2015 general elections is not evident in the Scottish constituency vote between 2011

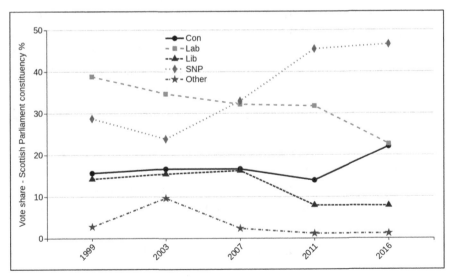

Figure 7.3
Vote share by party in Scottish Parliament elections
– constituency 1999 to 2016.

and 2016. Instead, the ascendance of the SNP is more gradual. Turnout, which is discussed later, may well play a role in this too.

A more recent divergence in voting for constituency MSPs and MPs is in the movement between SNP, Labour and Conservative vote shares. Whereas the SNP's gains in the 2015 general election mainly seem to be at Labour's expense, Labour's losses in the Scottish elections of 2016 appear to have benefited the Conservatives. In truth, the changes were more complex than this and to understand them involves an appreciation of the regional differences within Scotland.

In the North East of Scotland, the SNP lost votes in rural constituencies to the Conservatives possibly due to Scottish government delays in passing EU payments to farmers. Greater Glasgow, however, saw a shift from Labour to SNP but it was less dramatic than 2015 for several reasons. Firstly, the independence referendum was a further year into the past, but the shift to the SNP had begun well before 2014 in any case, being evident in the Scottish Parliament elections of both 2007 and 2011. But Labour may have also gained the vote of some left leaning independence supporters in Greater Glasgow due to Jeremy Corbyn becoming UK Labour party leader in September 2015. It's also probable that more centre ground voters who used to favour 'New Labour' under Blair and Brown were put off by the new leadership and moved to the Conservatives, with their unambiguous anti-independence stance perhaps attracted some No voters from the 2014 referendum. The net result was that Labour lost votes to both the SNP and Conservatives, and the Conservatives gained votes from both SNP and Labour.

The second vote on a Scottish Parliamentary election ballot paper is for the 56 MSPs to represent eight regions. Each region is represented by seven MSPs. These are: Central Scotland, Glasgow, Highland & Islands, Lothian, Mid Scotland & Fife, North East Scotland, South of Scotland and West of Scotland. These MSPs are sometimes referred to as list MSPs due to the way they are selected from regional party lists, which we'll describe shortly.

Figure 7.4 shows the shares of votes for regional MSPs.

At first sight, this graph looks very much like the constituency one, but there are three notable differences. The first is that the SNP lost regional vote share in 2016, and by more than they gained in the constituency vote.

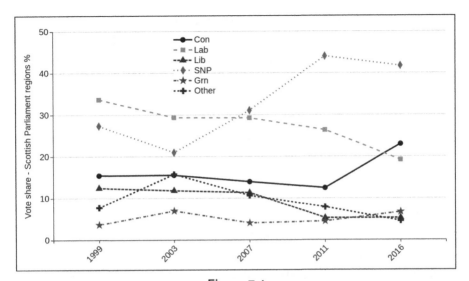

Figure 7.4

Vote share by party in Scottish Parliament elections – regional 1999 to 2016.

The second is that despite Labour coming second in the constituency vote, albeit very narrowly, the Conservatives were ahead in the regional vote, coming in second for the first time in a Scottish Parliament election. The final difference is that although the Green's vote share was negligible at 0.6% in 2016 for constituencies, and so not even shown on that graph, it was 6.6% in the regional vote, putting them ahead of the Liberal Democrats for the first time in any election.

The reasons why such differences matter requires an understanding of the type of proportional representation used in Scottish Parliament elections. The first past the post system in the first vote means that voters can identify one MSP with their local area. The second vote is then used to ensure that regional MSPs are selected so the overall number of MSPs reflects the vote share. This is achieved by applying what is known as the D'Hondt method[2] to make sure that if a party receives a disproportionately large number of constituency MSPs relative to its vote share, it will win fewer regional MSPs. Similarly, parties that win few or no constituency MSPs will be more likely to win regional MSPs.

With this in mind, it is understandable that smaller parties such as the Greens focus their electoral strategy on the regional vote. This, plus the fact that the Greens also took a pro-independence stance explains not only their gains in the regional 2016 vote, but also why the SNP lost regional votes. That said, the Liberal Democrats target their efforts on winning a few target constituency seats, much as they do in general elections. Whereas the Greens won six regional MSPs and no constituency MSPs, the Liberal Democrats won just one regional MSP but 4 constituency MSPs.

The SNP dominance also means that the next two largest parties in 2016, Labour and the Conservatives, also have to rely heavily on the regional vote to win most of their MSPs. In fact, this has always been the case for the Conservatives, and in 1999 they won all their MSPs from the regional vote.

In the general election of 2015, the battle in most constituencies was between Labour and the SNP. So it makes sense that pro-UK, Conservative supporters, at least those who understand the system, might give their regional vote to that party but then lend their constituency vote to whoever they perceive as mostly likely to beat the SNP. This is a likely explanation of why the Conservatives fared better than Labour in the regional vote as compared to the constituency vote.

Figure 7.5 shows the results of each Scottish Parliament election by the number of MSPs for each party.

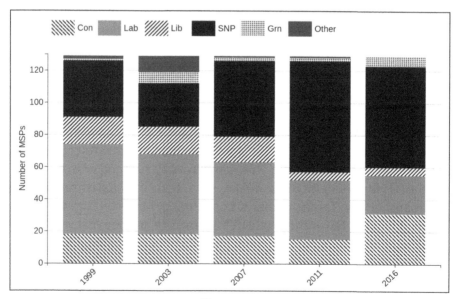

Figure 7.5
MSPs by party in Scottish Parliament elections – regional 1999 to 2016.

As expected, the share of MSPs reflects the vote shares in the previous graph, though the dominant party, currently the SNP, still benefit slightly. In 2011, this fact, together with some good luck, enabled the SNP to win an outright majority; that is, the SNP had 69 MSPs which was more than half of the 129 total. Although having such a majority is normal in the Westminster parliament under first past the post, this was thought to be a highly unlikely outcome in the Scottish Parliament with proportional representation.

The other notable change over time is that the make-up of smaller parties has shifted. The design of the voting system was supposed to make it easier for a few small parties to gain a few MSPs. But in 1999, 126 of 129 seats were won by the main parties with the Greens having one MSP, the Scottish Socialists having one MSP and one MSP being independent, that is affiliated to no party. All these were won on the regional vote.

Smaller parties fared much better in 2003 with seven Greens MSPs, six Scottish Socialist MSPs, three independent and one Scottish Senior Citizen MSP. Of these 17 MSPs, 15 were won on the regional vote but two independents won on constituency votes. With the rise of the SNP from 2007, the number of independent and smaller party MSPs dwindled in number to just three in 2007 and 2011. In 2016, there were six Green MSPs, but none from any other of these smaller parties, making the 2016 parliament the least diverse in terms of number of parties and independents. But that of course depends on what is meant by 'smaller party'. The Greens have two more MSPs than the Liberal Democrats so either both should both be classed as being 'smaller parties', or perhaps neither of them should.

Councillors

Since 1995, local government in Scotland has consisted of 32 Scottish councils. This replaced the previous system of a two tier council system that had a few, large regional councils and numerous smaller district councils. In one sense, this means that aside from a brief gap between 1995 and the formation of the modern Scottish Parliament in 1999, Scotland has had a three tier government structure since 1975.

Until the 2003 elections, councillors were elected using the first past the post system. After that, a flavour of proportional representation, called the Single Transferable Vote or STV, has been used. In this, a voter ranks candidates from their most preferred to their least preferred, though they do not need to rank all listed on the ballot paper. The voter indicates their preferred candidate by writing a 1, the next by a 2 and so on. Another important difference from the other elections is that a ward, the council equivalent of a constituency, has three or four councillors to represent it.

Although voting is simple, how votes produce the result is not. The first step is to work out a special threshold: this is equal to the number of valid votes cast divided by the number of councillors for the ward. If any candidate receives more first preference votes than this threshold they are elected as a councillor. For example, in a ward with four councillors in which there are 4000 first preference votes, any candidate who receives 1001 or more votes is elected. The winning candidate's second preference votes are then distributed amongst the remaining candidates and the procedure is repeated. If at any stage, no candidate exceeds the threshold, then the candidate with the lowest total at that stage is eliminated and their next preference votes are distributed amongst the remaining candidates.

Figure 7.6 shows the vote shares by party.

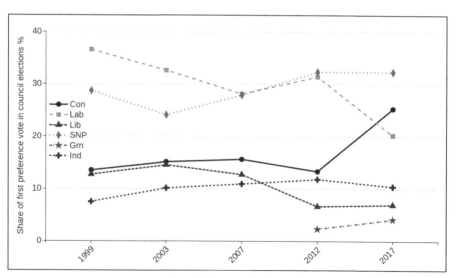

Figure 7.6
Vote share by party in council elections 1999 to 2017.

The trends are broadly similar to that for the Scottish Parliament regional vote shares in Figure 7.4. One difference is that the SNP are less dominant and, in 2017, the three largest parties had only a 12 percentage point spread in vote share, much less than the 20 percentage point spread for the Scottish Parliament region vote share.

The other difference is that independents have consistently attracted around 10% of the vote, exceeding that of the Liberal Democrats and the Greens in 2012 and 2017. This tells us that parties play a weaker role in council elections. Part of the reason for this is in how councils are controlled.

If a party has a majority of councillors then it effectively forms the government of that council, though the word 'government' is not used, instead one talks of who has control of the council. This is because the executive powers, that is the decision-making responsibilities of councillors controlling a council, are not like those of ministers in a government at Holyrood or Westminster.

Especially since the introduction of STV in 2007, it has been rare for any one party to win a majority. After the 2017 elections, no party had a majority in any council, and after the 2012 elections, only five of 32 councils had majorities, three Labour and two SNP. Instead, most councils are minority controlled by a single party with the most councillors, or else by a coalition of two or more parties together with independent councillors. There are several unusual situations with councils that have no analogues in Scottish or UK governments. For example, in West Lothian, despite the SNP having the most councillors, there is a Labour minority in control. Also, all three island council areas – the Western Isles, Orkney and Shetland – are controlled by independents because only a minority of councillors are affiliated with parties.

Members of the European Parliament

As of August 2018, Scotland, for the time being, is represented by six Members of the European Parliament or MEPs. From 1979 to 1994 eight MEPs were elected in constituencies using the first past the post system, but from 1999 MEPs have been selected using the D'Hondt proportional representation system. This is similar to that used in Scotland except there is no constituency element and all candidates are selected from a Scotland-wide list.

Figure 7.7 shows the vote share for MEPs by party since proportional representation was introduced in 1999.

The results of European elections differ from the elections discussed above in a number of respects. The SNP were dominant in 2009 but Labour closed the gap with a substantial rise in their vote in 2014. The other significant difference is that UKIP's share of the vote, which barely registers in any other Scottish election, achieved just over 10% in 2014, putting them in fourth place and giving them enough votes to win one MEP. In 2014, the SNP and Labour had two MEPs each and the Conservatives one. The low turnout in European elections is doubtless related to why their results differ from other elections in Scotland, which we'll return to later.

On 23 June 2016, the UK held a referendum with a single question regarding its EU membership:

> Should the United Kingdom remain a member of the European Union or leave the European Union?

Voters could choose between two answers on the ballot paper 'Remain' and 'Leave'. For the whole UK, 51.9% of voters chose Leave and 48.1% chose Remain. Of the three UK countries and nine regions of England involved in the vote, only Scotland, London and Northern Ireland showed

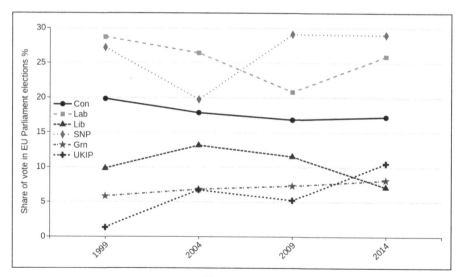

Figure 7.7
Vote share by party in European Parliament elections 1999 to 2016.

a majority for remain. In Scotland, 1.66 million people voted for Remain, and 1.02 million people voted for Leave meaning that 62.0% of votes were for Remain and 38.0% of votes were for Leave. Scotland had the second lowest turnout in this referendum at 67.2%, with the lowest being Northern Ireland at 62.7%. UK-wide turnout was 72.2% and the highest turnout was 76.7% in the South East region of England. The EU referendum was not binding, meaning that the government was under no legal compulsion to act on the result.

On 29 March 2017, the UK government triggered the formal process for leaving the EU by invoking Article 50 of its Lisbon Treaty. Unless other arrangements are agreed with the EU in the meantime, this commits the UK to leaving the European Union by 30 March 2019. At this point the UK will cease to have any MEPs.

The 2014 independence referendum

In 2012, the UK Prime Minister David Cameron and First Minister of Scotland Alex Salmond together with Secretary of State for Scotland Michael Moore and the Deputy First Minister Nicola Sturgeon signed the Edinburgh agreement. This provided a legal basis for the Scottish Parliament to hold a referendum on Scotland leaving the UK to form a separate state.

On 18 September 2014, residents aged 16 and over in Scotland were presented with a single question on the referendum ballot paper:

Should Scotland be an independent country?

The result was that 2.00 million people voted No and 1.62 million voted Yes, being 55.3% and 44.7% of votes respectively. Out of the total electorate, 46.7% voted No, 37.8% voted Yes and 15.5% did not vote.

There has only been one such referendum to date so unlike the various election results we can only track the public mood towards independence by examining opinion polls, and some care is required in comparing them with the actual result.

Although the No side were always expected to prevail, in the weeks leading up to the vote there was a widespread feeling, confirmed by several opinion polls, that the Yes side were gaining momentum and seeing their vote share increase. Novelist and Yes advocate Irvine Welsh summarised it as follows:[3]

The process and the subsequent debate, which they won handsomely, took support for independence from around 30% to 45% and heading north.

Similar statements have been made by prominent politicians, including former First Minister Alex Salmond. The 45% clearly refers to the referendum result itself, but the 30% can only refer to the result of some opinion poll at some unspecified time before the referendum.

Figure 7.8 shows results from opinion polls. Those from 2013 are from the What Scotland Thinks website[4] and those from 2012 are taken from primary sources.

The scatter on this graph is considerable. Most polls had a sample size of about 1000 and so this will generate a statistical uncertainty in which 97% of results are plus or minus 3 percentage points of the true value – a spread of 6 percentage points. We can never know the true value at any time other than at the actual referendum, but it is clear that the scatter at any given date covers a spread of more than the 6 percentage points we might expect. The extra scatter is most likely due to the way the question is asked. For example, some polls asked how the respondent would vote now, while others asked how they would vote on the day of the referendum. The latter may generate more responses for *Don't know*. Also, polls conducted online or by phone tend to generate lower percentages of *Don't know* than interviews conducted face to face.

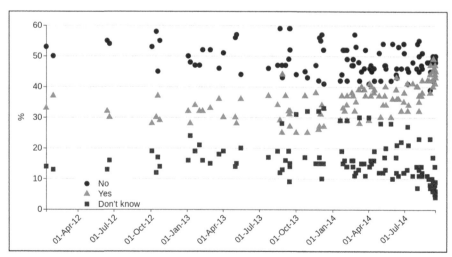

Figure 7.8
Opinion polling ahead of the 2014 referendum from January 2012.

Through 2012 and 2013, polls showed *Yes* ranging from 25% to 38% with one outlier at 44% which was a Panelbase poll commissioned by the SNP, and *No* ranged from 41% to 59% over this same time. The percentage for *Don't Know* was mostly between 10% and 20% but there were a few around 30% which were all face to face polls conducted by TNS-BMRB. Despite the scatter, it is clear that there was little change in 2012 and 2013.

During 2014, the Yes vote does appear to increase, but a closer look at the graph shows that in the weeks leading up to the referendum both the *Yes* and *No* percentages increase and *Don't know* percentages decrease. This is the opinion polls detecting that people are making up their minds as the referendum approaches.

To make more definite conclusions we need to look at statistics summarising periods of interest in the run up to the referendum. Table 7.1 shows the minimum, maximum and average (mean) for 2012, 2013, January to August 2014 and September 2014. Also shown in the 'exc' columns are the vote percentages excluding Don't Knows (DK) in the opinion polls and Did Not Votes (DNV) in the actual result.

These poll averages tell us that from 2012 to the month of the referendum, *No* declined from 53% to 47%, whereas *Yes* increased from 32% to 44%. This appears to confirm Irvine Welsh's quote, give or take a few percentage points. But, the opinion poll average for September 2014 does not reflect the result. The *No* lead of 3pp in the opinion poll average does not match the 9pp lead in the final result. Excluding DK and DNVs does not help because the result was 55%/45% but the

	No	Yes	DK or DNV	Number of polls	No exc	Yes exc
2012	53%	32%	15%	8	62%	38%
2013	50%	32%	19%	31	61%	39%
2012 & 2013	50%	32%	18%	39	61%	39%
Jan-Aug 2014	48%	36%	16%	51	57%	43%
Sep 2014	47%	44%	9%	19	52%	48%
Result	**47%**	**38%**	**15%**	-	**55%**	**45%**

Table 7.1
Statistics for opinion polls prior to the 2014 referendum.

September opinion poll average is statistically significantly different at 52%/48%. (The average of 19 polls with plus or minus 3pp uncertainty will have a much lower uncertainty than 3, theoretically about plus or minus 0.7pp.)

Based on all of this, my equivalent of Irvine Welsh's statement would be the more precise, but much less pithy:

> Opinion polls from 2012, the year of the Edinburgh agreement, until the end of 2013 show a support for Yes mostly in the range 25% to 40%, averaging 32%, and No between 40% and 60%, averaging 50%, with Don't Knows averaging 18%. The result of the referendum on 18 September 2014 was that of all registered voters, 38% voted Yes, 47% No, and 15% did not vote.

Similar conclusions are arrived at by John Curtice from his analysis of results from the Scottish Social Attitudes Survey between 2013 and 2015.[5]

With the above table and graph, together with the cautionary notes on comparing polls with the actual results, there are a couple of further observations we can make. Firstly, the drift towards Yes began *before* the official campaigns got underway on 30 May 2014. This can be interpreted as an effect of pre-campaign activity in local meetings and in social media such as Facebook and Twitter, but also, as you'll see below, there's historical evidence that shows a rise in support for independence whenever Scottish constitutional issues, or even policies specific to Scotland are raised in the public consciousness.

Secondly, there is little correlation with high profile announcements and events that attracted much attention in both traditional and social media, notably the high profile TV debates that took place in August, and the hurried visits and 'the vow' of the Westminster party leaders.

In fact, the only sudden change that can be seen in the above graphs is the narrowing of the gap between Yes and No at the start of September 2014, which took most people by surprise precisely because it wasn't obviously prompted by any event or disclosure of information. With hindsight, the change seems more likely to be a change in how people responded to polls than an actual shift in voting intention.

Figure 7.9 shows the history of Scottish independence support according to results from the polling company Ipsos Mori (formerly called just Mori) and data collected as part of the Scottish Social Attitudes survey.[6]

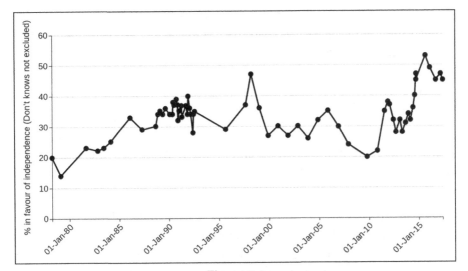

Figure 7.9

Opinion polling on Scottish independence 1978 to 2017.

Data from 2012 onwards are from individual polls published by Ipsos Mori.[7] The same caveat applies as for previous graphs in that the question and methods of polling have varied.

In taking such a long view of data, it's important to remember that we are not simply looking at the shift of a similar group of people as we have done in previous graphs. Most folk over 60 who expressed an opinion in 1978 will not be alive in 2017, and many folk who answered an opinion poll in 2017 were not of voting age in 1978, and some would not even have been born. With such long term data we are looking at how opinion changes between generations as well as shifts amongst a common group of people.

The first hump in the early 1990s coincides with the introduction of the poll tax. Polling data is sparse in the mid-1990s but it appears support for independence fell, but was revived to reach 37% at the time of the devolution referendum in September 1997. The peak of 47% is from a poll in the spring of 1998. A year later it had fallen to 36% and fell to just under 30% where it remained until another peak in late 2005 which does not appear to correspond to any particular event.

The trough in which support for independence dropped to 20% in late 2009, the lowest level since the 1970s, was most likely due to the uncertainty generated by the 2008 financial crisis and the ensuing recession.

Following the May 2011 election, which resulted in the SNP majority government, independence rose to 35% in the summer and peaked at 38% in late 2011 before falling back to around 30% in 2012 and 2013.

The next rise occurred ahead of the 2014 referendum, but the all-time record peak of 53% is after the referendum in August 2015, and three months after the SNP's successful performance in that year's general election. Polls from other companies at about the same time show support for independence at similar levels to what was found just prior to the referendum, and Ipsos Mori found the same in subsequent polls, so it's likely this result is an outlier.

The last three points on this graph are for polls that took place after the EU referendum. Other polling companies found a short-lived surge in support for independence in the weeks following the 2016 referendum but most polls since have returned to roughly where they were in September 2014.

Turnout

Figure 7.10 shows the Scottish turnout – the percentage of registered voters who made valid votes at an election or referendum.

Through most of the 20th century turnout varied between 70% and 80% in general elections. It declined to 58% in 2001 but rose to 71% in 2015

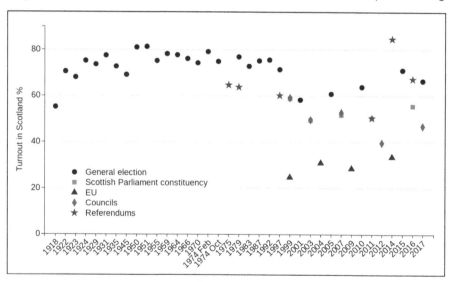

Figure 7.10
Turnout at Scottish elections 1918 to 2017.

before falling back to 66% in 2017. These trends are broadly similar to those of the whole UK except turnout increased by a few percentage points between 2015 and 2017 in all other parts of the UK.

Turnouts in Scottish Parliament elections have been much lower than general elections, with the highest turnout of 59% being for the first one in 1999, and the lowest being for the 2011 election at 50%. Council elections used to have the same turnouts as Scottish Parliament elections until 2007 because both took place on the same day. However, after this caused problems in 2007, council elections have taken place the year after Scottish Parliament elections and their turnouts has been markedly lower, being only 40% in 2012.

European elections have seen the lowest turnouts, being only 25% in 1999. In the most recent one in 2014, which is likely to be the last, turnout was only 34%. This is in stark contrast to the independence referendum which took place later in the same year for which turnout was 85% – higher than any other shown on this graph. Other referendums have had much lower turnouts than this with the EU referendum being 67% in Scotland, somewhat lower than the 72% UK-wide turnout. The referendum on the Alternative Vote in 2011 had a turnout of only 50% which was identical to the Scottish Parliament turnout because they took place on the same day.

The 1997 devolution referendum had a turnout of 60% which was similar to the turnout of the first Scottish Parliament elections that took place two years later. It found 74% of voters supported devolution and 63% wanted a Scottish Parliament with its own powers to set rates of taxation. The previous devolution referendum of 1979 had a slightly higher turnout of 64% with 52% of votes for devolution and 48% against. This meant that only 33% of the electorate had shown approval and because the associated 1978 Act of Parliament stipulated that a 40% level was required, devolution was not implemented and the act was repealed.

Turnout is sometimes used indirectly to highlight that only a minority of the population voted to bring about a particular outcome. We can divide recent elections and referendums each into three groups:

- those who voted for the winning outcome or party
- those who voted for the losing outcome or parties
- those who did not vote at all

7

And for each group we can calculate its share of the registered electorate at the election or referendum in question. The results of doing this and ranking by share in descending order is shown in Table 7.2.

	Share of electorate
2014 independence referendum – No	46.7%
2016 Scottish Parliament – Did not vote	44.3%
2015 General Election – Non-Conservative	41.7%
2017 General Election – Non-Conservative	39.5%
2014 independence referendum – Yes	37.8%
EU referendum – Leave	37.4%
EU referendum – Remain	34.7%
2015 General Election – Did not vote	33.9%
2017 General Election – Did not vote	31.3%
2016 Scottish Parliament – Non-SNP	31.1%
2017 General Election – Conservative	29.2%
EU referendum – Did not vote	27.8%
2016 Scottish Parliament – SNP	24.6%
2015 General Election – Conservative	24.4%
2014 independence referendum – Did not vote	15.5%

Table 7.2
Shares of the electorate in recent elections and referendums 2014 to 2017.

The first point is that no recent exercise in voting has found a majority in favour of any outcome. The highest was the No vote in the 2014 independence referendum, but even this fell short of attracting votes from 50% of the electorate. In a close second place is the share of the electorate that did not vote in the Scottish Parliament elections in 2016. The next two are for UK-wide votes for parties other than the Conservatives in 2015 and 2017. In both cases, the Conservative party went on to form the government, though without a majority of MPs in 2017.

The shares of the electorate for Conservatives in government at Westminster and the SNP in government at Holyrood languish near the bottom of the table. The share that gave these governments their mandate is roughly a quarter of the electorate, though this did not give either government an overall majority in 2016 or 2017.

Of course, one can argue that elections and referendums are about the relative share of votes and that absolute share of the electorate is irrelevant. However, many decisions based on voting in society require a quorum, that is a minimum number of members present at a meeting before a vote can be deemed valid. This is common for companies and committees operating in public life. In fact, examples exist at both Westminster and Holyrood, with the House of Commons having a quorum of 40 MPs, and there being a quorum of 5 MSPs on Scottish Parliament committees. There also exist examples of votes that require minimum turnouts or shares of the electorate, the 1979 devolution referendum being one such example, as mentioned above.

An alternative to turnout limits is to require super-majorities on certain votes. This is commonly stipulated for certain types of resolutions requiring a vote at a company's board meeting, and is often required by countries in amending their constitutions. Another method to ensure there is strong mandate for change is to ask for a double majority. This is a common procedure in referendums in Switzerland in which a majority is required in the overall vote and also all cantons, administrative regions of Switzerland, each have to achieve a majority. In the UK, this could have been applied in the EU referendum vote, either for all four countries, or across Scotland, Wales, Northern Ireland and all nine regions of England. Similarly, in the independence referendum, a double majority might have required all eight Scottish Parliament regions, or even all 32 council areas to show a majority for Yes before independence could be pursued.

Recent research suggests that statisticians in many countries may be underestimating turnout because current methods overestimate the number of eligible voters.[8] Although this would raise the turnout percentages mentioned above by as much as 10pp, it cannot by itself help with the issue of the very different turnouts for different elections.

Some thoughts
Winston Churchill once quipped that 'Democracy is the worst form of government, except for all the others.' But there are many ways to realise democracy, some that merely involve variations in how elections are

conducted, but others that seek to give citizens' rights and responsibilities that extend beyond the casting of a simple vote.

In the last 20 years, proportional representation or PR in its different guises has been introduced for electing MSPs, MEPs and councillors in Scotland. By design, this has led to the distribution of seats amongst parties being a fairer reflection of their shares of the vote, but hopes that PR would help smaller parties and independents have only been partly realised. It is notable that around 10% of councillors are independents but this was true too in 2003 before PR was introduced in council elections.

When millions of people vote in an election for MPs or MSPs, the outcome is that they indirectly hand all executive power to a very small group of individuals – the government. In most cases, the ministers who wield such power are drawn from a single party, but usually, as illustrated for the 2015, 2016 and 2017 elections in Table 7.2, the electorate casts more votes for all the parties that do not form the government. In other words, the government is chosen by the largest minority of voters rather than a majority. Even if you are comfortable with this situation, it is worth considering how things might be done differently.

The first problem that a single party government presents is that the First or Prime Minister has a restricted pool from which to choose ministers. When one whittles down the list according to competency, availability and internal party politics, the choice can become very limited indeed. One solution to this is to appoint ministers from other parties, but usually this only happens either during a crisis, such as the National Government of 1931, or in war-time, or because the major governing party lacks a majority by itself and so enters into a coalition. This happened with the UK government in the 2010–2015 Conservative-Liberal Democrat coalition, and coalitions were formed between Labour and Liberal Democrats from 1999 to 2007 at Holyrood.

Alternatives are available. In other countries, ministers are routinely chosen from outside the small group of governing party MPs (Germany, Italy, Spain and Poland) and in some countries MPs are even forbidden from becoming ministers (France, the Netherlands and Sweden). In fact, the only other EU member that insists on ministers also being MPs is Ireland. The main advantage of relaxing such a requirement is that ministers can be chosen from a much wider pool and so people with the appropriate experience and skills can be recruited into government.

Another approach is to make the government more accountable to the rest of parliament. To do this, both Westminster and Holyrood have cross-party committees of MPs and MSPs that can examine government policy and question ministers. For this to be effective, the committees cannot be mostly chaired or dominated by the governing party. The result of the 2011 Scottish election caused problems because the Scottish parliamentary committee system was, unlike its Westminster equivalent, not designed for a situation where a single party ran a majority government.

One problem with our current electoral system is that we often seem to forget how it is meant to function. An MP or MSP is sometimes seen by the public as a delegate who is expected to put the views of her or his constituents to parliament. This is in fact impossible because the views of many thousands of people are much too varied. Instead, the election is meant to be a process where the public chooses the candidate they trust the most to *represent* them in parliament in finding ways to fit their local issues into those of the whole country. This is why our system is called a representative democracy. Misunderstandings of how representation is meant to work in our political system are in part why recent referendums have caused so much political turbulence.

But none of the above ideas address the problem of turnout. That roughly one in three people do not vote in a typical general election, or half of the electorate do not vote in Scottish Parliament or council elections should, I think, be of serious concern. The introduction of PR was expected to help with this as it would eliminate the concept of a 'wasted vote' under the first part the post system. That is, why bother voting for the Nice party if you live in a Naughty party safe seat? But you can see from Figure 7.10 that PR has not helped at all with turnout.

A radical proposal is that of sortition. This extends the idea of the parliamentary committee out into the general public. In it, members of the public are selected at random to serve on committees that can help form, scrutinise and criticise government policy. This would not be a light undertaking, but civil servants could provide plain-English briefings and papers to help the members of such committees acquaint themselves with the pertinent facts. Parallels can be drawn with the jury system, in which jurors are drawn together, informed on complex legal matters and expected to deliberate and come to a definitive conclusion.

The idea of sortition is not simply to give the government a larger arena in which to form and test policy, though that could be a likely result. It would also cause members of such committees to become more engaged in politics. At any one time, only a small fraction of the population would serve on them, but over the years a greater share of the electorate will build up some such experience, or at least know a friend or family member who has. In short, the idea of sortition is to encourage citizens to engage in the politics of government rather than being limited to a vote on choosing the party or parties of government.

Some questions to ponder:

- Is Scotland in any sense more left-wing than other parts of the UK?
- Given Scotland is not too dissimilar to the rest of the UK in attitudes on the EU and immigration (see Chapter 1), how do we explain the much higher remain vote share in the EU referendum?
- How meaningful are mandates from mass voting when no party or electoral option has ever achieved support from more than 50% of the electorate?
- Has the introduction of proportional representation delivered the benefits that were expected?
- What ideas other than sortition can help improve turnout and encourage more interaction between politicians and their electorate?

Final thoughts

There may have been some parts where you nodded along, and others where you learned something new and were perhaps surprised. But the most valuable parts will be those that challenged your existing beliefs. Perhaps you felt annoyed at me for letting an opinion creep in too strongly, or perhaps I made a mistake, or maybe it was reality that jarred with your preconceptions, or my values might clash with yours. Regardless, it is my hope that what I have written will, along with some reflection, help you form a view about the state of the society around you and how you may act to improve it. To conclude this book I would like to tell you how my thoughts have evolved over the three years I spent writing it.

I found some of my preconceptions about Scotland were wrong. The thing that surprised me the most was the significant real terms rise in everyone's incomes over the last two decades. Also, income inequality has hardly changed in recent years, and, if anything, was slightly reduced during the post-2008 recession.

I'm not saying we do not have a significant problem with inequality, nor that inequalities have not increased in recent decades. I am saying that reality is more nuanced than the views I had formed from popular discourse in the media, on Twitter and in pub conversations.

The data in Chapter 3 provides evidence that income inequality increased, decreased or stayed the same, depending on how you measure it. But what's clear is that from 1995 to 2008 incomes rose and poverty rates fell and that, despite the recession, people still have higher real incomes now than in 1995. Yet, poverty rates have risen in recent years and there's good evidence that the poorest are facing an increasing struggle with housing costs and debt. Reality is complex.

And I was not expecting to discover that Scotland is one of the most prosperous parts of the UK, being on a par with the south east of England in terms of income (Chapter 6) and poverty rates (Chapter 3). This is not the impression I had gained from listening to Scottish political debates in recent years. That said, I'm sure this is of no comfort at all to the 15-20% of Scotland's population who are living in some kind of poverty.

Another surprise was that despite the overall level of public sector debt doubling over the last decade, the interest on that debt was the only area of public spending to see a long-term fall. I've given a partial account of the counter-intuitive nature of public debt and money, but a separate book would be needed to do it justice.

The 2008 financial crisis is, with little doubt, the most important event in recent times. It is visible on almost every graph in this book. Its most curious effect was on air freight in Scotland, which appeared to drop markedly *before* the financial crisis. Could such a drop be an early warning of the next crisis? I'm not sure. It may have been related to climbing oil prices, but that too, in retrospect, seems to have been a proxy for the financial crisis.

It's hard to see obvious features in the graphs that reflect the significant changes in the parties of government in Scotland and the UK over the last decade. The effect of the UK government's austerity since 2010 can be seen, though there has not been a dramatic fall in public spending in Scotland as often claimed by the Scottish government, but instead, after many years of spending growth, it has remained flat in real terms since 2010 (Chapter 5).

But, constant public spending, even in real terms, when you have a growing and aging population means that public services, especially health, will be put under increasing pressure and if nothing is done the quality of those services is bound to decline. Education spending, which is also devolved, has fallen in Scotland since 2007–08 (Chapter 5) and now that school pupil numbers are rising, that too is a cause for concern in coming years.

It's very hard to retain strong political or economic prejudices and be honest with such public data because there is so much apparently paradoxical complexity. Inequality, as described above, provides a good example.

Looking at the numbers and combining and slicing them with spreadsheets and equations can reveal a lot, but it has no purpose without a moral context: a poverty rate can never tell you what it is like to look into a seemingly empty future. Number games can also lead to a false sense that everything is quantifiable, explicable and even predictable.

But reality is not like that. It is uncertain. A society, just like the individuals that form it, is quite capable of behaving irrationally and might react to similar circumstances in surprisingly different ways at different times. Even a well-intentioned government that takes an evidenced-based approach to policy cannot be sure that its actions will fulfill its aims.

Bertrand Russell probably best explained how we should deal with uncertainty:

> I think nobody should be certain of anything. If you're certain, you're certainly wrong because nothing deserves certainty. So one ought to hold all one's beliefs with a certain element of doubt, and one ought to be able to act vigorously in spite of the doubt... One has in practical life to act upon probabilities, and what I should look to philosophy to do is to encourage people to act with vigour without complete certainty.

I believe it should be the task of all citizens to try and think through the reality of their society and face up to uncertainty without letting it cloud what can be established with some certainty. If you don't attempt to do this then you're effectively placing blind trust in your peers, or worse still, in your government. Either way, you may well regret it when they begin acting with vigour in a way that you do not like.

Glossary

Absolute poverty

Despite its name, this is the same as relative poverty (see below) except that the median household income is fixed at that for a recent reference year and inflated for use in the current year. As such, comparing absolute and relative poverty rates shows how inflation has affected those on the lowest incomes. In the UK, absolute poverty is defined and measured by the ONS and should not be confused with the UN or world bank definitions relating to more severe international poverty.

Average

A number that gives a typical or middle value for a collection of numbers. Usually it is synonymous with the mean but it can refer to the median. See below for definitions of mean and median.

Census

A record of the entire population and where they reside on a particular date. The census takes place in the second year of each decade (2021, 2011, 2001, 1991 etc) across the UK but it is administered separately in each country.

Councillors

There are 1,227 councillors in Scotland, each one representing a ward. There are 354 wards across Scotland's 32 councils. Three or four councillors represent each ward and are selected using the Single Transferrable Vote system of Proportional Representation.

Deficit

The deficit is public expenditure less the total of tax and other public revenue. It is often referred to as the budget deficit or fiscal deficit and it is equal to the negative of the net fiscal balance.

Devolution

This refers to the fact that the Scottish Parliament, Welsh Assembly, Northern Irish Assembly and London Assembly have powers previously held by the UK parliament. Any powers retained by the UK parliament, such as for defence and foreign affairs, are said to be reserved, and those held by the Scottish Parliament and the assemblies are said to be devolved. Powers can also be thought of as being devolved to councils or reserved to the Scottish Parliament but for mainly historical and political reasons the terminology of devolution is not often used.

Fiscal

This refers to matters relating to tax and public spending. Economic policies are sometimes referred to as fiscal to distinguish them from monetary policies which concern currency and interest rates.

GDP

Gross Domestic Product. This is the value created in production (hence product) by all economic activities taking place within a country (hence domestic) excluding any element of depreciation (hence gross). It can be interpreted as the sum of all incomes which is mostly composed of wages and profits.

GNI
Gross National Income. Similar to GDP but adjusted to allow for the fact that income from some activities will flow out to foreign owners and flow in to those who own foreign assets. GDP is calculated according to where the economic activity (eg making steel) takes place and GNI according to ownership (eg who owns the steel company).

GVA
Gross Value Added. This is similar to GDP but excludes taxes on products and production, notably VAT. GVA is useful in regional breakdowns of GDP for which taxes cannot easily be estimated or apportioned. The term output is sometimes used interchangeably with GVA but it can also mean GDP.

Growth rate
Sometimes referred to as just growth and it often refers to the growth of GDP, usually in real terms. The annual growth rate involves taking this year's number, subtracting last year's number and dividing by last year's number and multiplying by 100 to make it a percentage. For example, if a quantity was 100 last year and is 105 this year, then the growth rate is 105 less 100, divided by 100, which gives 0.05 or 5%.

Inflation
The growth of prices without any corresponding change in the measurable value of goods or services. Inflation of prices paid by consumers is measured by the CPI or CPIH index published by the ONS. Inflation associated with UK macro-economic figures such as GDP are measured by deflators and published by the UK's HM Treasury.

MP
Member of Parliament. There are currently 650 MPs in the UK, one for each constituency; Scotland has 59 MPs. They are elected using the first past the post system.

MEP
Member of the European Parliament. There are 6 MEPs for Scotland elected using the D'Hondt proportional representation system.

MSP
Member of the Scottish Parliament. There are 129 MSPs selected using a hybrid proportional representation system. First past the post is used to select 73 constituency MSPs and the remaining 56 are chosen by the D'Hondt method to bring the numbers of MSPs for each party roughly in line with their vote shares.

Mean
Often synonymous with average. For a collection of numbers, you can calculate

the mean by adding them all up and dividing by the number of them. For 4, 5, 6 the sum is 4+5+6=15, and dividing by three gives the mean, which is 5.

Median
The number that divides a group of numbers so that half are larger, and the other half is smaller. For 4, 5, 6, the median is 5, because one number (4) is smaller, and one number is larger (6). For 4, 5, 6, 7, the median would be 5.5, so that two numbers are smaller and two are larger.

ONS
The UK's Office for National Statistics publishes datasets and statistical reports describing the UK.

Poll
This often refers to a survey of voting intention but can also refer to the vote itself (eg polling station). See survey.

Relative poverty
This is a UK definition of poverty from the ONS that measures the percentage of the population that are below 60% of the median household income for that year.

Reserved
See devolution.

SIMD
Scottish Index of Multiple Deprivation. This takes many measures of poverty and deprivation and uses them to create a single index, or score. This is done for thousands of small areas that cover all of Scotland's population so that they can be ranked and used to construct, for example, a list of the 20% most deprived areas in Scotland.

Survey
in contrast to the census, a survey only seeks to interview a relatively small sample of the population, typically 1 in a 1,000 people or less. These results can then be scaled up to reflect the entire population but are subject to greater uncertainties than a census. A survey of voting intention is often called a poll.

Endnotes

Chapter 1

1   www.scotlandscensus.gov.uk
2   www.nrscotland.gov.uk/statistics-and-data/statistics/statistics-by-theme/
     population/population-estimates/mid-year-population-estimates/mid-2017
3   data.worldbank.org/indicator/SP.POP.TOTL.FE.ZS
4   www.scotlandscensus.gov.uk
5   www.scotlandscensus.gov.uk/results-glance
6   www.scotlandscensus.gov.uk/census-releases
7   www.ons.gov.uk/ons/rel/regional-trends/region-and-country-profiles/
     key-statistics-and-profiles---august-2012/key-statistics---scotland--
     august-2012.html
8   www.scotlandscensus.gov.uk/documents/censusresults/release1a/rel1asb.
     pdf
9   www.scotlandscensus.gov.uk/documents/censusresults/release1a/rel1asb.
     pdf
10   www.scotlandscensus.gov.uk/documents/censusresults/release1b/rel1bsb.
     pdf
11   www.scotlandscensus.gov.uk/documents/censusresults/release1a/rel1asb.
     pdf
12   www.nrscotland.gov.uk/statistics-and-data/statistics/statistics-by-theme/
     population/2011-census-reconciliation-report
13   www.scotlandscensus.gov.uk/documents/censusresults/release2a/
     StatsBulletin2A.pdf
14   www.ons.gov.uk/peoplepopulationandcommunity/populationand migration/
     populationestimates/datasets/populationestimatesfor
     ukenglandandwalesscotlandandnorthernireland
15   www.scotlandscensus.gov.uk/documents/censusresults/release1a/
     rel1asbtable2.xls
16   www.scotlandscensus.gov.uk/documents/censusresults/release1a/
     rel1asbtable3.pdf
17   www.nrscotland.gov.uk/statistics-and-data/statistics/statistics-by-theme/
     population/population-projections/population-projections-scotland/
     population-pyramids-of-scotland
18   www.nrscotland.gov.uk/statistics-and-data/statistics/stats-at-a-glance/
     time-series-datasets
19   www.nrscotland.gov.uk/statistics-and-data/statistics/statistics-by-theme/
     population/population-estimates/mid-year-population-estimates/mid-
     2016/list-of-figures
20   www.nrscotland.gov.uk/statistics-and-data/statistics/statistics-by-theme/
     population/population-estimates/mid-year-population-estimates/mid-
     2016/list-of-figures
21   www.ipsos.com/ipsos-mori/en-uk/shifting-ground-attitudes-towards-
     immigration-and-brexit
22   www.imf.org/en/Publications/Staff-Discussion-Notes/Issues/2016/
     12/31/Emigration-and-Its-Economic-Impact-on-Eastern-Europe-42896

23   blog.whatscotlandthinks.org/2017/03/what-do-voters-in-scotland-want-from-brexit/
24   www.scotlandscensus.gov.uk/documents/censusresults/release1b/rel1bsb.pdf
25   www.ros.gov.uk
26   www.gov.scot/Topics/Statistics/16002
27   www.scotlandscensus.gov.uk/documents/censusresults/release2a/rel2asbtable7.xls

Chapter 2

1   www.npr.org/2014/05/02/309040279/in-4-000-years-one-thing-hasnt-changed-it-takes-time-to-buy-light
2   www.gov.scot/Topics/Statistics/Browse/Business/Energy
3   www.npr.org/2016/09/27/495671385/how-an-engineers-desperate-experiment-created-fracking
4   www.bbc.co.uk/news/uk-scotland-scotland-politics-41484153
5   www.bbc.co.uk/news/uk-scotland-37474396
6   www.bbc.co.uk/news/uk-scotland-40953427
7   www.scottishshale.co.uk/HistoryPages/index.html
8   www.theguardian.com/uk/2010/dec/20/why-so-cold-winter
9   www.gov.uk/government/statistics/electricity-chapter-5-digest-of-united-kingdom-energy-statistics-dukes
10   www.emrdeliverybody.com/Capacity%20Markets%20Document%20Library/Electricity%20Capacity%20Report%202015.pdf
11   www.gov.scot/Topics/Business-Industry/Energy/Energy-sources/19185
12   www.gov.scot/Topics/Business-Industry/Energy/RoutemapUpdate2015
13   www.gridwatch.templar.co.uk/
14   www.gov.uk/government/statistics/electricity-chapter-5-digest-of-united-kingdom-energy-statistics-dukes
15   www.scottishwater.co.uk/About-Us/Publications/Annual-Reports/Annual-Report-1617
16   beta.gov.scot/news/water-contract-brings-40m-in-savings/
17   www.bbc.co.uk/news/uk-scotland-scotland-business-36605882
18   www.gov.uk/government/speeches/ons-decision-on-the-classification-of-network-rail
19   www.bbc.co.uk/news/uk-scotland-41388672
20   www.transport.gov.scot/publication/scottish-transport-statistics-no-35-2016-edition/
21   www.gov.scot/Topics/Statistics/16002
22   www.gov.uk/government/uploads/system/uploads/attachment_data/file/385918/aviation-notes.pdf
23   www.gov.scot/Publications/2017/09/9979
24   www.ons.gov.uk/peoplepopulationandcommunity/householdcharacteristics/homeinternetandsocialmediausage/bulletins/internetaccesshouseholdsandindividuals/2017
25   www.gov.scot/simd
26   research.un.org/en/climate-change/reports

Chapter 3

1   www.gov.scot/Publications/2017/03/2213
2   www.gov.uk/government/collections/households-below-average-income-hbai--2
3   visual.ons.gov.uk/household-income-and-inequality-where-do-you-fit-in/
4   www.ifs.org.uk/wheredoyoufitin/
5   www.gov.scot/About/Performance/scotPerforms/purpose/solidarity
6   www.gov.uk/government/statistics/households-below-average-income-199495-to-201516
7   piketty.pse.ens.fr/en/
8   www.ifs.org.uk/publications/7274
9   blogs.worldbank.org/developmenttalk/international-poverty-line-has-just-been-raised-190-day-global-poverty-basically-unchanged-how-even
10 data.worldbank.org/indicator/PA.NUS.PRVT.PP
11 www.gov.uk/government/statistics/households-below-average-income-199495-to-201516
12 data.worldbank.org/indicator/NY.GNP.PCAP.PP.KD?order=wbapi_data_value_2011+wbapi_data_value+wbapi_data_value-first&sort=asc
13 www.gov.scot/Publications/2017/02/6032/0
14 www.bankofengland.co.uk/monetarypolicy/Pages/qe/qe_faqs.aspx
15 www.ons.gov.uk/peoplepopulationandcommunity/personalandhouseholdfinances/incomeandwealth/bulletins/theeffectsoftaxesandbenefitsonhouseholdincome/financialyearending2016

Chapter 4

1   www.nfer.ac.uk/nfer/index.cfm?9B1C0068-C29E-AD4D-0AEC-8B4F43F54A28
2   www.gov.uk/know-when-you-can-leave-school
3   www.gov.scot/Topics/Statistics/Browse/School-Education/Summarystatsforschools
4   www.gov.scot/Publications/2014/12/7590/4
5   www.gov.scot/Topics/Education/Schools/FAQs
6   www.gov.scot/Topics/Statistics/Browse/School-Education/TrendData
7   www.gov.scot/Topics/Statistics/Browse/School-Education/HistoricDatasets/PupilTeacherHistoric
8   www.ssln.org.uk
9   www.gov.scot/Topics/Statistics/Browse/School-Education/PISA
10 scqf.org.uk/
11 www.audit-scotland.gov.uk/report/scotlands-colleges-2017
12 www.sfc.ac.uk/publications-statistics/statistical-publications/statistical-publications-2017/SFCST032017.aspx
13 andrewmcgettigan.org/2017/07/13/fiscal-illuions/
14 adventuresinevidence.com/2017/05/30/student-debt-and-grants-in-scotland-a-summary/
15 fullfact.org/education/are-poor-scots-half-likely-get-university-poor-english-pupils/

16 www.gov.scot/Topics/Statistics/SIMD
17 www.ecu.ac.uk/publications/intersectionality-scottish-heis/
18 www.isdscotland.org/Health-Topics/Hospital-Care/Hospitals/
19 www.isdscotland.org/Health-Topics/Hospital-Care/Inpatient-and-Day-Case-Activity/
20 www.isdscotland.org/Health%2DTopics/Waiting%2DTimes/Publications/
21 www.isdscotland.org/Health-Topics/General-Practice/Workforce-and-Practice-Populations/
22 www.health.org.uk/sites/health/files/TheImpactOfPerformanceTargetsWithinTheNHSAndInternationally_0.pdf
23 www.abdn.ac.uk/news/11451/
24 www.scotcourts.gov.uk/the-courts/sheriff-court/find-a-court
25 www.parliament.scot/Budget/TracktheBudget2017-18/stackedbar.html#
26 www.lawscot.org.uk/news-and-events/news/slab-annual-report-2017/
27 www.gov.scot/Topics/Statistics/Browse/Crime-Justice/TrendData
28 www.gov.scot/Publications/2002/05/14636/3952
29 history.fnal.gov/testimony.html

Chapter 5

1   www.gov.scot/Topics/Statistics/Browse/Economy/GERS
2   www.gov.uk/government/statistics/gdp-deflators-at-market-prices-and-money-gdp-september-2017-quarterly-national-accounts-september-2017
3   www.gov.scot/Publications/2017/08/7201/7
4   budgetresponsibility.org.uk/forecasts-in-depth/tax-by-tax-spend-by-spend/national-insurance-contributions/#policy_costings
5   www.gov.scot/Publications/2017/08/7201/4
6   www.eia.gov/dnav/pet/hist/LeafHandler.ashx?n=pet&s=rbrte&f=a
7   ec.europa.eu/eurostat/tgm/table.do?tab=table&init=1&language=en&pcode=tec00127&plugin=1
8   www.gov.scot/Publications/2013/11/9348/7
9   www.scottish.parliament.uk/parliamentarybusiness/CurrentCommittees/93867.aspx
10 www.parliament.scot/parliamentarybusiness/Bills/103199.aspx
11 www.gov.scot/Publications/2017/12/8959
12 www.parliament.scot/parliamentarybusiness/17534.aspx
13 www.gov.uk/government/publications/how-to-understand-public-sector-spending/how-to-understand-public-sector-spending#departmental-expenditure-limits-del
14 www.legislation.gov.uk/asp/2014/6/schedule/1
15 www.gov.scot/Publications/2014/10/7445/1
16 fraserofallander.org/2017/12/14/todays-scottish-budget-a-brief-review/
17 www.gov.scot/Publications/2017/12/8959/20
18 www.gov.uk/government/publications/spending-review-and-autumn-statement-2015-documents
19 fraserofallander.org/2017/12/11/an-introductory-guide-to-this-weeks-scottish-budget/

20   www.gov.uk/browse/tax/income-tax
21   www.gov.uk/government/publications/the-agreement-between-the-scottish-government-and-the-united-kingdom-government-on-the-scottish-governments- fiscal-framework
22   www.gov.scot/Publications/2017/02/1688
23   www.audit-scotland.gov.uk/report/local-government-in-scotland-financial-overview-201516
24   www.gov.uk/government/publications/annual-report-and-accounts-2014-15
25   www.gov.scot/Publications/2016/03/4517
26   www.gov.scot/Resource/0049/00494765.pdf
27   publications.parliament.uk/pa/cm201516/cmselect/cmscotaf/660/66005.htm
28   www.gov.uk/government/collections/hmt-central-funds
29   www.nao.org.uk/wp-content/uploads/2018/01/PFI-and-PF2.pdf
30   www.architectsjournal.co.uk/news/poor-construction-and-lack-of-scrutiny-caused-scottish-schools-defects/10017249.article
31   pdfs.semanticscholar.org/1b34/c11aa1323040956d6609bccbdf24c264260e.pdf
32   www.audit-scotland.gov.uk/uploads/docs/report/2015/s22_151001_scottish_gov_esa10briefing.pdf

Chapter 6

1   www.gov.scot/Topics/Statistics/Browse/Economy/QNAS
2   www.bbc.co.uk/news/world-us-canada-41889787
3   www.gov.scot/Topics/Statistics/Browse/Economy/SNAP/expstats/aggregates/GNI
4   bankunderground.co.uk/2016/06/10/rewriting-history-understanding-revisions-to-uk-gdp/
5   www.gov.scot/topics/statistics/browse/economy/QNA2016Q1
6   www.oecd.org/std/understanding-national-accounts-9789264214637-en.htm
7   www.gov.uk/government/statistics/gdp-deflators-at-market-prices-and-money-gdp-september-2017-quarterly-national-accounts-september-2017
8   www.gov.scot/Publications/2014/06/5184/4
9   www.ons.gov.uk/employmentandlabourmarket
10   www.ons.gov.uk/employmentandlabourmarket/peopleinwork/employmentandemployeetypes/methodologies/aguidetolabourmarketstatistics
11   www.strath.ac.uk/business/economics/fraserofallanderinstitute/labourmarkettrends/
12   www.ons.gov.uk/employmentandlabourmarket/peopleinworkearningsandworkinghours/bulletins/annualsurveyofhoursandearnings/2017provisionaland 2016revisedresults
13   www.gov.uk/government/collections/trade-union-statistics
14   www.gla.ac.uk/media/media_167194_en.pdf
15   www.gov.scot/Topics/Statistics/Browse/Economy/Exports/ESSPublication

16   webarchive.nationalarchives.gov.uk/20160105193307/www.ons.gov.uk/ons/
     rel/elmr/longer-term-trends/public-sector-fianaces/art-ltt-psf.html#tab-
     Trends-in-Public-Sector-Finances
17   www.lisbon-treaty.org
18   www.ons.gov.uk/economy/governmentpublicsectorandtaxes/
     publicsectorfinance/bulletins/publicsectorfinances/november2017#how-
     big-is-public-sector-debt
19   www.coppolacomment.com/2013/01/government-debt-isnt-what-you-think-it.
     html
20   www.bankofengland.co.uk/quarterly-bulletin/2014/q1/money-creation-in-
     the-modern-economy
21   adamtooze.com/books/crashed-2018/
22   www.activecitizen.scot/2016/10/balances-and-north-sea-exports.html

Chapter 7

1   researchbriefings.parliament.uk/ResearchBriefing/Summary/CBP-
    7529#fullreport
2   www.parliament.scot/Research%20briefings%20and%20fact%20sheets/
    Scottish_Parliament_Electoral_System.pdf
3   www.theguardian.com/commentisfree/2014/sep/20/irvine-welsh-scottish-
    independence-glorious-failure
4   whatscotlandthinks.org
5   www.research.aqmen.ac.uk/files/2017/07/PostGE2015Scotland_
    Referendum-Impact.pdf
6   www.ipsos.com/ipsos-mori/en-uk/35-years-scottish-attitudes-towards-
    independence
7   www.ipsos.com/ipsos-mori/en-uk
8   www.economist.com/news/britain/21734359-britain-it-almost-ten-
    percentage-points-higher-previously-thought-new-paper

Index

London 27, 83, 89, 92, 98, 108, 111, 118, 123, 239, 245, 265, 278, 296

Luath Press Limited

committed to publishing well written books worth reading

LUATH PRESS takes its name from Robert Burns, whose little collie Luath (*Gael.*, swift or nimble) tripped up Jean Armour at a wedding and gave him the chance to speak to the woman who was to be his wife and the abiding love of his life. Burns called one of 'The Twa Dogs' Luath after Cuchullin's hunting dog in Ossian's *Fingal*. Luath Press was established in 1981 in the heart of Burns country, and now resides a few steps up the road from Burns' first lodgings on Edinburgh's Royal Mile.
Luath offers you distinctive writing with a hint of unexpected pleasures.

Most bookshops in the UK, the US, Canada, Australia, New Zealand and parts of Europe either carry our books in stock or can order them for you. To order direct from us, please send a £sterling cheque, postal order, international money order or your credit card details (number, address of cardholder and expiry date) to us at the address below. Please add post and packing as follows: UK – £1.00 per delivery address; overseas surface mail – £2.50 per delivery address; overseas airmail – £3.50 for the first book to each delivery address, plus £1.00 for each additional book by airmail to the same address. If your order is a gift, we will happily enclose your card or message at no extra charge.

Luath Press Limited
543/2 Castlehill
The Royal Mile
Edinburgh EH1 2ND
Scotland
Telephone: 0131 225 4326 (24 hours)
email: sales@luath.co.uk
Website: www.luath.co.uk